RYAN **PARROTT** • MARCO **RENNA** • WALTER **BAIAMONTE**

# MIGHTY MORPHIN

## VOLUME ONE

Published by

BOOM!
S T U D I O S

DESIGNER
**SCOTT NEWMAN**

ASSISTANT EDITOR
**GWEN WALLER**

EDITOR
**DAFNA PLEBAN**

HASBRO SPECIAL THANKS
**ED LANE**, **BETH ARTALE**,
AND **MICHAEL KELLY**

**Ross Richie** CEO & Founder
**Joy Huffman** CFO
**Matt Gagnon** Editor-in-Chief
**Filip Sablik** President, Publishing & Marketing
**Stephen Christy** President, Development
**Lance Kreiter** Vice President, Licensing & Merchandising
**Bryce Carlson** Vice President, Editorial & Creative Strategy
**Kate Henning** Director, Operations
**Spencer Simpson** Director, Sales
**Scott Newman** Manager, Production Design
**Elyse Strandberg** Manager, Finance
**Sierra Hahn** Executive Editor
**Jeanine Schaefer** Executive Editor
**Dafna Pleban** Senior Editor
**Shannon Watters** Senior Editor
**Eric Harburn** Senior Editor
**Sophie Philips-Roberts** Associate Editor
**Amanda LaFranco** Associate Editor
**Jonathan Manning** Associate Editor
**Gavin Gronenthal** Assistant Editor
**Gwen Waller** Assistant Editor
**Allyson Gronowitz** Assistant Editor
**Ramiro Portnoy** Assistant Editor
**Kenzie Rzonca** Assistant Editor
**Shelby Netschke** Editorial Assistant
**Michelle Ankley** Design Lead
**Marie Krupina** Production Designer
**Grace Park** Production Designer
**Chelsea Roberts** Production Designer
**Samantha Knapp** Production Design Assistant
**José Meza** Live Events Lead
**Stephanie Hocutt** Digital Marketing Lead
**Esther Kim** Marketing Lead
**Breanna Sarpy** Live Events Coordinator
**Amanda Lawson** Marketing Assistant
**Morgan Perry** Retail Sales Lead
**Holly Aitchison** Digital Sales Coordinator
**Megan Christopher** Operations Coordinator
**Rodrigo Hernandez** Operations Coordinator
**Zipporah Smith** Operations Coordinator
**Jason Lee** Senior Accountant
**Sabrina Lesin** Accounting Assistant
**Lauren Alexander** Administrative Assistant

Licensed by:

WRITTEN BY
**RYAN PARROTT**

ILLUSTRATED BY
**MARCO RENNA**

COLORS BY
**WALTER BAIAMONTE**
WITH ASSISTANCE BY **KATIA RANALLI**

LETTERS BY
**ED DUKESHIRE**

COVER BY
**INHYUK LEE**

ELTARIAN AND GREEN RANGER
CHARACTER DESIGNS BY
**DAN MORA**

# CHAPTER ONE

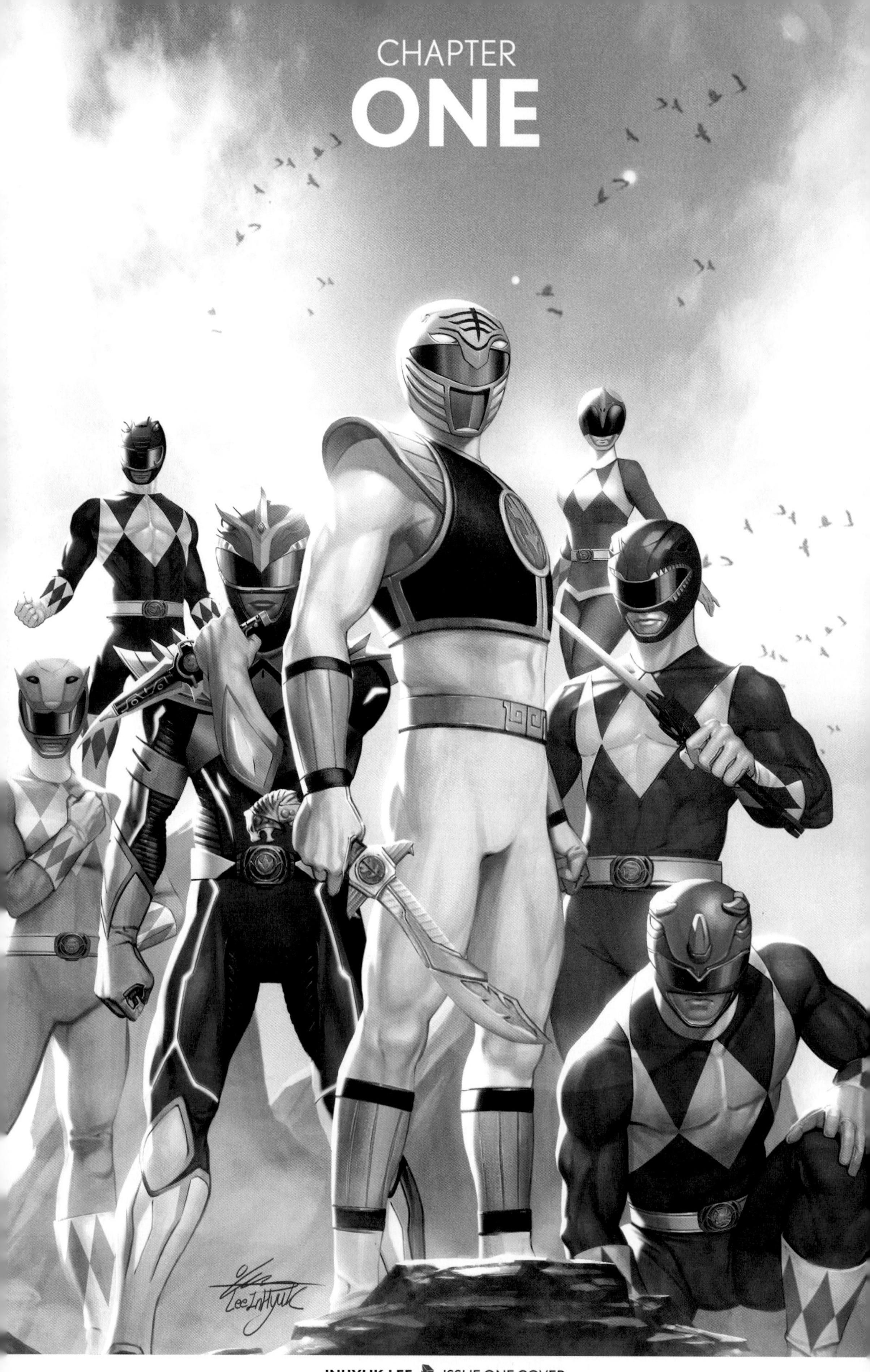

**INHYUK LEE** ISSUE ONE COVER

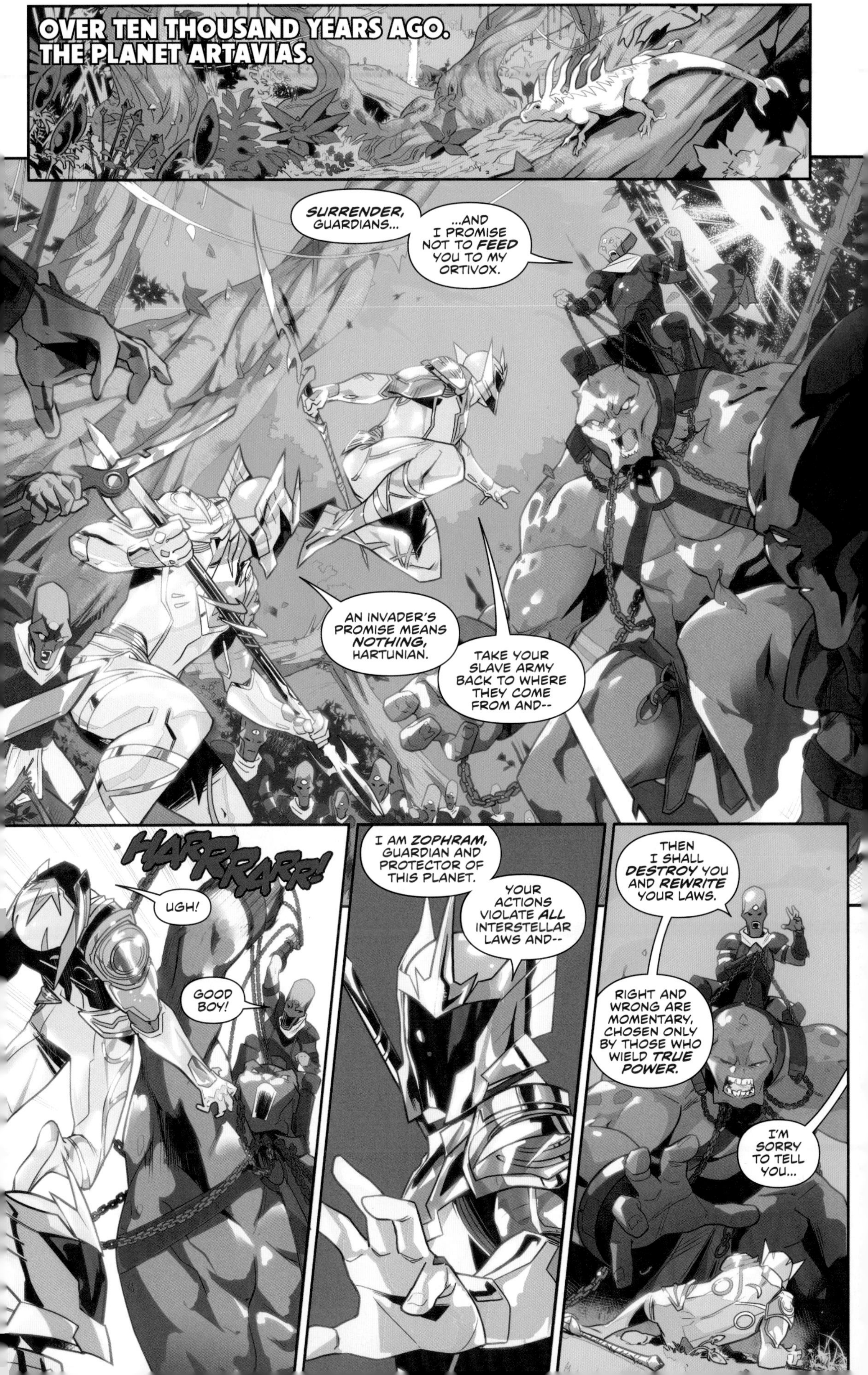
OVER TEN THOUSAND YEARS AGO. THE PLANET ARTAVIAS.
SURRENDER, GUARDIANS...
...AND I PROMISE NOT TO FEED YOU TO MY ORTIVOX.
AN INVADER'S PROMISE MEANS NOTHING, HARTUNIAN.
TAKE YOUR SLAVE ARMY BACK TO WHERE THEY COME FROM AND--
HARRRARR!
UGH!
GOOD BOY!
I AM ZOPHRAM, GUARDIAN AND PROTECTOR OF THIS PLANET.
YOUR ACTIONS VIOLATE ALL INTERSTELLAR LAWS AND--
THEN I SHALL DESTROY YOU AND REWRITE YOUR LAWS.
RIGHT AND WRONG ARE MOMENTARY, CHOSEN ONLY BY THOSE WHO WIELD TRUE POWER.
I'M SORRY TO TELL YOU...

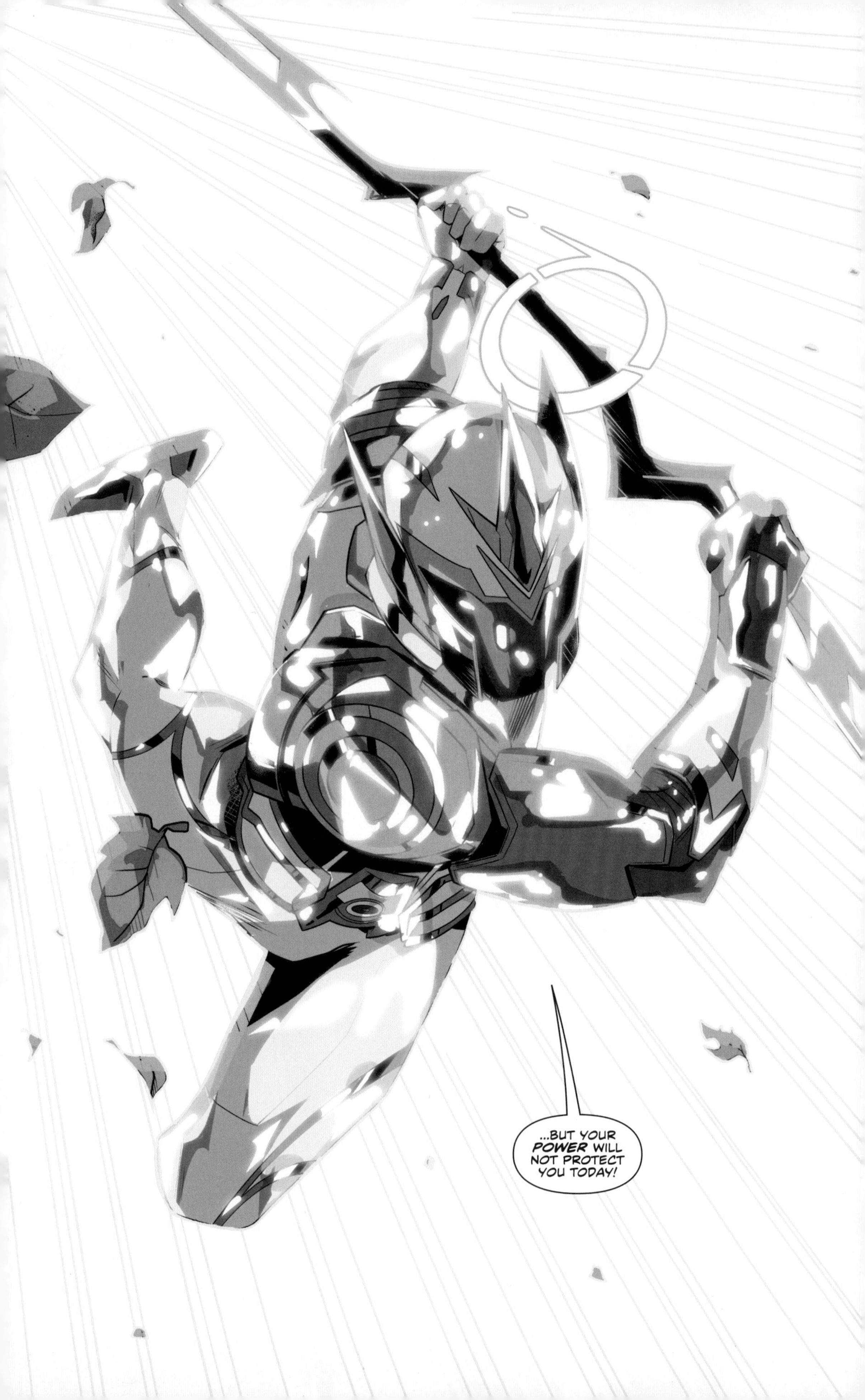
...BUT YOUR POWER WILL NOT PROTECT YOU TODAY!

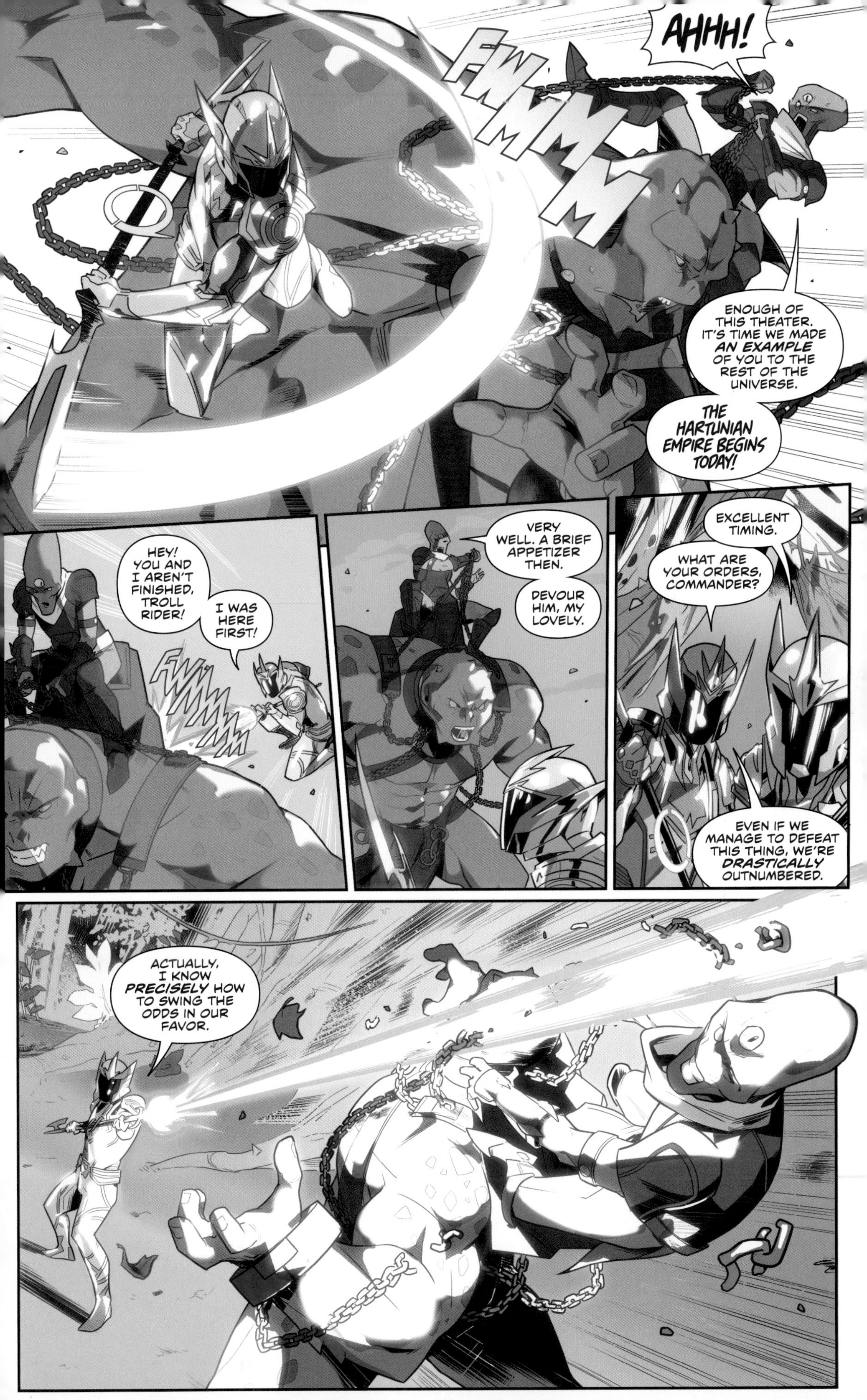
AHHH!
FWMMM
ENOUGH OF THIS THEATER. IT'S TIME WE MADE AN EXAMPLE OF YOU TO THE REST OF THE UNIVERSE.
THE HARTUNIAN EMPIRE BEGINS TODAY!
HEY! YOU AND I AREN'T FINISHED, TROLL RIDER!
I WAS HERE FIRST!
FWMMM
VERY WELL. A BRIEF APPETIZER THEN.
DEVOUR HIM, MY LOVELY.
EXCELLENT TIMING.
WHAT ARE YOUR ORDERS, COMMANDER?
EVEN IF WE MANAGE TO DEFEAT THIS THING, WE'RE DRASTICALLY OUTNUMBERED.
ACTUALLY, I KNOW PRECISELY HOW TO SWING THE ODDS IN OUR FAVOR.

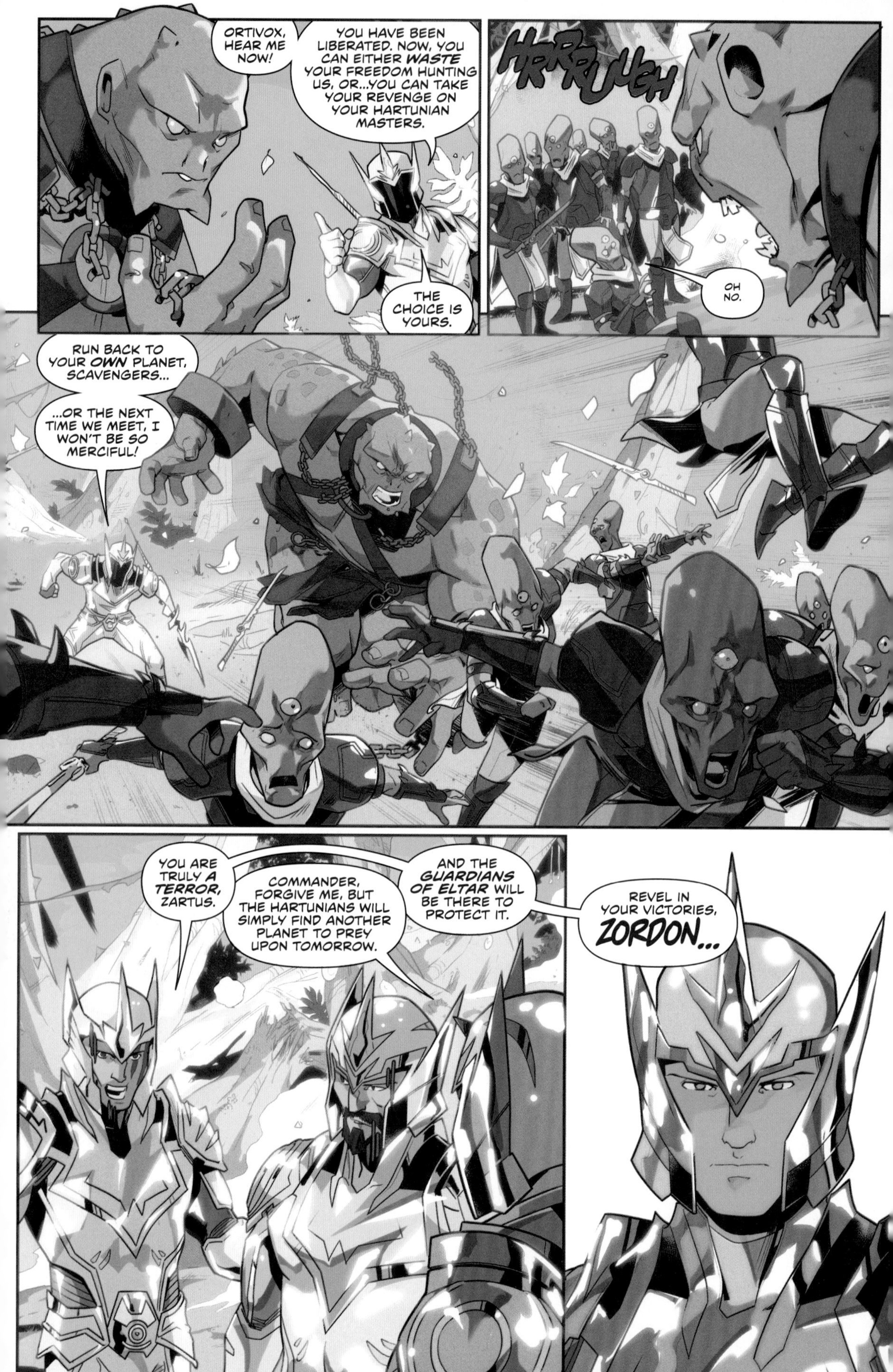
ORTIVOX, HEAR ME NOW!
YOU HAVE BEEN LIBERATED. NOW, YOU CAN EITHER WASTE YOUR FREEDOM HUNTING US, OR...YOU CAN TAKE YOUR REVENGE ON YOUR HARTUNIAN MASTERS.
THE CHOICE IS YOURS.
HRRRRUUGH
OH NO.
RUN BACK TO YOUR OWN PLANET, SCAVENGERS...
...OR THE NEXT TIME WE MEET, I WON'T BE SO MERCIFUL!
YOU ARE TRULY A TERROR, ZARTUS.
COMMANDER, FORGIVE ME, BUT THE HARTUNIANS WILL SIMPLY FIND ANOTHER PLANET TO PREY UPON TOMORROW.
AND THE GUARDIANS OF ELTAR WILL BE THERE TO PROTECT IT.
REVEL IN YOUR VICTORIES, ZORDON...

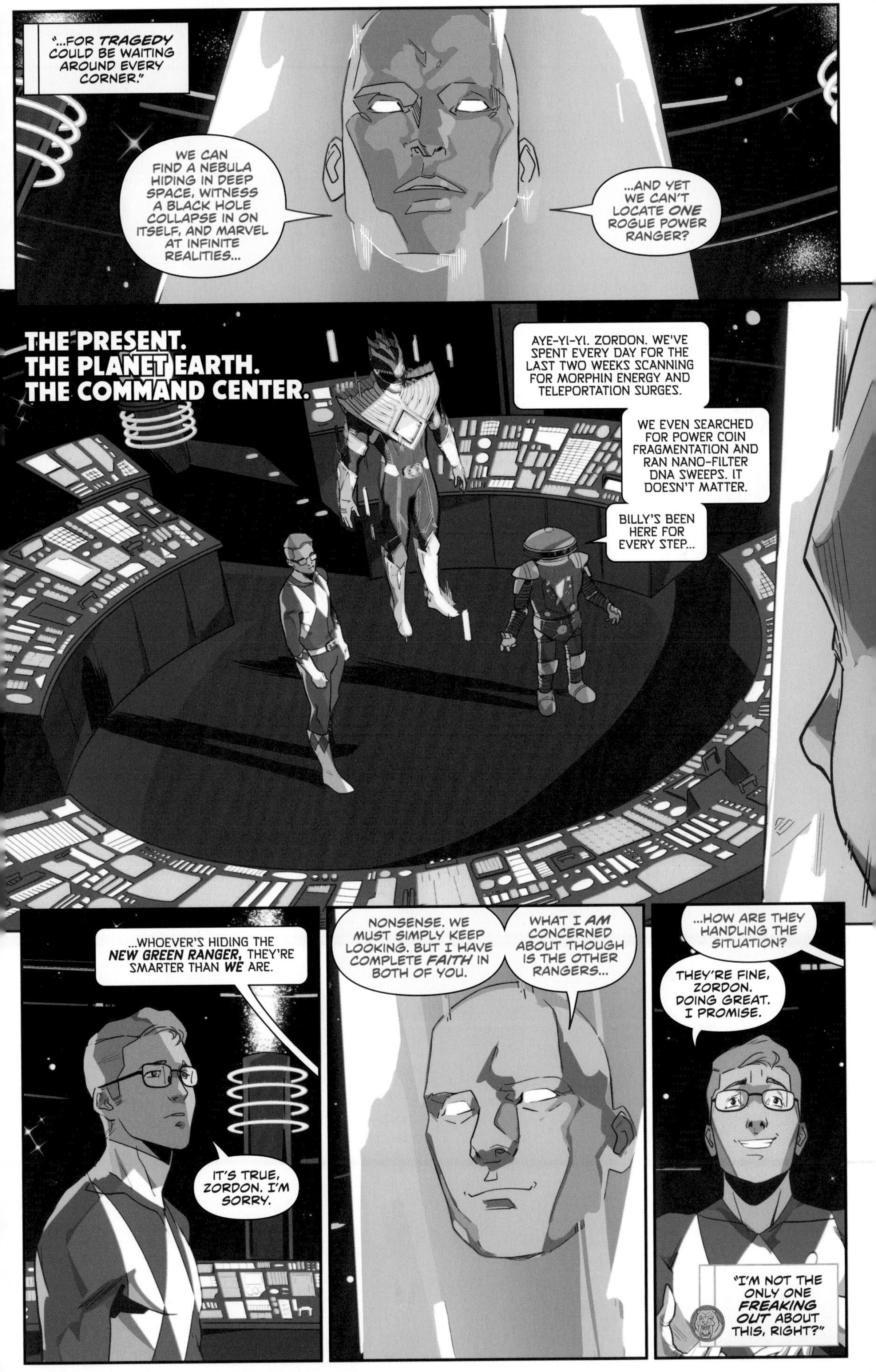
"...FOR TRAGEDY COULD BE WAITING AROUND EVERY CORNER."
WE CAN FIND A NEBULA HIDING IN DEEP SPACE, WITNESS A BLACK HOLE COLLAPSE IN ON ITSELF, AND MARVEL AT INFINITE REALITIES...
...AND YET WE CAN'T LOCATE ONE ROGUE POWER RANGER?
THE PRESENT. THE PLANET EARTH. THE COMMAND CENTER.
AYE-YI-YI. ZORDON. WE'VE SPENT EVERY DAY FOR THE LAST TWO WEEKS SCANNING FOR MORPHIN ENERGY AND TELEPORTATION SURGES.
WE EVEN SEARCHED FOR POWER COIN FRAGMENTATION AND RAN NANO-FILTER DNA SWEEPS. IT DOESN'T MATTER.
BILLY'S BEEN HERE FOR EVERY STEP...
...WHOEVER'S HIDING THE NEW GREEN RANGER, THEY'RE SMARTER THAN WE ARE.
IT'S TRUE, ZORDON. I'M SORRY.
NONSENSE. WE MUST SIMPLY KEEP LOOKING. BUT I HAVE COMPLETE FAITH IN BOTH OF YOU.
WHAT I AM CONCERNED ABOUT THOUGH IS THE OTHER RANGERS...
...HOW ARE THEY HANDLING THE SITUATION?
THEY'RE FINE, ZORDON. DOING GREAT. I PROMISE.
"I'M NOT THE ONLY ONE FREAKING OUT ABOUT THIS, RIGHT?"

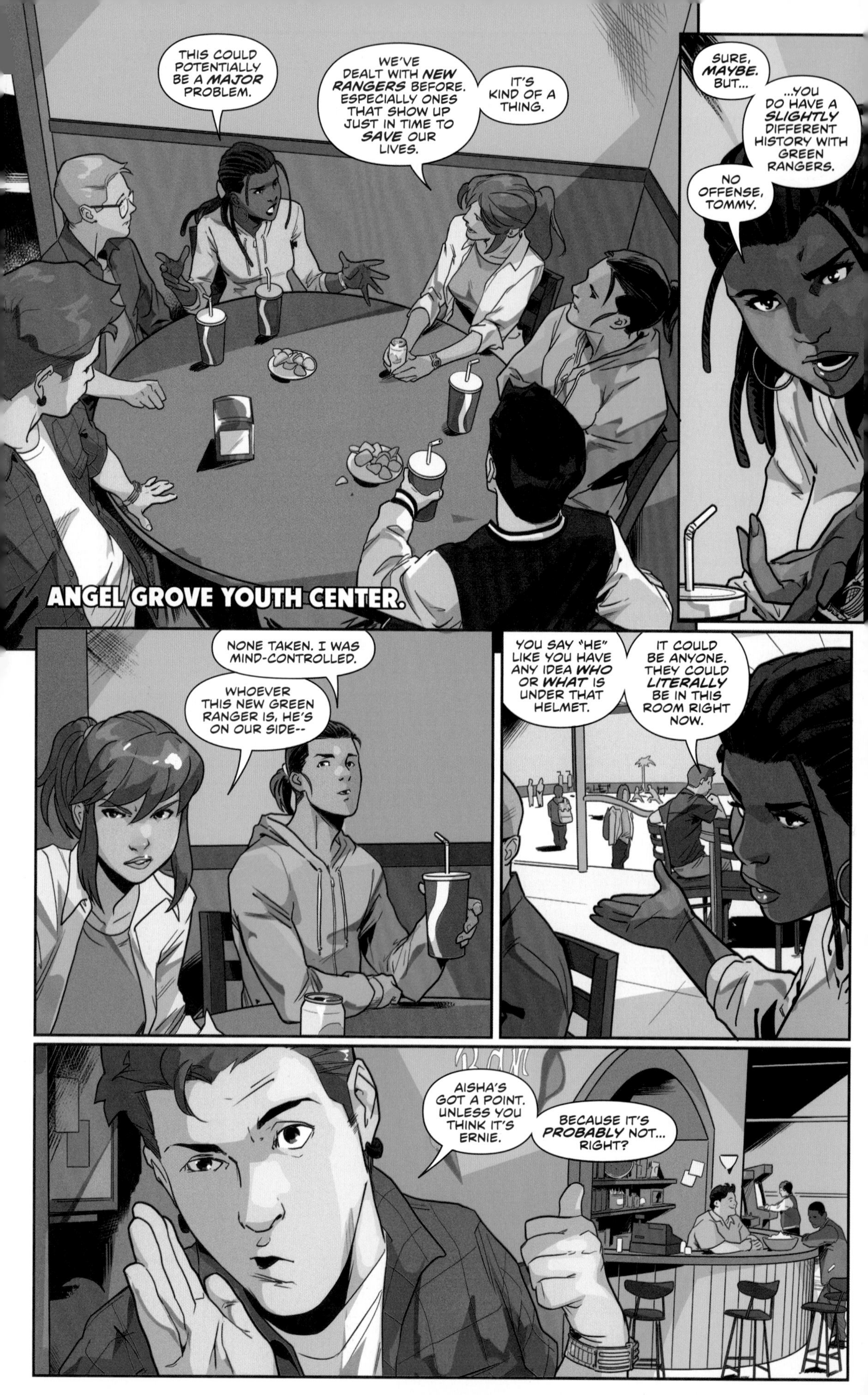
THIS COULD POTENTIALLY BE A MAJOR PROBLEM.
WE'VE DEALT WITH NEW RANGERS BEFORE. ESPECIALLY ONES THAT SHOW UP JUST IN TIME TO SAVE OUR LIVES.
IT'S KIND OF A THING.
ANGEL GROVE YOUTH CENTER.
SURE, MAYBE. BUT...
...YOU DO HAVE A SLIGHTLY DIFFERENT HISTORY WITH GREEN RANGERS.
NO OFFENSE, TOMMY.
NONE TAKEN. I WAS MIND-CONTROLLED.
WHOEVER THIS NEW GREEN RANGER IS, HE'S ON OUR SIDE--
YOU SAY "HE" LIKE YOU HAVE ANY IDEA WHO OR WHAT IS UNDER THAT HELMET.
IT COULD BE ANYONE. THEY COULD LITERALLY BE IN THIS ROOM RIGHT NOW.
AISHA'S GOT A POINT. UNLESS YOU THINK IT'S ERNIE.
BECAUSE IT'S PROBABLY NOT... RIGHT?

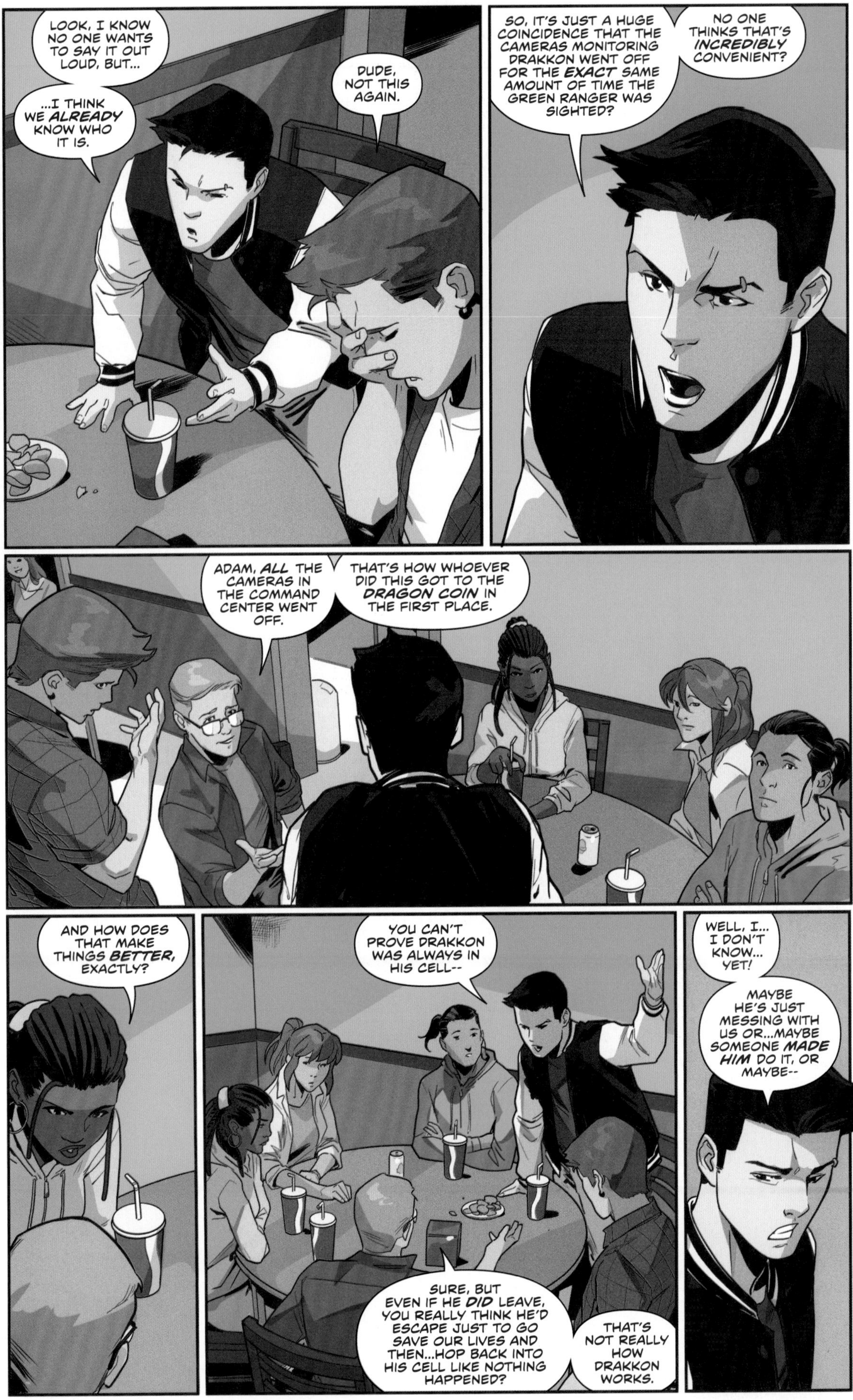
LOOK, I KNOW NO ONE WANTS TO SAY IT OUT LOUD, BUT...
...I THINK WE *ALREADY* KNOW WHO IT IS.
DUDE, NOT THIS AGAIN.
SO, IT'S JUST A HUGE COINCIDENCE THAT THE CAMERAS MONITORING DRAKKON WENT OFF FOR THE *EXACT* SAME AMOUNT OF TIME THE GREEN RANGER WAS SIGHTED?
NO ONE THINKS THAT'S *INCREDIBLY* CONVENIENT?
ADAM, *ALL* THE CAMERAS IN THE COMMAND CENTER WENT OFF.
THAT'S HOW WHOEVER DID THIS GOT TO THE *DRAGON COIN* IN THE FIRST PLACE.
AND HOW DOES THAT MAKE THINGS *BETTER,* EXACTLY?
YOU CAN'T PROVE DRAKKON WAS ALWAYS IN HIS CELL--
SURE, BUT EVEN IF HE *DID* LEAVE, YOU REALLY THINK HE'D ESCAPE JUST TO GO SAVE OUR LIVES AND THEN...HOP BACK INTO HIS CELL LIKE NOTHING HAPPENED?
THAT'S NOT REALLY HOW DRAKKON WORKS.
WELL, I... I DON'T KNOW... YET!
MAYBE HE'S JUST MESSING WITH US OR...MAYBE SOMEONE *MADE HIM* DO IT, OR MAYBE--

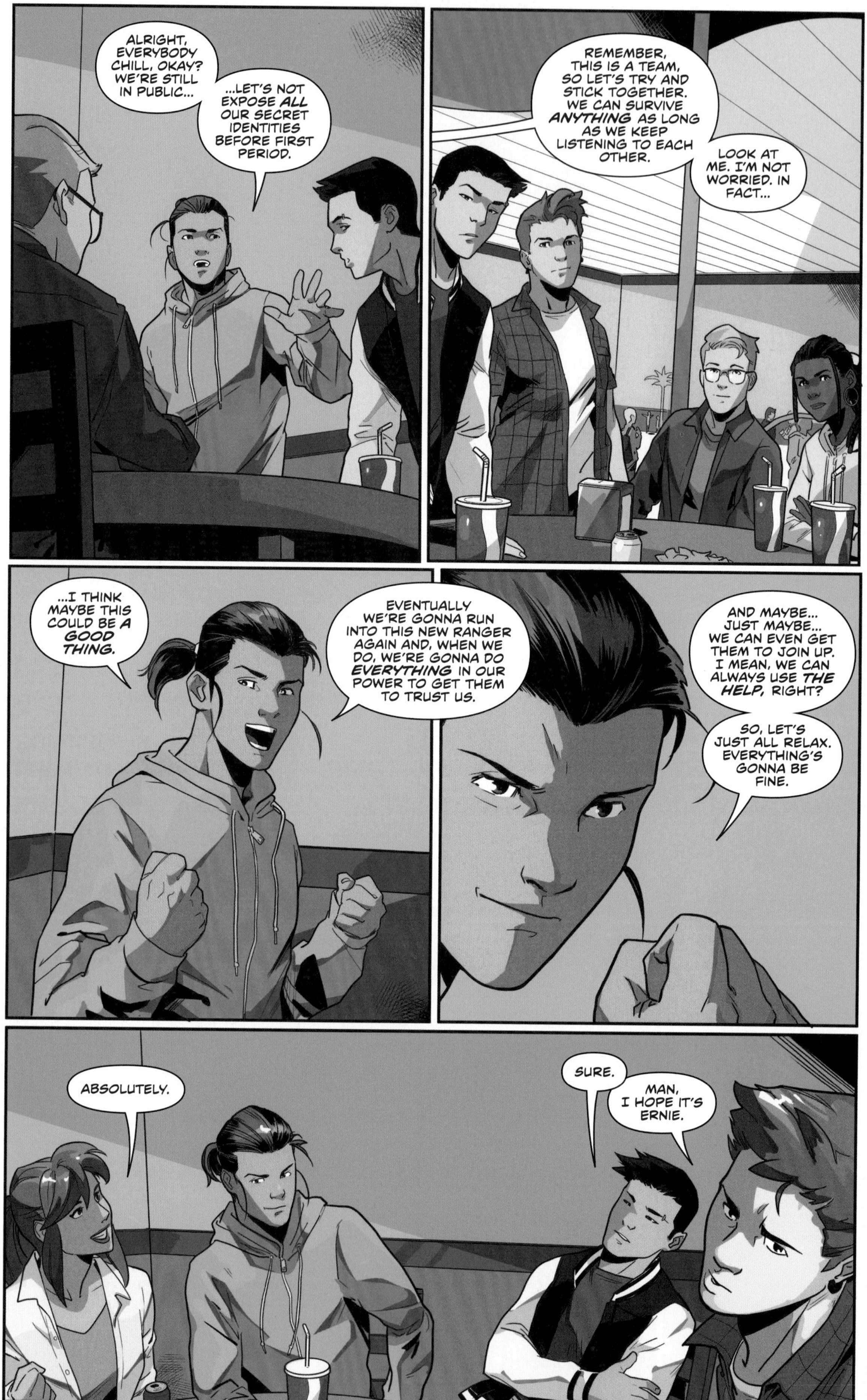
ALRIGHT, EVERYBODY CHILL, OKAY? WE'RE STILL IN PUBLIC...
...LET'S NOT EXPOSE ALL OUR SECRET IDENTITIES BEFORE FIRST PERIOD.
REMEMBER, THIS IS A TEAM, SO LET'S TRY AND STICK TOGETHER. WE CAN SURVIVE ANYTHING AS LONG AS WE KEEP LISTENING TO EACH OTHER.
LOOK AT ME. I'M NOT WORRIED. IN FACT...
...I THINK MAYBE THIS COULD BE A GOOD THING.
EVENTUALLY WE'RE GONNA RUN INTO THIS NEW RANGER AGAIN AND, WHEN WE DO, WE'RE GONNA DO EVERYTHING IN OUR POWER TO GET THEM TO TRUST US.
AND MAYBE... JUST MAYBE... WE CAN EVEN GET THEM TO JOIN UP. I MEAN, WE CAN ALWAYS USE THE HELP, RIGHT?
SO, LET'S JUST ALL RELAX. EVERYTHING'S GONNA BE FINE.
ABSOLUTELY.
SURE.
MAN, I HOPE IT'S ERNIE.

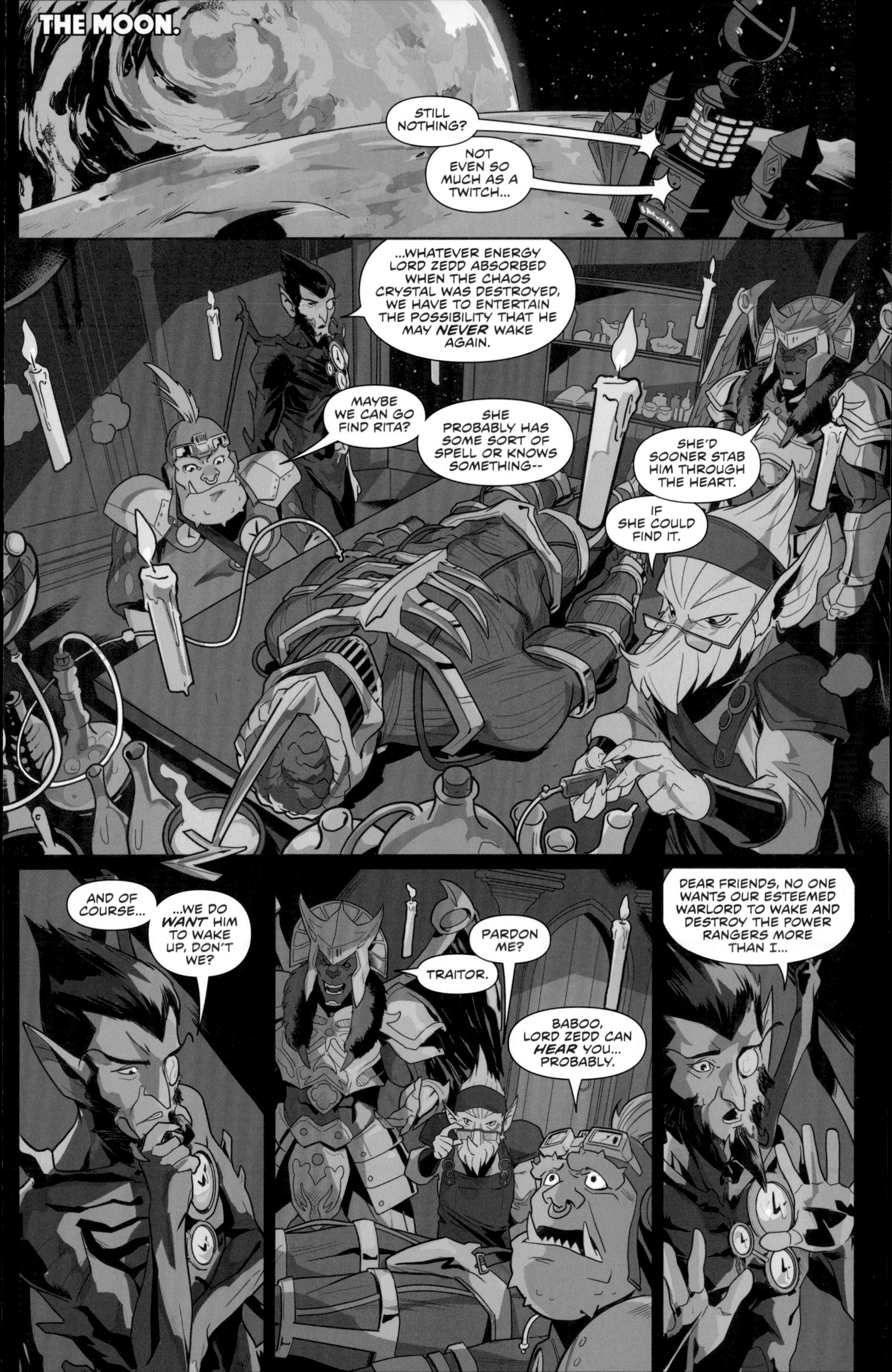
THE MOON.
STILL NOTHING?
NOT EVEN SO MUCH AS A TWITCH...
...WHATEVER ENERGY LORD ZEDD ABSORBED WHEN THE CHAOS CRYSTAL WAS DESTROYED, WE HAVE TO ENTERTAIN THE POSSIBILITY THAT HE MAY NEVER WAKE AGAIN.
MAYBE WE CAN GO FIND RITA?
SHE PROBABLY HAS SOME SORT OF SPELL OR KNOWS SOMETHING--
SHE'D SOONER STAB HIM THROUGH THE HEART.
IF SHE COULD FIND IT.
AND OF COURSE...
...WE DO WANT HIM TO WAKE UP, DON'T WE?
PARDON ME?
TRAITOR.
BABOO, LORD ZEDD CAN HEAR YOU... PROBABLY.
DEAR FRIENDS, NO ONE WANTS OUR ESTEEMED WARLORD TO WAKE AND DESTROY THE POWER RANGERS MORE THAN I...

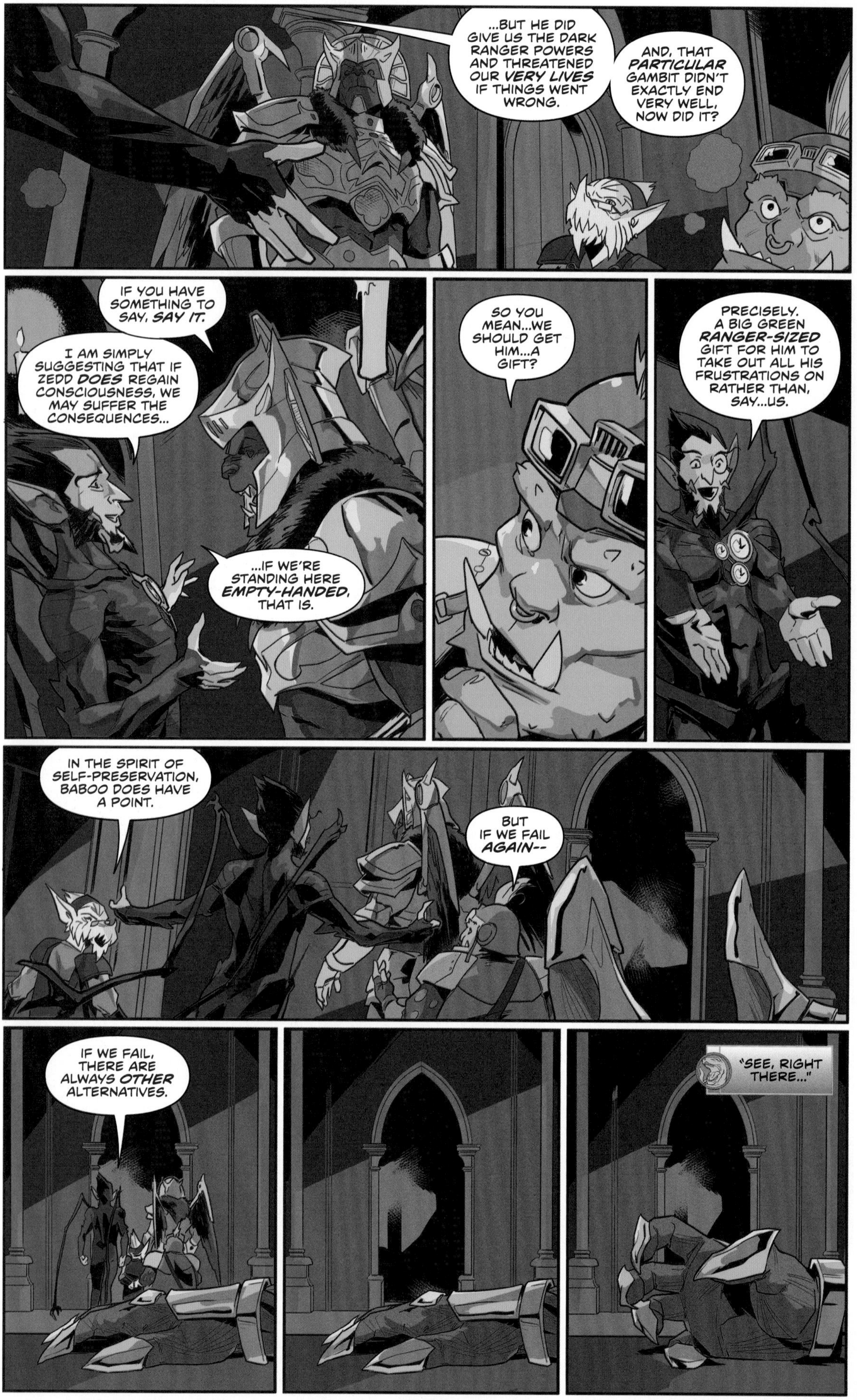
...BUT HE DID GIVE US THE DARK RANGER POWERS AND THREATENED OUR *VERY LIVES* IF THINGS WENT WRONG.
AND, THAT *PARTICULAR* GAMBIT DIDN'T EXACTLY END VERY WELL, NOW DID IT?
IF YOU HAVE SOMETHING TO SAY, *SAY IT.*
I AM SIMPLY SUGGESTING THAT IF ZEDD *DOES* REGAIN CONSCIOUSNESS, WE MAY SUFFER THE CONSEQUENCES...
...IF WE'RE STANDING HERE *EMPTY-HANDED,* THAT IS.
SO YOU MEAN...WE SHOULD GET HIM...A GIFT?
PRECISELY. A BIG GREEN *RANGER-SIZED* GIFT FOR HIM TO TAKE OUT ALL HIS FRUSTRATIONS ON RATHER THAN, SAY...US.
IN THE SPIRIT OF SELF-PRESERVATION, BABOO DOES HAVE A POINT.
BUT IF WE FAIL *AGAIN--*
IF WE FAIL, THERE ARE ALWAYS *OTHER* ALTERNATIVES.
"SEE, RIGHT THERE..."

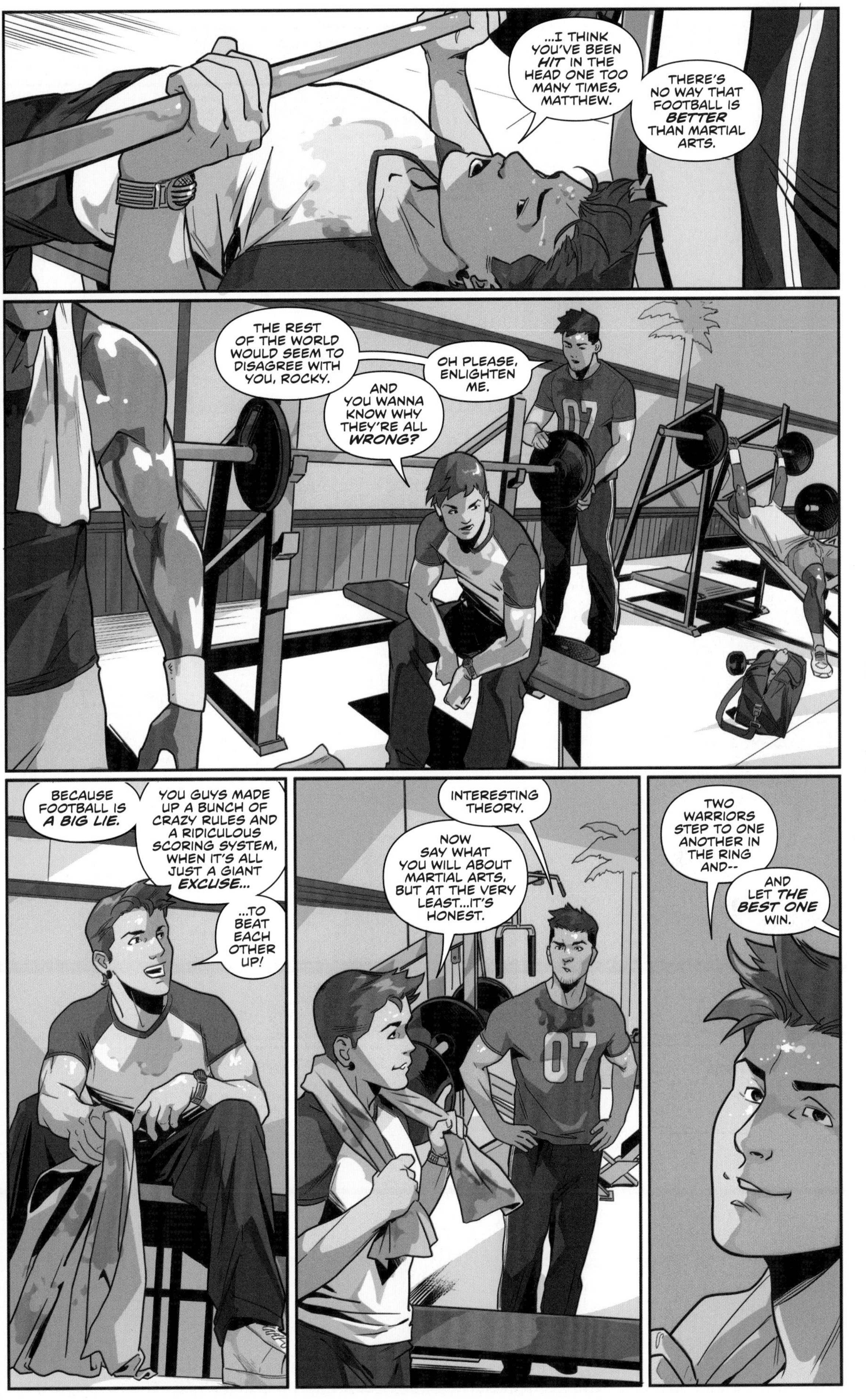
...I THINK YOU'VE BEEN *HIT* IN THE HEAD ONE TOO MANY TIMES, MATTHEW.
THERE'S NO WAY THAT FOOTBALL IS *BETTER* THAN MARTIAL ARTS.
THE REST OF THE WORLD WOULD SEEM TO DISAGREE WITH YOU, ROCKY.
OH PLEASE, ENLIGHTEN ME.
AND YOU WANNA KNOW WHY THEY'RE ALL *WRONG?*
BECAUSE FOOTBALL IS *A BIG LIE.*
YOU GUYS MADE UP A BUNCH OF CRAZY RULES AND A RIDICULOUS SCORING SYSTEM, WHEN IT'S ALL JUST A GIANT *EXCUSE...*
...TO BEAT EACH OTHER UP!
INTERESTING THEORY.
NOW SAY WHAT YOU WILL ABOUT MARTIAL ARTS, BUT AT THE VERY LEAST...IT'S HONEST.
TWO WARRIORS STEP TO ONE ANOTHER IN THE RING AND--
AND LET *THE BEST ONE* WIN.
07

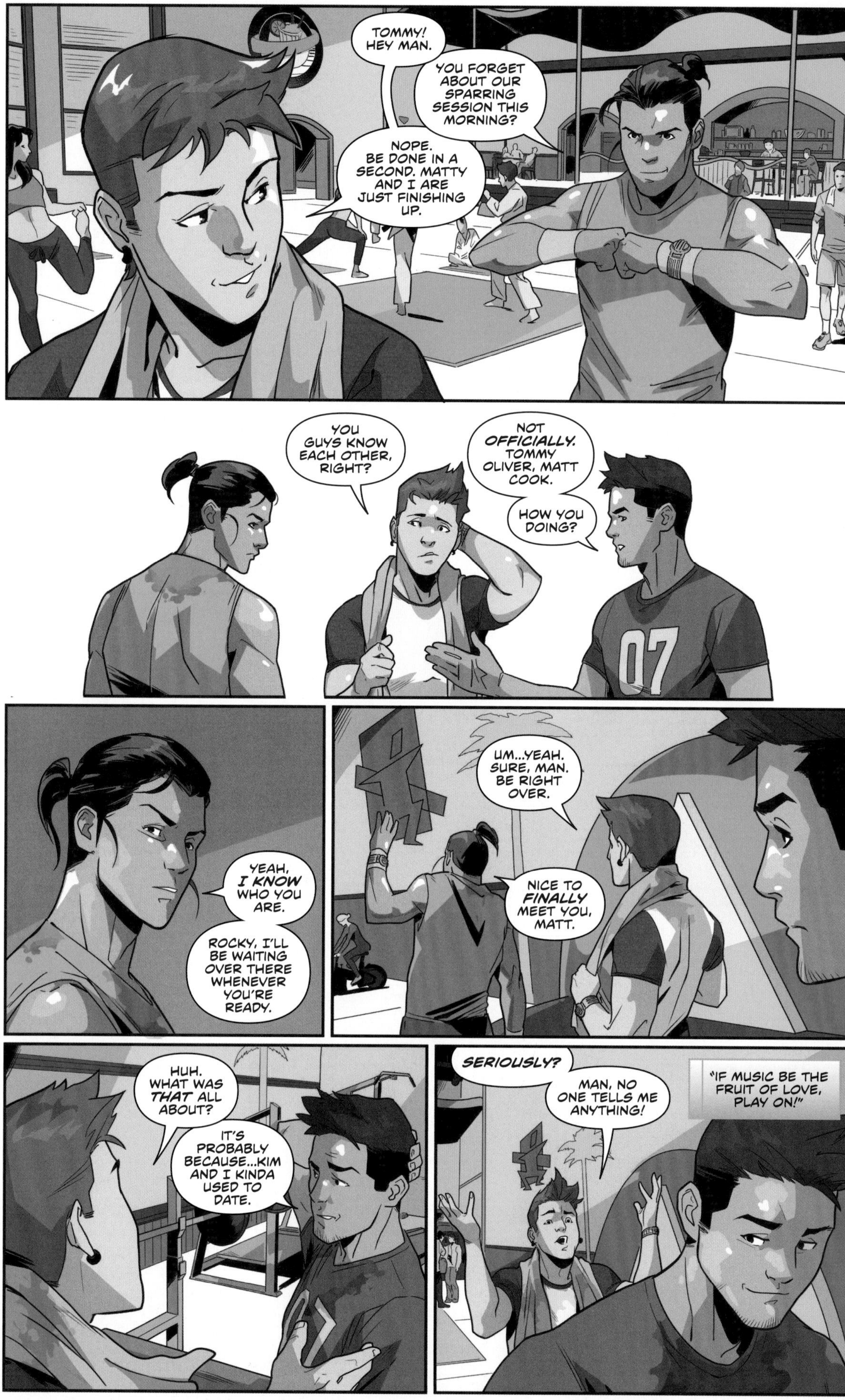
TOMMY! HEY MAN.
YOU FORGET ABOUT OUR SPARRING SESSION THIS MORNING?
NOPE. BE DONE IN A SECOND. MATTY AND I ARE JUST FINISHING UP.
YOU GUYS KNOW EACH OTHER, RIGHT?
NOT *OFFICIALLY*. TOMMY OLIVER, MATT COOK.
HOW YOU DOING?
07
YEAH, ***I KNOW*** WHO YOU ARE.
ROCKY, I'LL BE WAITING OVER THERE WHENEVER YOU'RE READY.
UM...YEAH. SURE, MAN. BE RIGHT OVER.
NICE TO ***FINALLY*** MEET YOU, MATT.
HUH. WHAT WAS ***THAT*** ALL ABOUT?
IT'S PROBABLY BECAUSE...KIM AND I KINDA USED TO DATE.
***SERIOUSLY?***
MAN, NO ONE TELLS ME ANYTHING!
"IF MUSIC BE THE FRUIT OF LOVE, PLAY ON!"

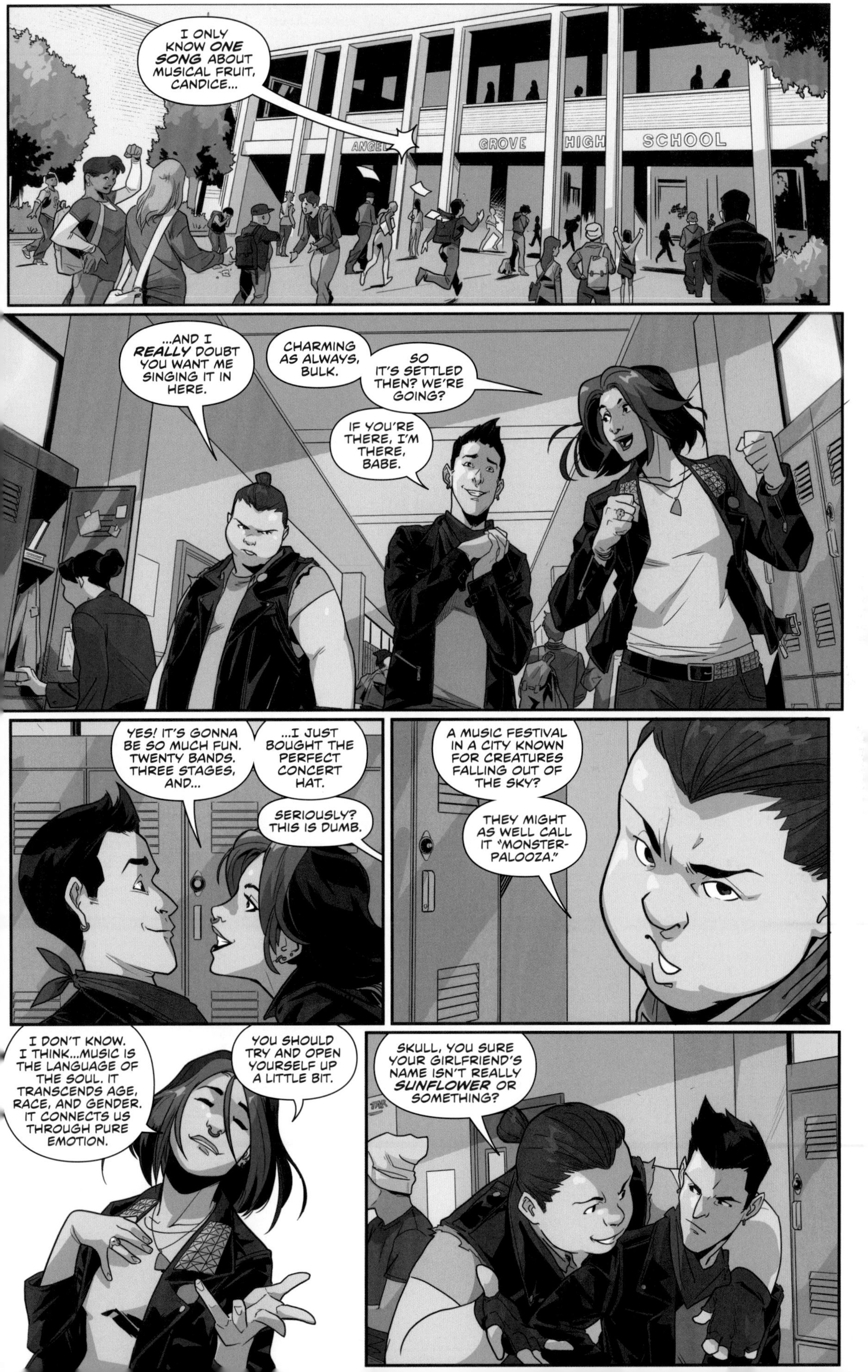
I ONLY KNOW ONE SONG ABOUT MUSICAL FRUIT, CANDICE...
ANGEL GROVE HIGH SCHOOL
...AND I REALLY DOUBT YOU WANT ME SINGING IT IN HERE.
CHARMING AS ALWAYS, BULK.
SO IT'S SETTLED THEN? WE'RE GOING?
IF YOU'RE THERE, I'M THERE, BABE.
YES! IT'S GONNA BE SO MUCH FUN. TWENTY BANDS. THREE STAGES, AND...
...I JUST BOUGHT THE PERFECT CONCERT HAT.
SERIOUSLY? THIS IS DUMB.
A MUSIC FESTIVAL IN A CITY KNOWN FOR CREATURES FALLING OUT OF THE SKY?
THEY MIGHT AS WELL CALL IT "MONSTER-PALOOZA."
I DON'T KNOW. I THINK...MUSIC IS THE LANGUAGE OF THE SOUL. IT TRANSCENDS AGE, RACE, AND GENDER. IT CONNECTS US THROUGH PURE EMOTION.
YOU SHOULD TRY AND OPEN YOURSELF UP A LITTLE BIT.
SKULL, YOU SURE YOUR GIRLFRIEND'S NAME ISN'T REALLY SUNFLOWER OR SOMETHING?

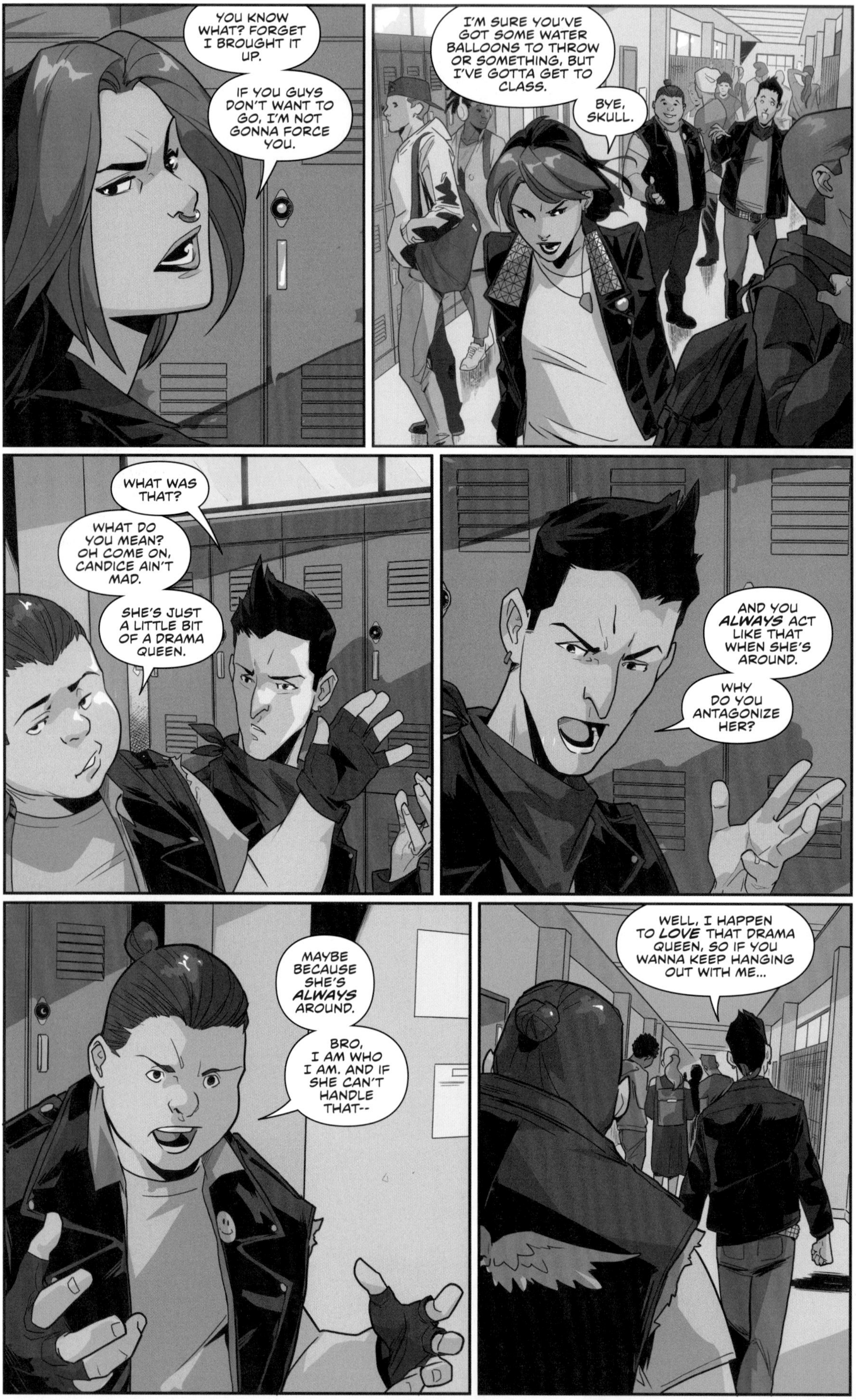
YOU KNOW WHAT? FORGET I BROUGHT IT UP.
IF YOU GUYS DON'T WANT TO GO, I'M NOT GONNA FORCE YOU.
I'M SURE YOU'VE GOT SOME WATER BALLOONS TO THROW OR SOMETHING, BUT I'VE GOTTA GET TO CLASS.
BYE, SKULL.
WHAT WAS THAT?
WHAT DO YOU MEAN? OH COME ON, CANDICE AIN'T MAD.
SHE'S JUST A LITTLE BIT OF A DRAMA QUEEN.
AND YOU ALWAYS ACT LIKE THAT WHEN SHE'S AROUND.
WHY DO YOU ANTAGONIZE HER?
MAYBE BECAUSE SHE'S ALWAYS AROUND.
BRO, I AM WHO I AM. AND IF SHE CAN'T HANDLE THAT--
WELL, I HAPPEN TO LOVE THAT DRAMA QUEEN, SO IF YOU WANNA KEEP HANGING OUT WITH ME...

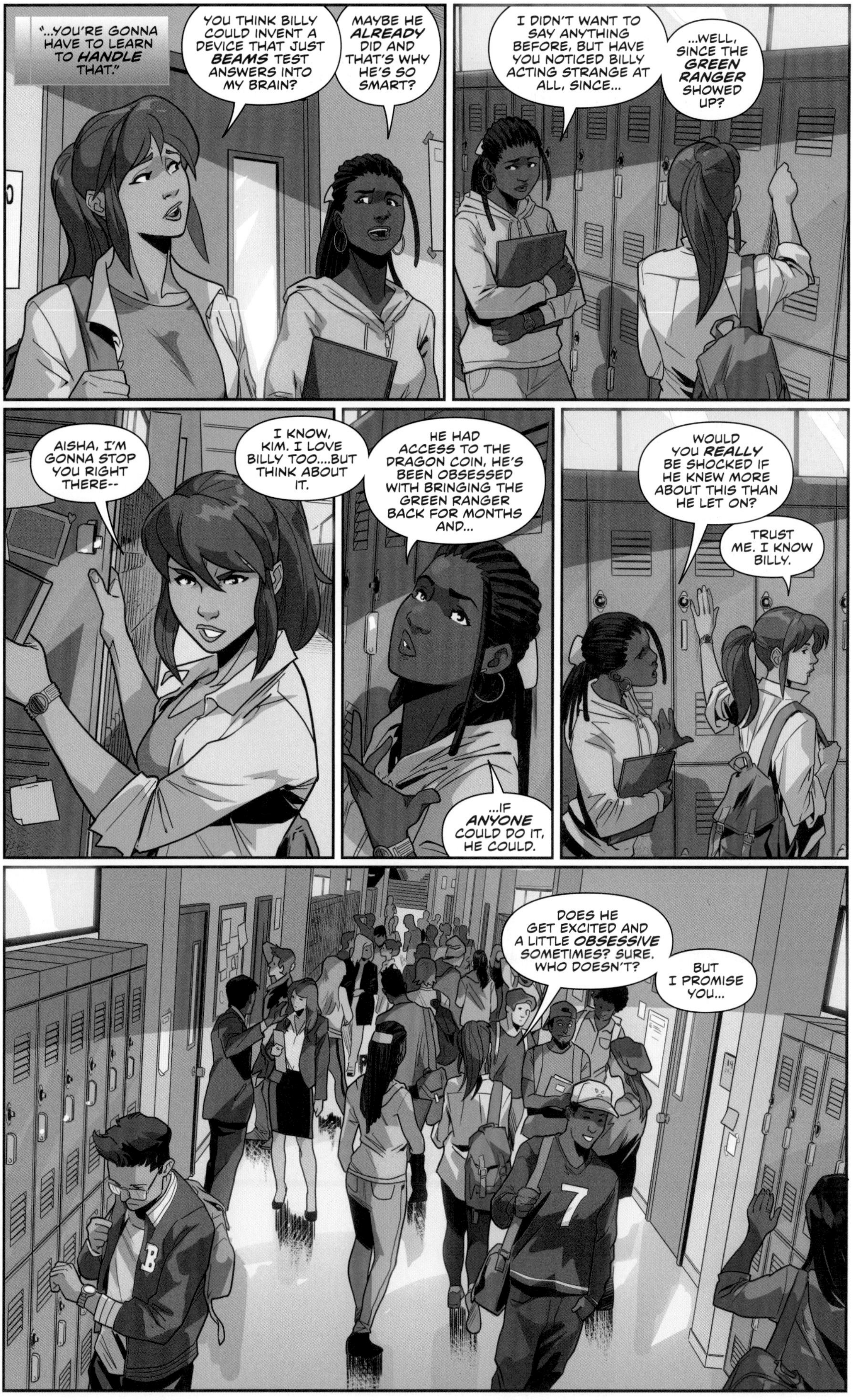
"...YOU'RE GONNA HAVE TO LEARN TO *HANDLE* THAT."
YOU THINK BILLY COULD INVENT A DEVICE THAT JUST *BEAMS* TEST ANSWERS INTO MY BRAIN?
MAYBE HE *ALREADY* DID AND THAT'S WHY HE'S SO SMART?
I DIDN'T WANT TO SAY ANYTHING BEFORE, BUT HAVE YOU NOTICED BILLY ACTING STRANGE AT ALL, SINCE...
...WELL, SINCE THE *GREEN RANGER* SHOWED UP?
AISHA, I'M GONNA STOP YOU RIGHT THERE--
I KNOW, KIM. I LOVE BILLY TOO....BUT THINK ABOUT IT.
HE HAD ACCESS TO THE DRAGON COIN, HE'S BEEN OBSESSED WITH BRINGING THE GREEN RANGER BACK FOR MONTHS AND...
...IF *ANYONE* COULD DO IT, HE COULD.
WOULD YOU *REALLY* BE SHOCKED IF HE KNEW MORE ABOUT THIS THAN HE LET ON?
TRUST ME. I KNOW BILLY.
DOES HE GET EXCITED AND A LITTLE *OBSESSIVE* SOMETIMES? SURE. WHO DOESN'T?
BUT I PROMISE YOU...

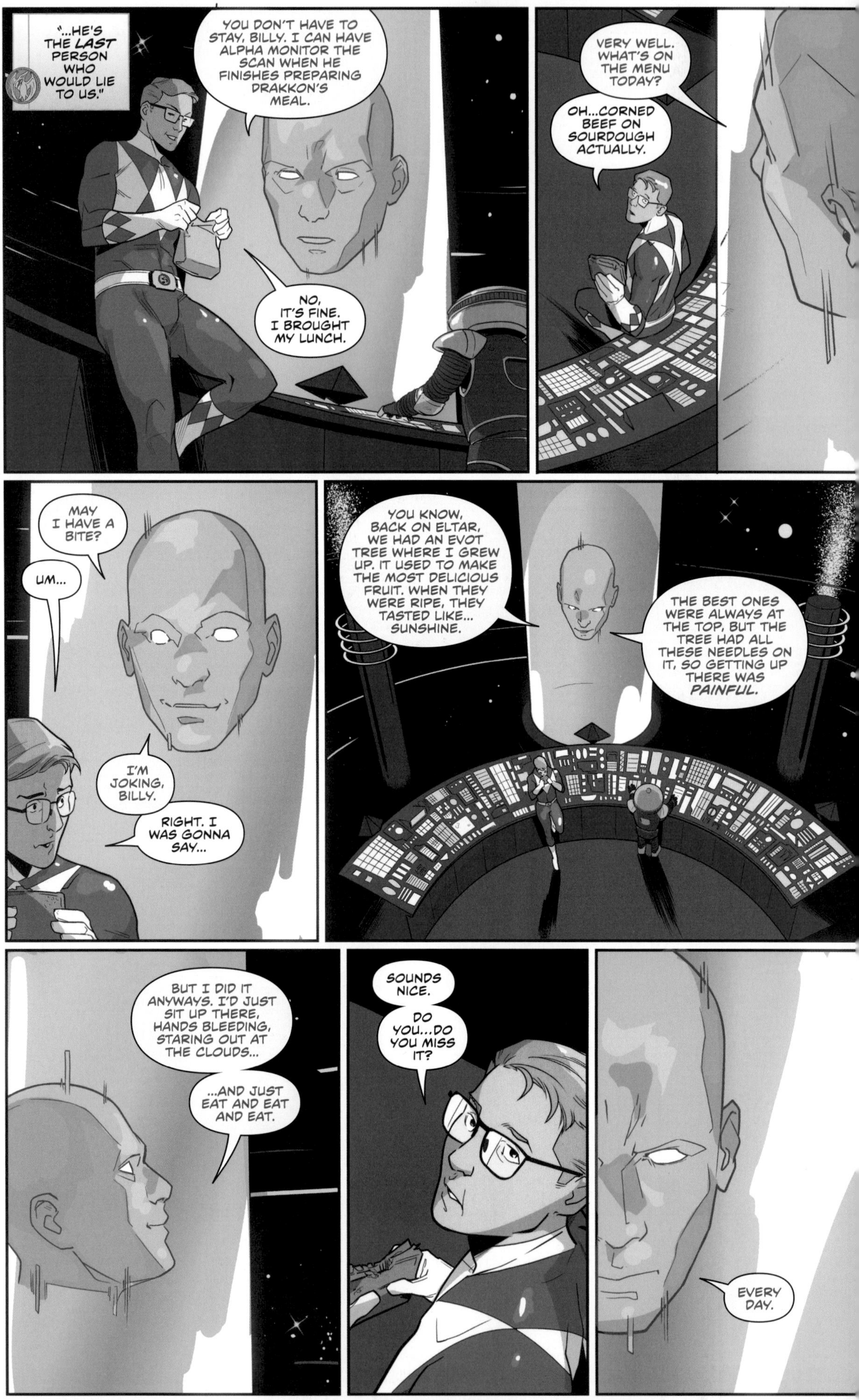

"...HE'S THE LAST PERSON WHO WOULD LIE TO US."
YOU DON'T HAVE TO STAY, BILLY. I CAN HAVE ALPHA MONITOR THE SCAN WHEN HE FINISHES PREPARING DRAKKON'S MEAL.
NO, IT'S FINE. I BROUGHT MY LUNCH.
VERY WELL. WHAT'S ON THE MENU TODAY?
OH...CORNED BEEF ON SOURDOUGH ACTUALLY.
MAY I HAVE A BITE?
UM...
I'M JOKING, BILLY.
RIGHT. I WAS GONNA SAY...
YOU KNOW, BACK ON ELTAR, WE HAD AN EVOT TREE WHERE I GREW UP. IT USED TO MAKE THE MOST DELICIOUS FRUIT. WHEN THEY WERE RIPE, THEY TASTED LIKE... SUNSHINE.
THE BEST ONES WERE ALWAYS AT THE TOP, BUT THE TREE HAD ALL THESE NEEDLES ON IT, SO GETTING UP THERE WAS PAINFUL.
BUT I DID IT ANYWAYS. I'D JUST SIT UP THERE, HANDS BLEEDING, STARING OUT AT THE CLOUDS...
...AND JUST EAT AND EAT AND EAT.
SOUNDS NICE.
DO YOU...DO YOU MISS IT?
EVERY DAY.

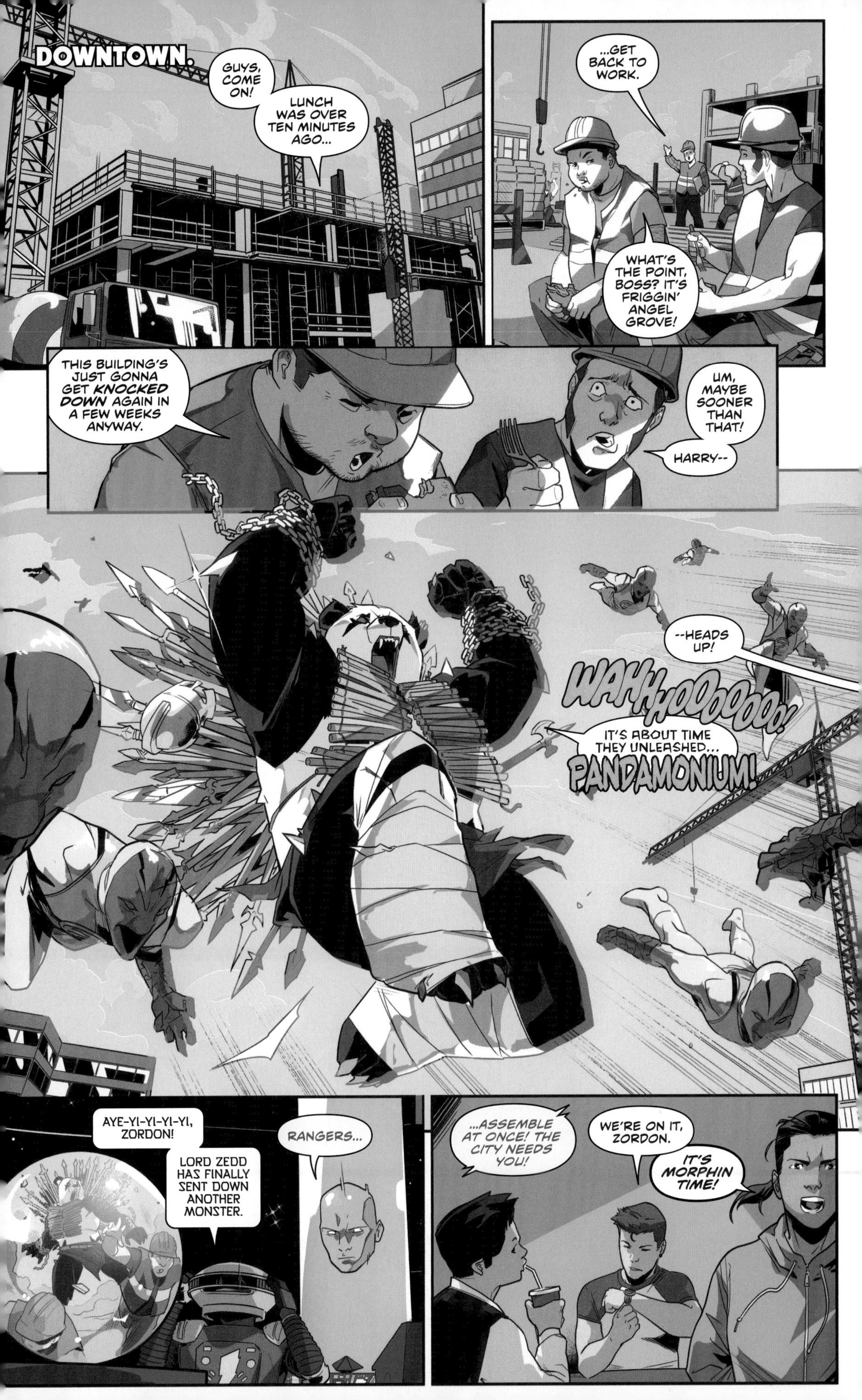
DOWNTOWN.
GUYS, COME ON!
LUNCH WAS OVER TEN MINUTES AGO...
...GET BACK TO WORK.
WHAT'S THE POINT, BOSS? IT'S FRIGGIN' ANGEL GROVE!
THIS BUILDING'S JUST GONNA GET KNOCKED DOWN AGAIN IN A FEW WEEKS ANYWAY.
UM, MAYBE SOONER THAN THAT!
HARRY--
--HEADS UP!
WAHHOOOOOOO!
IT'S ABOUT TIME THEY UNLEASHED... PANDAMONIUM!
AYE-YI-YI-YI-YI, ZORDON!
LORD ZEDD HAS FINALLY SENT DOWN ANOTHER MONSTER.
RANGERS...
...ASSEMBLE AT ONCE! THE CITY NEEDS YOU!
WE'RE ON IT, ZORDON.
IT'S MORPHIN TIME!

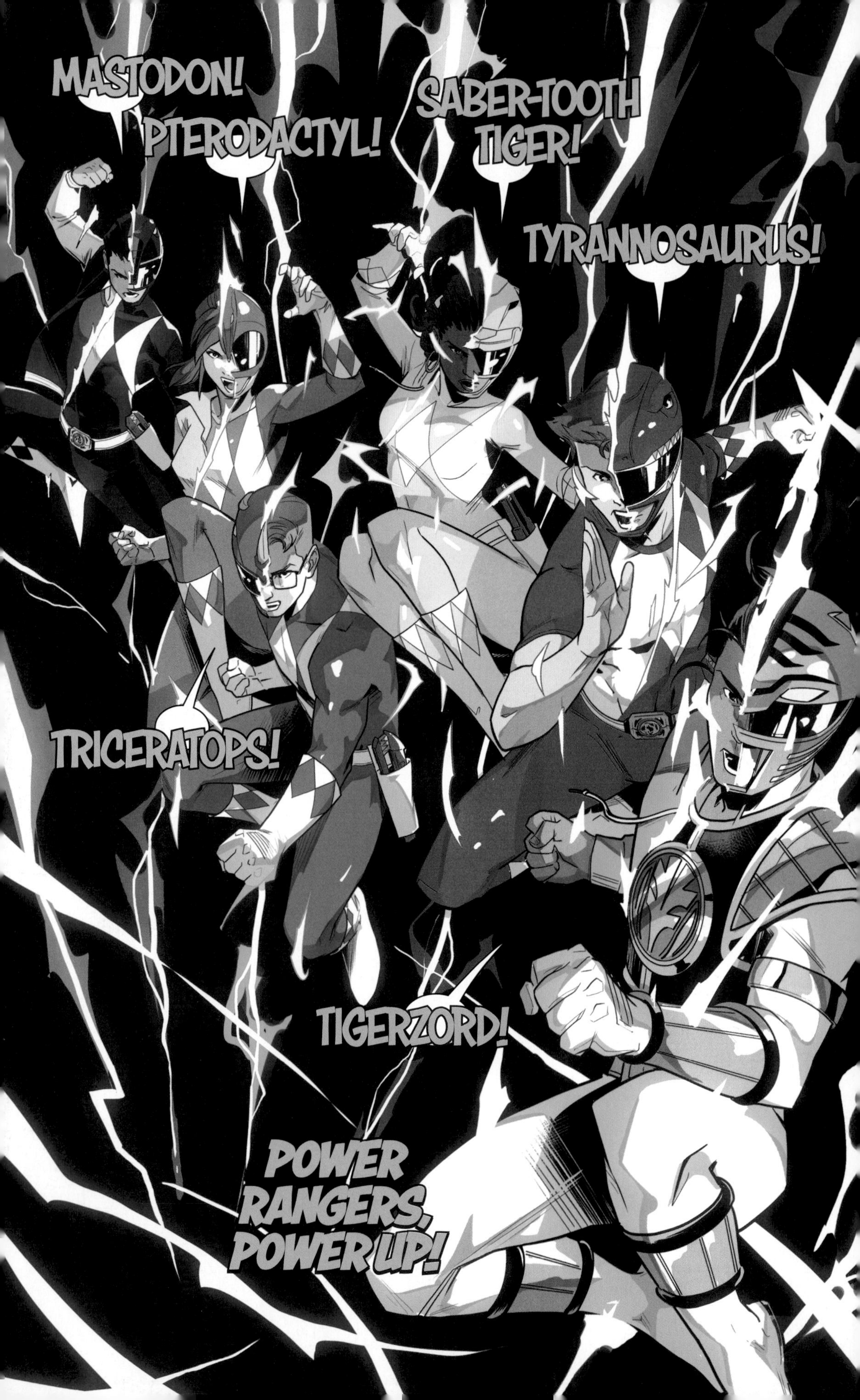
MASTODON!
PTERODACTYL!
SABER-TOOTH TIGER!
TYRANNOSAURUS!
TRICERATOPS!
TIGERZORD!
POWER RANGERS, POWER UP!

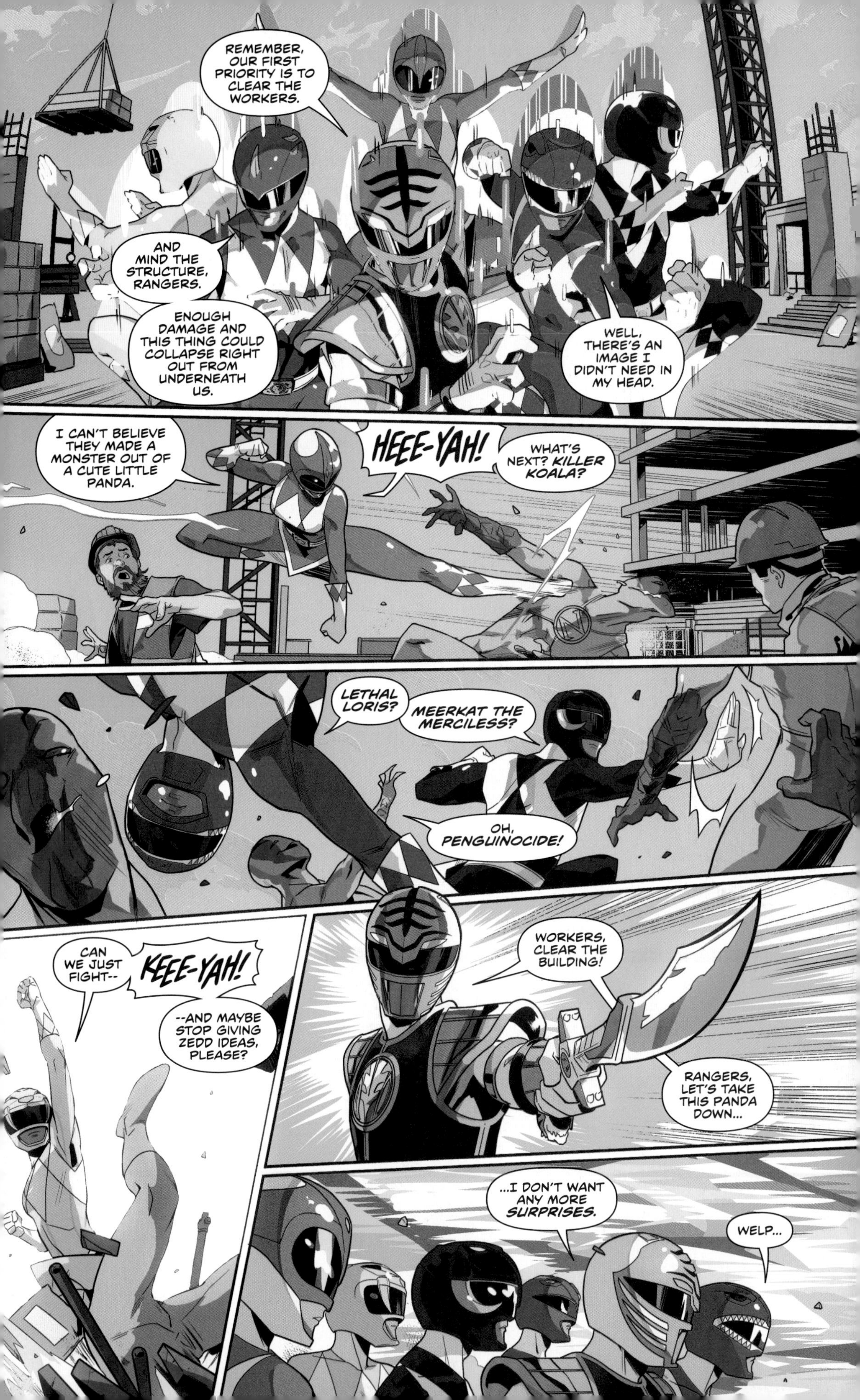
REMEMBER, OUR FIRST PRIORITY IS TO CLEAR THE WORKERS.
AND MIND THE STRUCTURE, RANGERS.
ENOUGH DAMAGE AND THIS THING COULD COLLAPSE RIGHT OUT FROM UNDERNEATH US.
WELL, THERE'S AN IMAGE I DIDN'T NEED IN MY HEAD.
I CAN'T BELIEVE THEY MADE A MONSTER OUT OF A CUTE LITTLE PANDA.
HEEE-YAH!
WHAT'S NEXT? KILLER KOALA?
LETHAL LORIS?
MEERKAT THE MERCILESS?
OH, PENGUINOCIDE!
CAN WE JUST FIGHT--
KEEE-YAH!
--AND MAYBE STOP GIVING ZEDD IDEAS, PLEASE?
WORKERS, CLEAR THE BUILDING!
RANGERS, LET'S TAKE THIS PANDA DOWN...
...I DON'T WANT ANY MORE SURPRISES.
WELP...

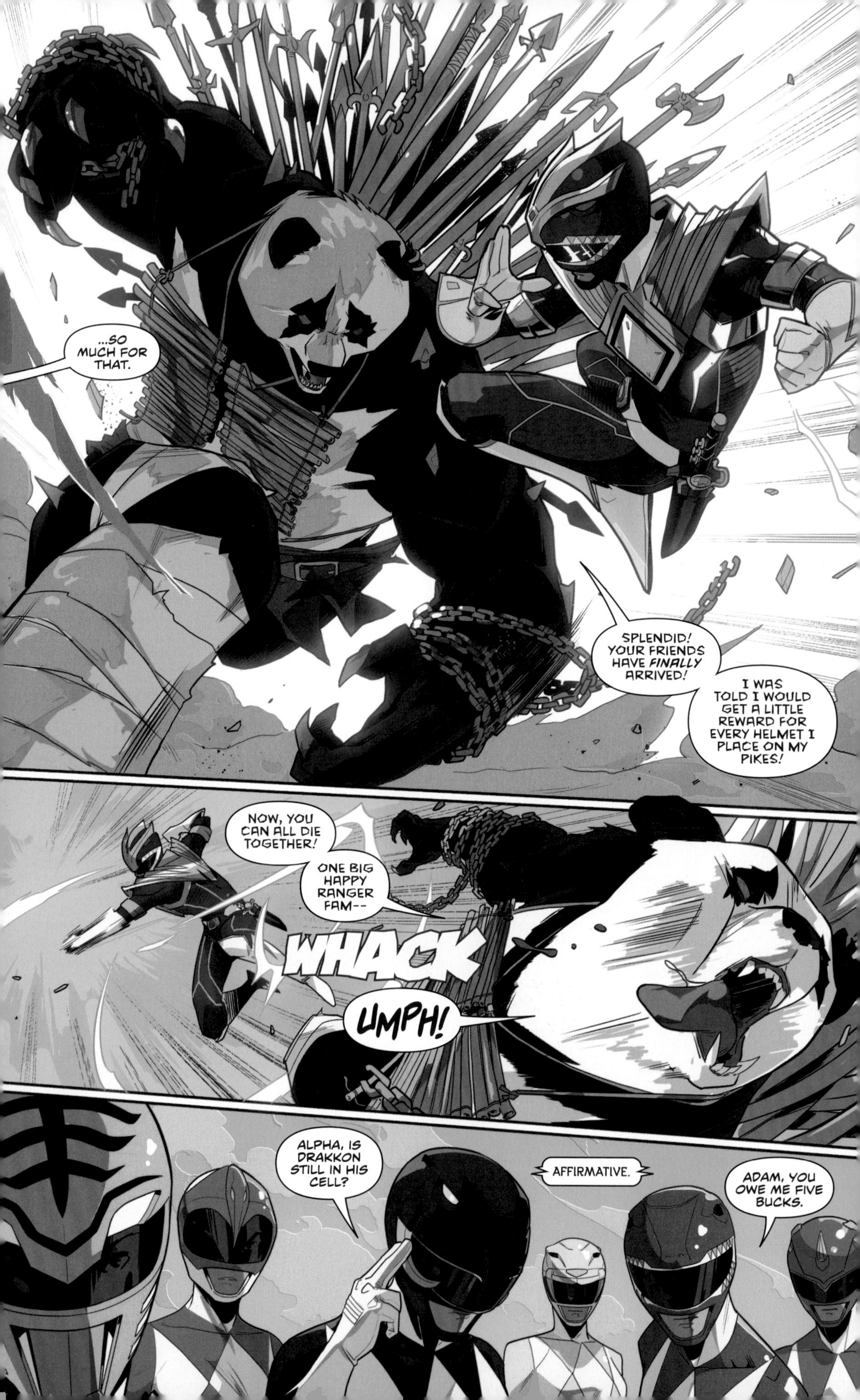
...SO MUCH FOR THAT.
SPLENDID! YOUR FRIENDS HAVE *FINALLY* ARRIVED!
I WAS TOLD I WOULD GET A LITTLE REWARD FOR EVERY HELMET I PLACE ON MY PIKES!
NOW, YOU CAN ALL DIE TOGETHER!
ONE BIG HAPPY RANGER FAM--
WHACK
UMPH!
ALPHA, IS DRAKKON STILL IN HIS CELL?
AFFIRMATIVE.
ADAM, YOU OWE ME FIVE BUCKS.

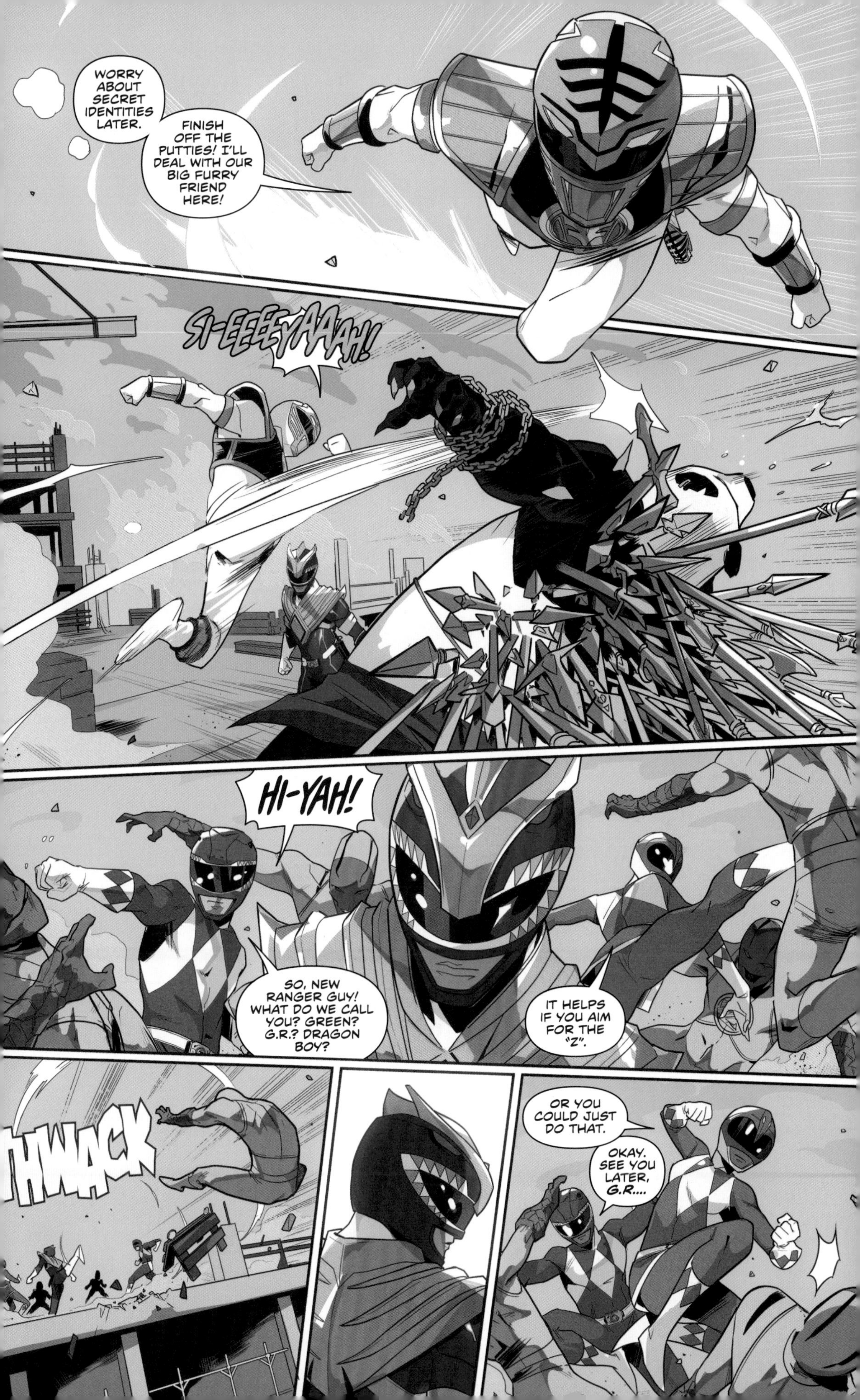
WORRY ABOUT SECRET IDENTITIES LATER.
FINISH OFF THE PUTTIES! I'LL DEAL WITH OUR BIG FURRY FRIEND HERE!
SI-EEEEYAAAAH!
HI-YAH!
SO, NEW RANGER GUY! WHAT DO WE CALL YOU? GREEN? G.R.? DRAGON BOY?
IT HELPS IF YOU AIM FOR THE "Z".
THWACK
OR YOU COULD JUST DO THAT.
OKAY. SEE YOU LATER, G.R....

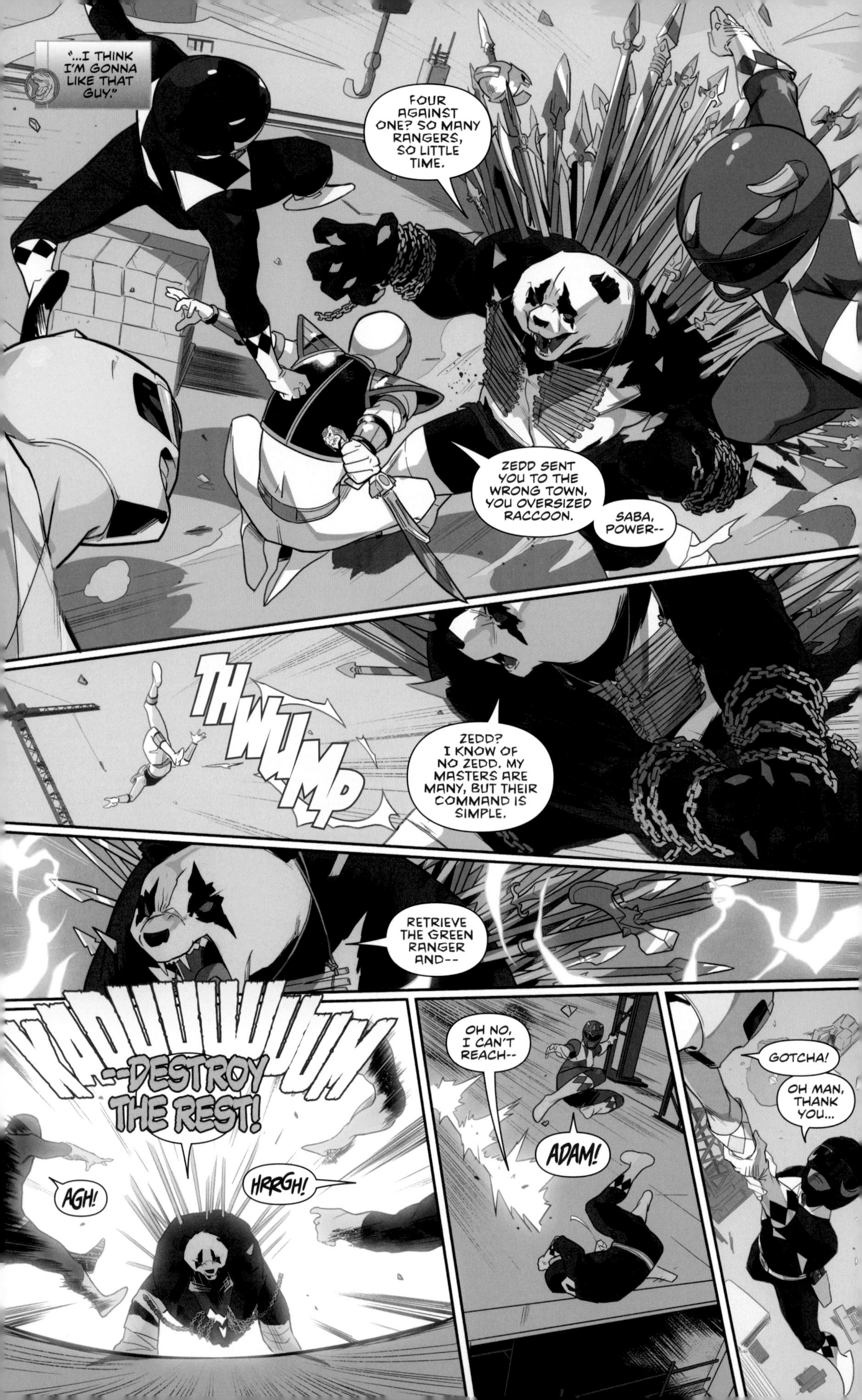
"...I THINK I'M GONNA LIKE THAT GUY."
FOUR AGAINST ONE? SO MANY RANGERS, SO LITTLE TIME.
ZEDD SENT YOU TO THE WRONG TOWN, YOU OVERSIZED RACCOON.
SABA, POWER--
THWUMP
ZEDD? I KNOW OF NO ZEDD. MY MASTERS ARE MANY, BUT THEIR COMMAND IS SIMPLE.
RETRIEVE THE GREEN RANGER AND--
--DESTROY THE REST!
AGH!
HRRGH!
OH NO, I CAN'T REACH--
ADAM!
GOTCHA!
OH MAN, THANK YOU...

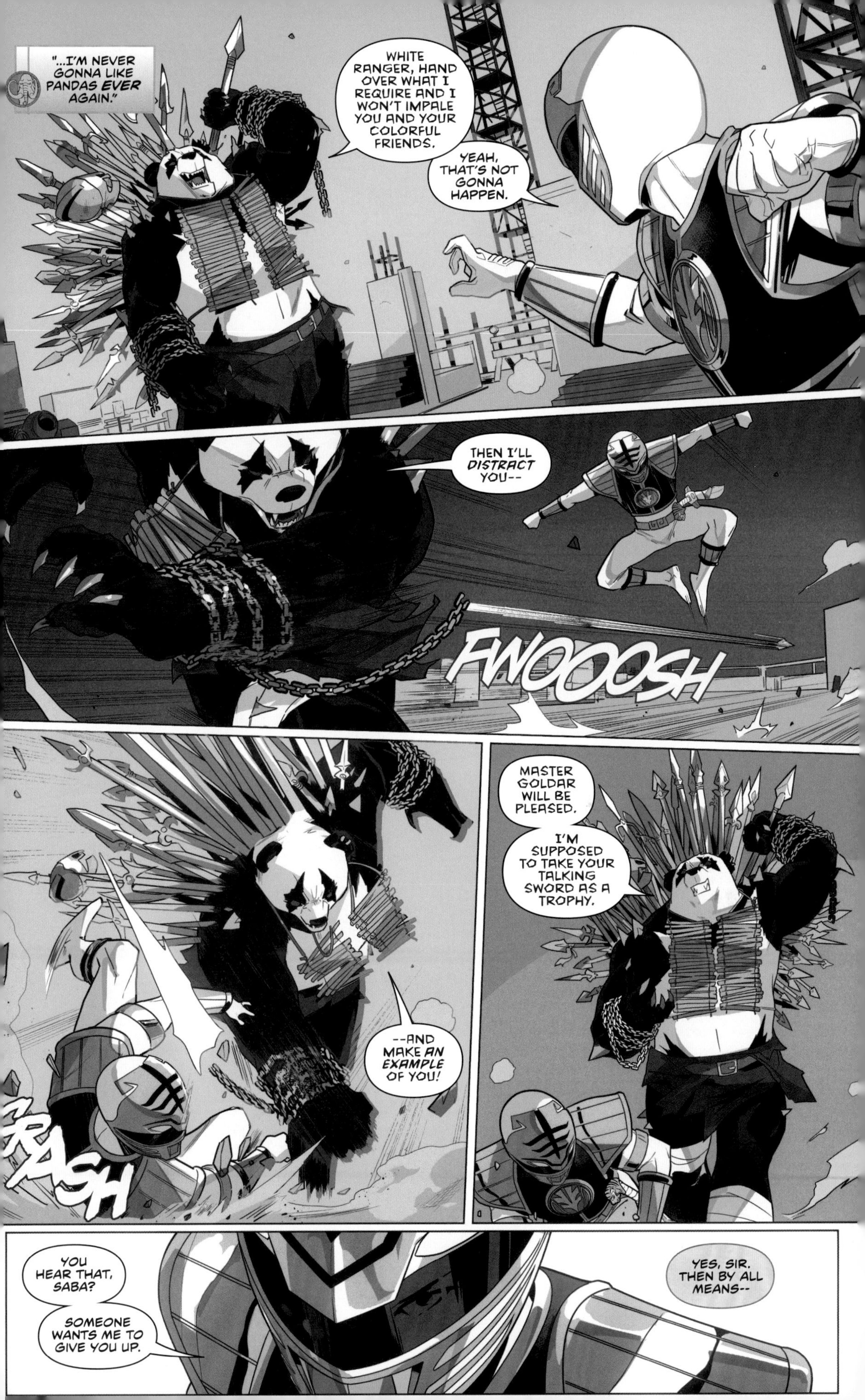
"...I'M NEVER GONNA LIKE PANDAS EVER AGAIN."
WHITE RANGER, HAND OVER WHAT I REQUIRE AND I WON'T IMPALE YOU AND YOUR COLORFUL FRIENDS.
YEAH, THAT'S NOT GONNA HAPPEN.
THEN I'LL DISTRACT YOU--
FWOOOSH
--AND MAKE AN EXAMPLE OF YOU!
CRASH
MASTER GOLDAR WILL BE PLEASED.
I'M SUPPOSED TO TAKE YOUR TALKING SWORD AS A TROPHY.
YOU HEAR THAT, SABA?
SOMEONE WANTS ME TO GIVE YOU UP.
YES, SIR. THEN BY ALL MEANS--

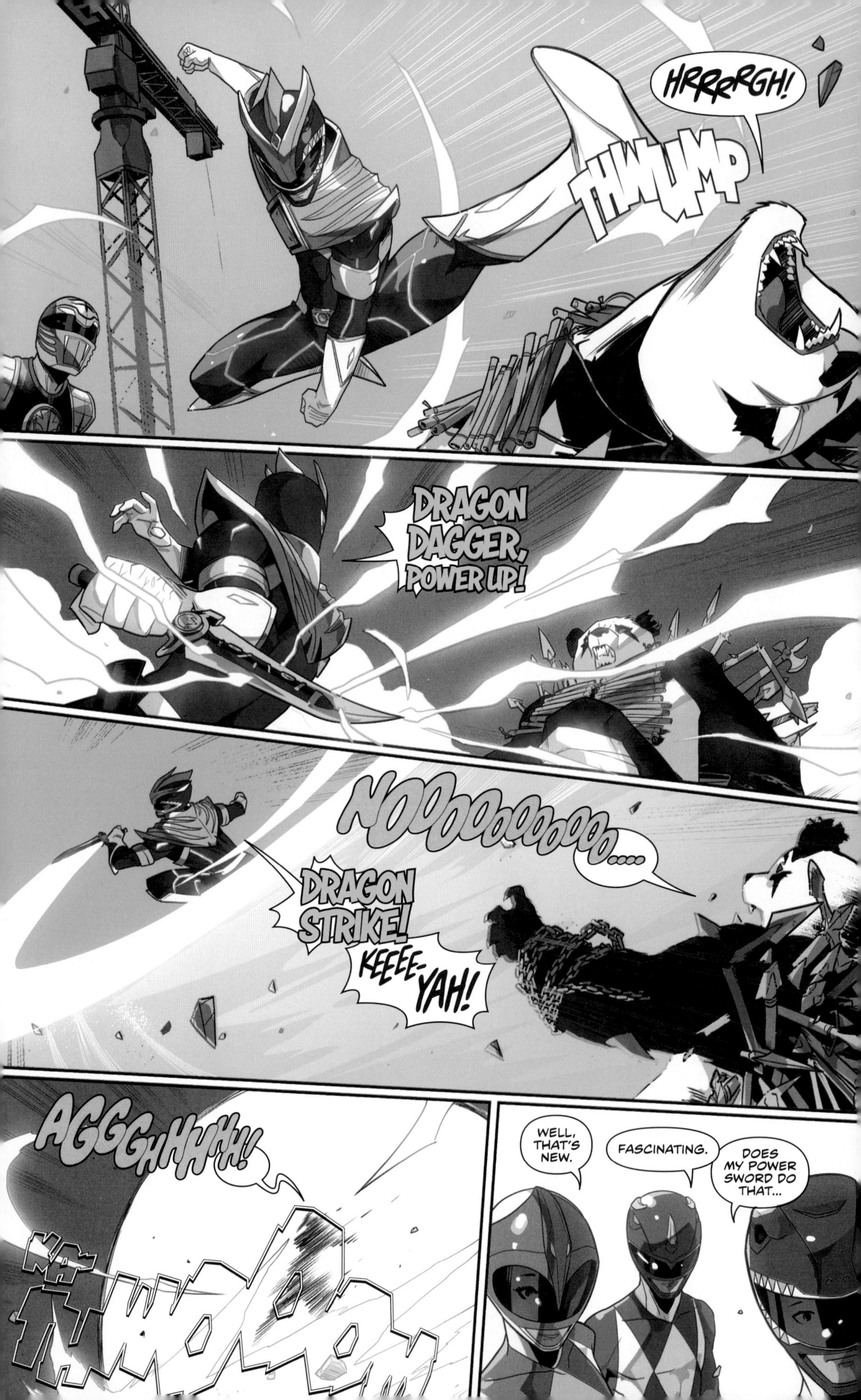
HRRRRGH!
THWUMP
DRAGON DAGGER, POWER UP!
NOOOOOOOOOOOO....
DRAGON STRIKE!
KEEEE-YAH!
AGGGHHHHH!
KA THWOOM
WELL, THAT'S NEW.
FASCINATING.
DOES MY POWER SWORD DO THAT...

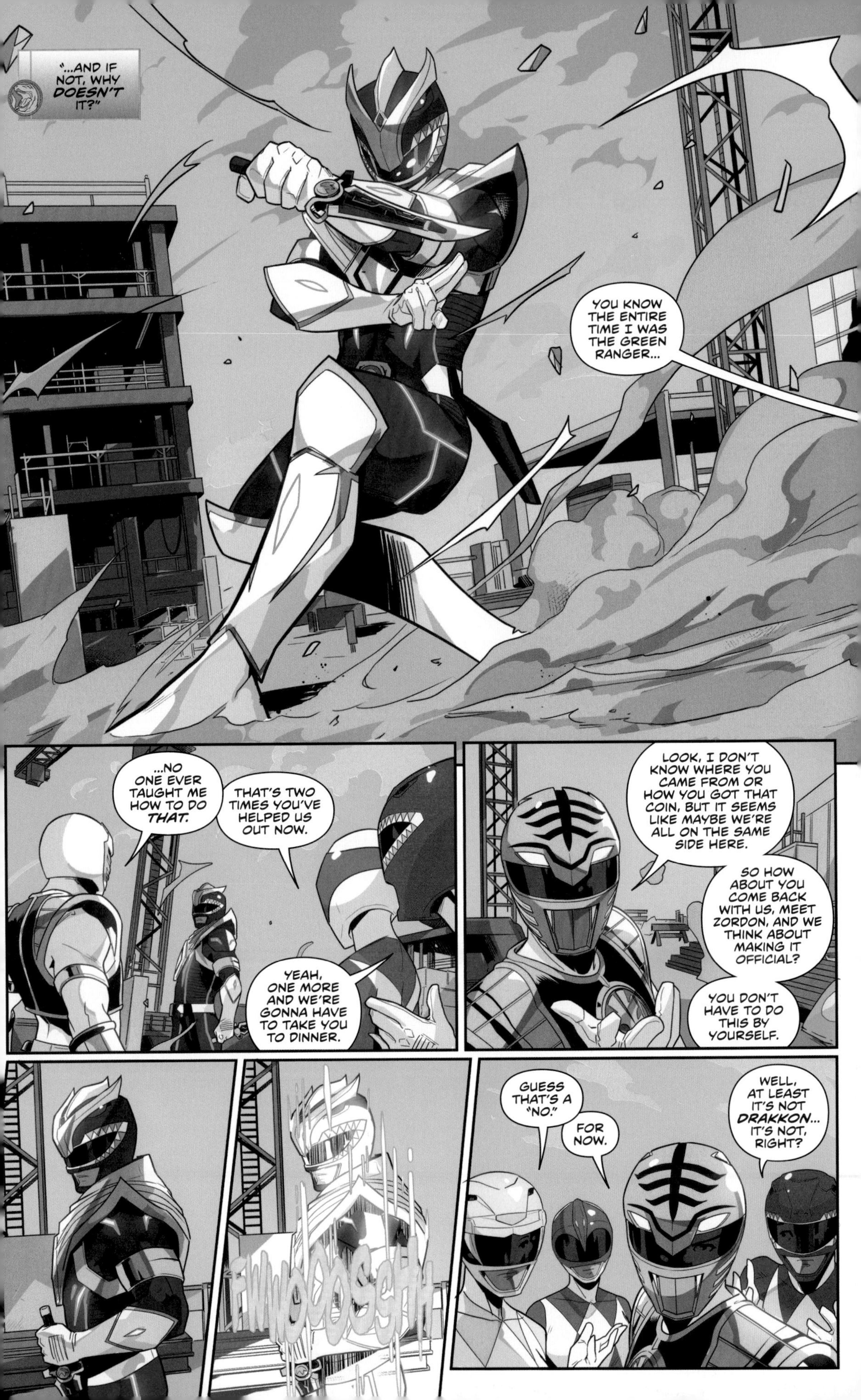
"...AND IF NOT, WHY DOESN'T IT?"
YOU KNOW THE ENTIRE TIME I WAS THE GREEN RANGER...
...NO ONE EVER TAUGHT ME HOW TO DO THAT.
THAT'S TWO TIMES YOU'VE HELPED US OUT NOW.
YEAH, ONE MORE AND WE'RE GONNA HAVE TO TAKE YOU TO DINNER.
LOOK, I DON'T KNOW WHERE YOU CAME FROM OR HOW YOU GOT THAT COIN, BUT IT SEEMS LIKE MAYBE WE'RE ALL ON THE SAME SIDE HERE.
SO HOW ABOUT YOU COME BACK WITH US, MEET ZORDON, AND WE THINK ABOUT MAKING IT OFFICIAL?
YOU DON'T HAVE TO DO THIS BY YOURSELF.
FWWOOOSSHH
GUESS THAT'S A "NO."
FOR NOW.
WELL, AT LEAST IT'S NOT DRAKKON... IT'S NOT, RIGHT?

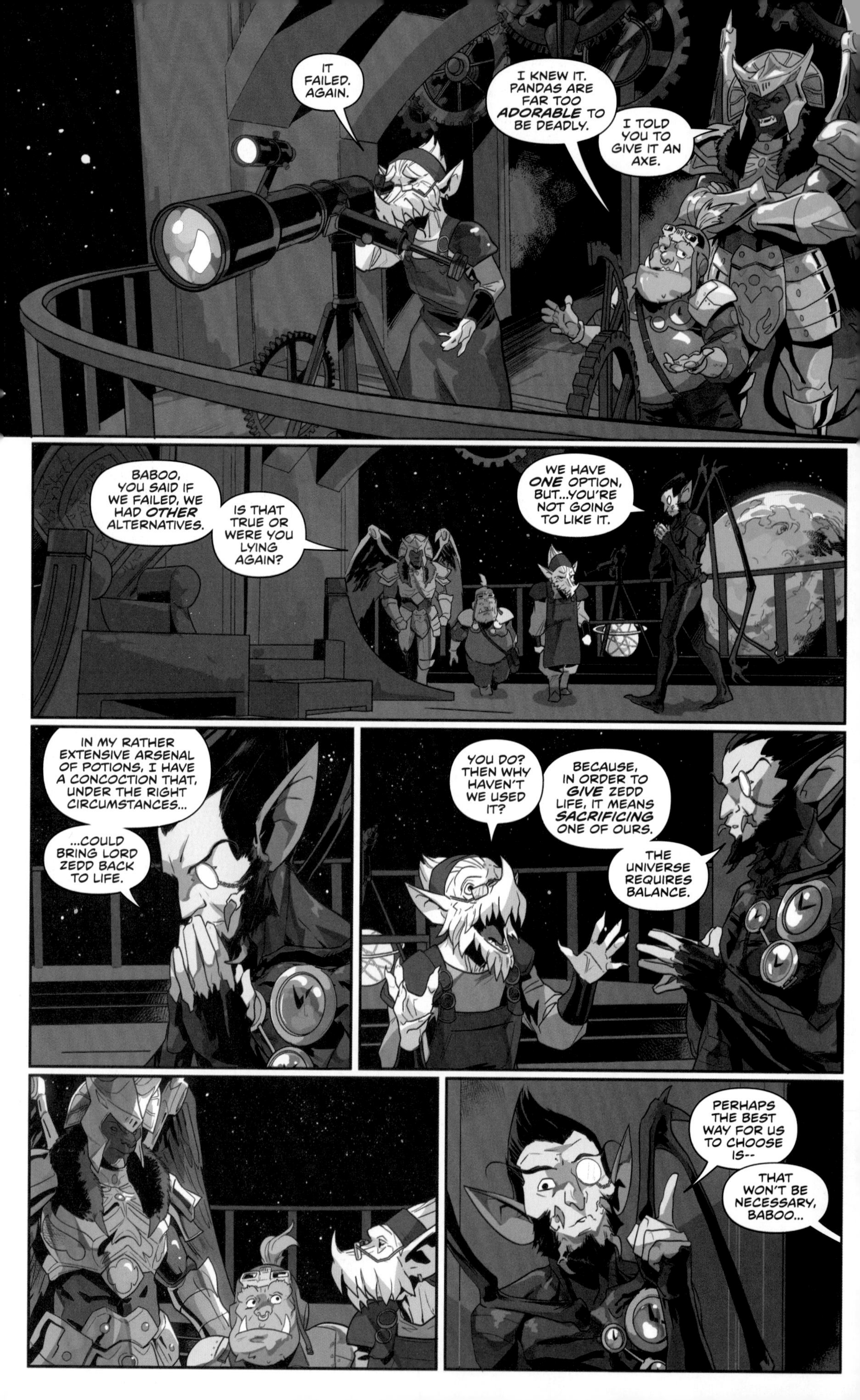
IT FAILED. AGAIN.
I KNEW IT. PANDAS ARE FAR TOO *ADORABLE* TO BE DEADLY.
I TOLD YOU TO GIVE IT AN AXE.
BABOO, YOU SAID IF WE FAILED, WE HAD *OTHER* ALTERNATIVES.
IS THAT TRUE OR WERE YOU LYING AGAIN?
WE HAVE *ONE* OPTION, BUT...YOU'RE NOT GOING TO LIKE IT.
IN MY RATHER EXTENSIVE ARSENAL OF POTIONS, I HAVE A CONCOCTION THAT, UNDER THE RIGHT CIRCUMSTANCES...
...COULD BRING LORD ZEDD BACK TO LIFE.
YOU DO? THEN WHY HAVEN'T WE USED IT?
BECAUSE, IN ORDER TO *GIVE* ZEDD LIFE, IT MEANS *SACRIFICING* ONE OF OURS.
THE UNIVERSE REQUIRES BALANCE.
PERHAPS THE BEST WAY FOR US TO CHOOSE IS--
THAT WON'T BE NECESSARY, BABOO...

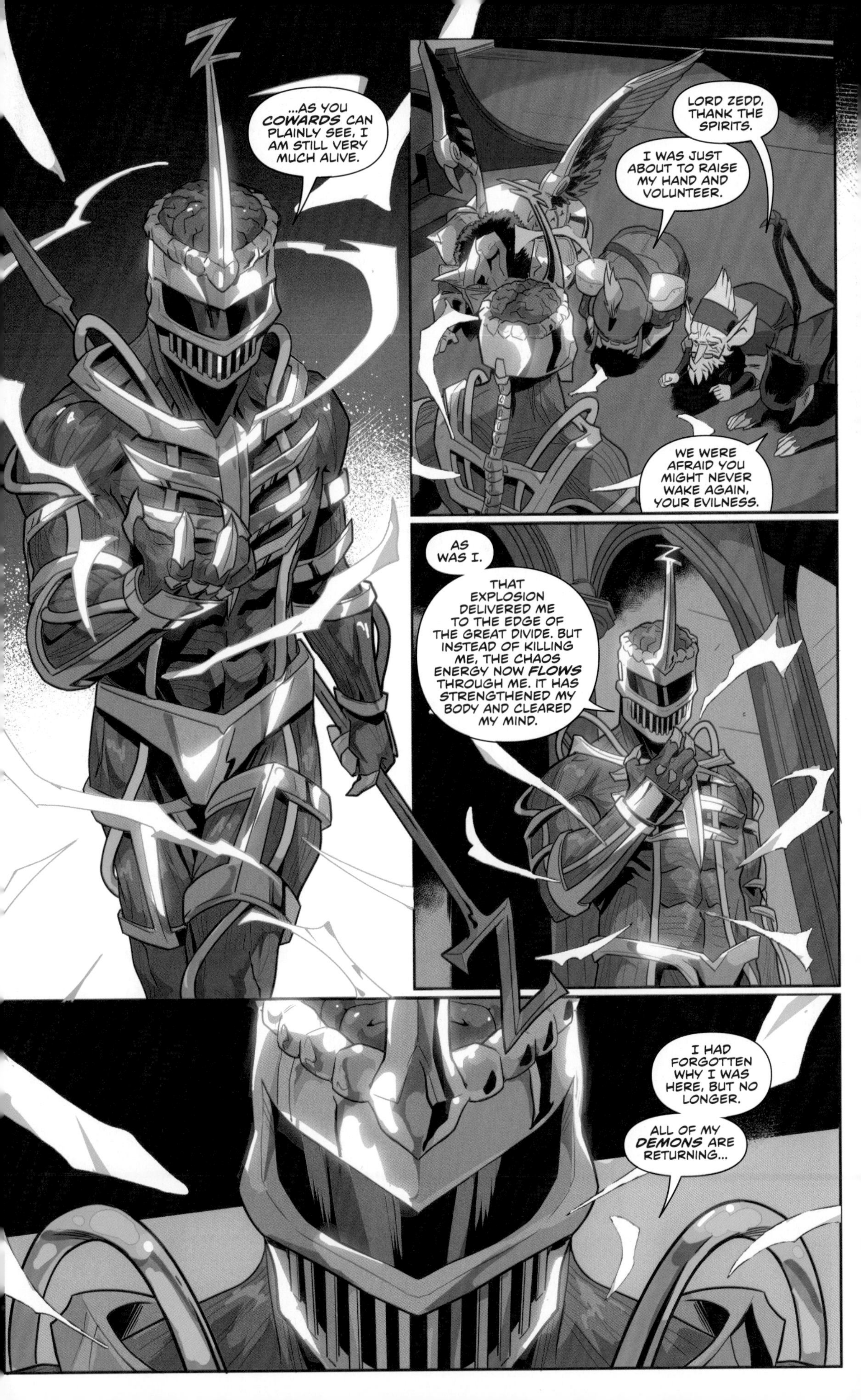
...AS YOU COWARDS CAN PLAINLY SEE, I AM STILL VERY MUCH ALIVE.
LORD ZEDD, THANK THE SPIRITS.
I WAS JUST ABOUT TO RAISE MY HAND AND VOLUNTEER.
WE WERE AFRAID YOU MIGHT NEVER WAKE AGAIN, YOUR EVILNESS.
AS WAS I.
THAT EXPLOSION DELIVERED ME TO THE EDGE OF THE GREAT DIVIDE. BUT INSTEAD OF KILLING ME, THE CHAOS ENERGY NOW FLOWS THROUGH ME. IT HAS STRENGTHENED MY BODY AND CLEARED MY MIND.
I HAD FORGOTTEN WHY I WAS HERE, BUT NO LONGER.
ALL OF MY DEMONS ARE RETURNING...

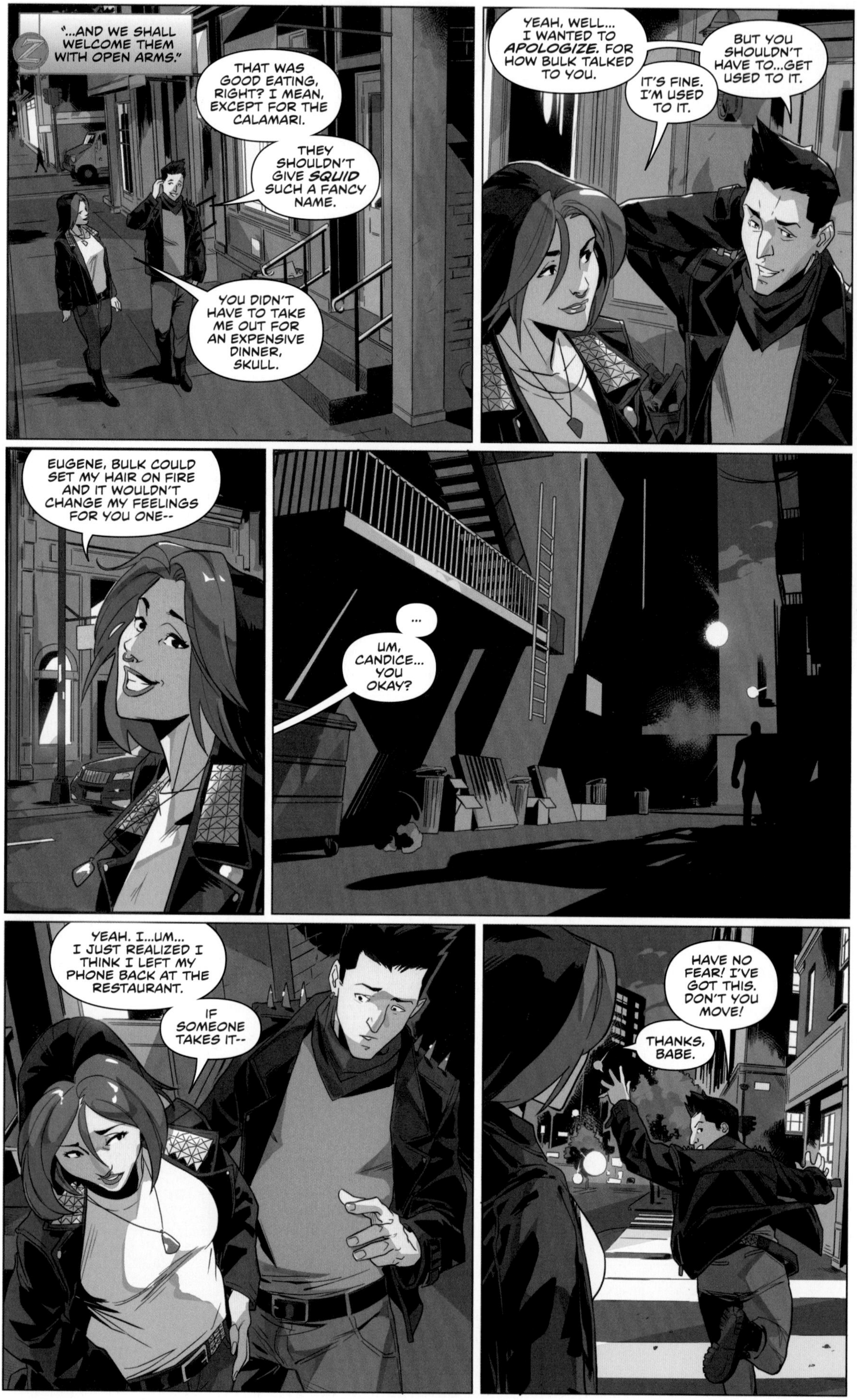
"...AND WE SHALL WELCOME THEM WITH OPEN ARMS."
THAT WAS GOOD EATING, RIGHT? I MEAN, EXCEPT FOR THE CALAMARI.
THEY SHOULDN'T GIVE SQUID SUCH A FANCY NAME.
YOU DIDN'T HAVE TO TAKE ME OUT FOR AN EXPENSIVE DINNER, SKULL.
YEAH, WELL... I WANTED TO APOLOGIZE. FOR HOW BULK TALKED TO YOU.
IT'S FINE. I'M USED TO IT.
BUT YOU SHOULDN'T HAVE TO...GET USED TO IT.
EUGENE, BULK COULD SET MY HAIR ON FIRE AND IT WOULDN'T CHANGE MY FEELINGS FOR YOU ONE--
...
UM, CANDICE... YOU OKAY?
YEAH. I...UM... I JUST REALIZED I THINK I LEFT MY PHONE BACK AT THE RESTAURANT.
IF SOMEONE TAKES IT--
HAVE NO FEAR! I'VE GOT THIS. DON'T YOU MOVE!
THANKS, BABE.

I'M ALONE.

WE ONLY HAVE A FEW MOMENTS UNTIL HE RETURNS.

I HOPE YOU HAD A LOVELY MEAL.

IT WAS VERY PLEASANT.

GOOD. BECAUSE WE RECEIVED THE MESSAGE.

ALREADY? I WAS TOLD I WOULD HAVE MONTHS, MAYBE EVEN A YEAR BEFORE--

I'M AFRAID NOT. THINGS ARE MOVING QUICKLY NOW.

I UNDERSTAND...

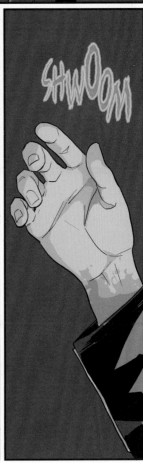

SHWOOM

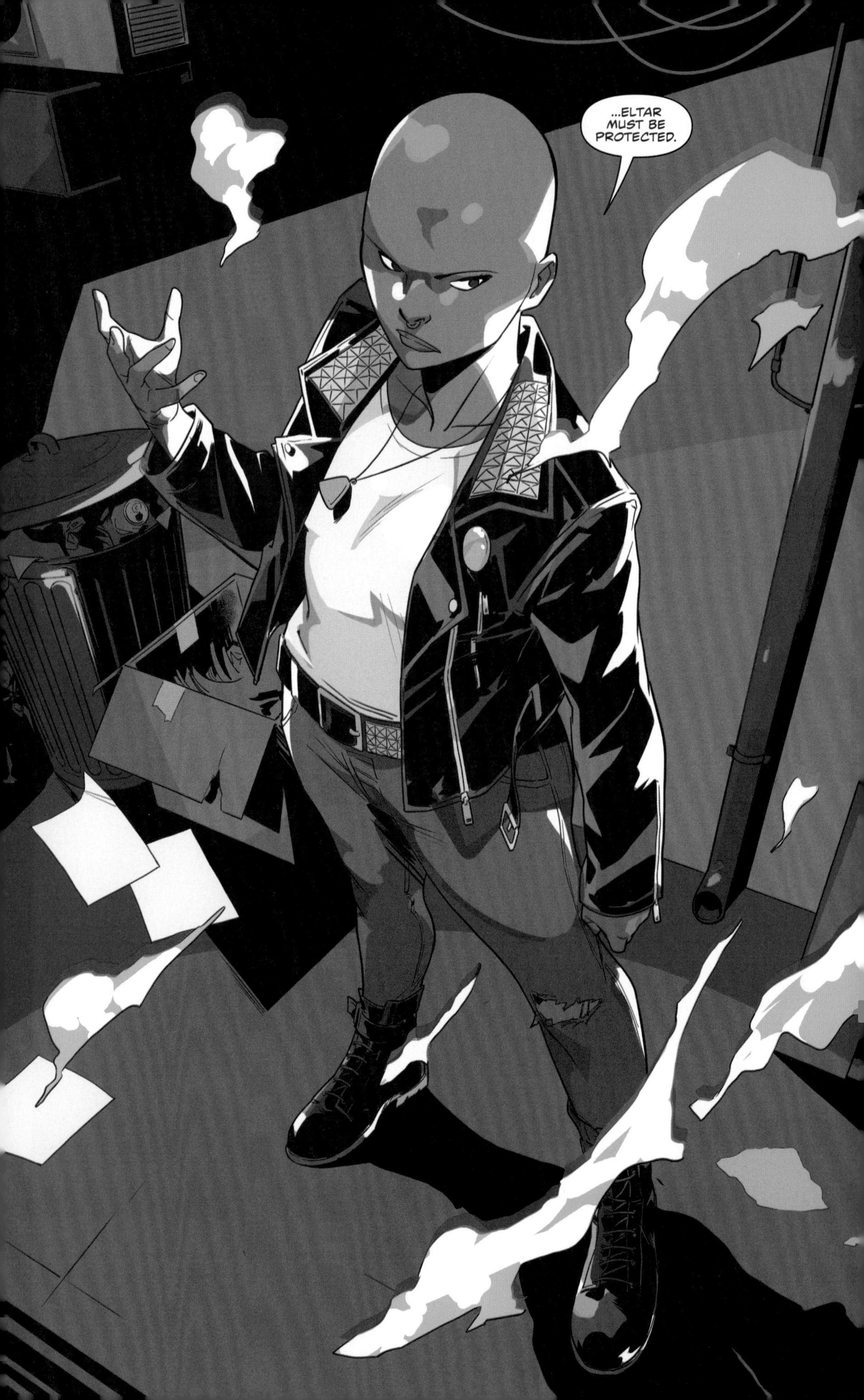
...ELTAR MUST BE PROTECTED.

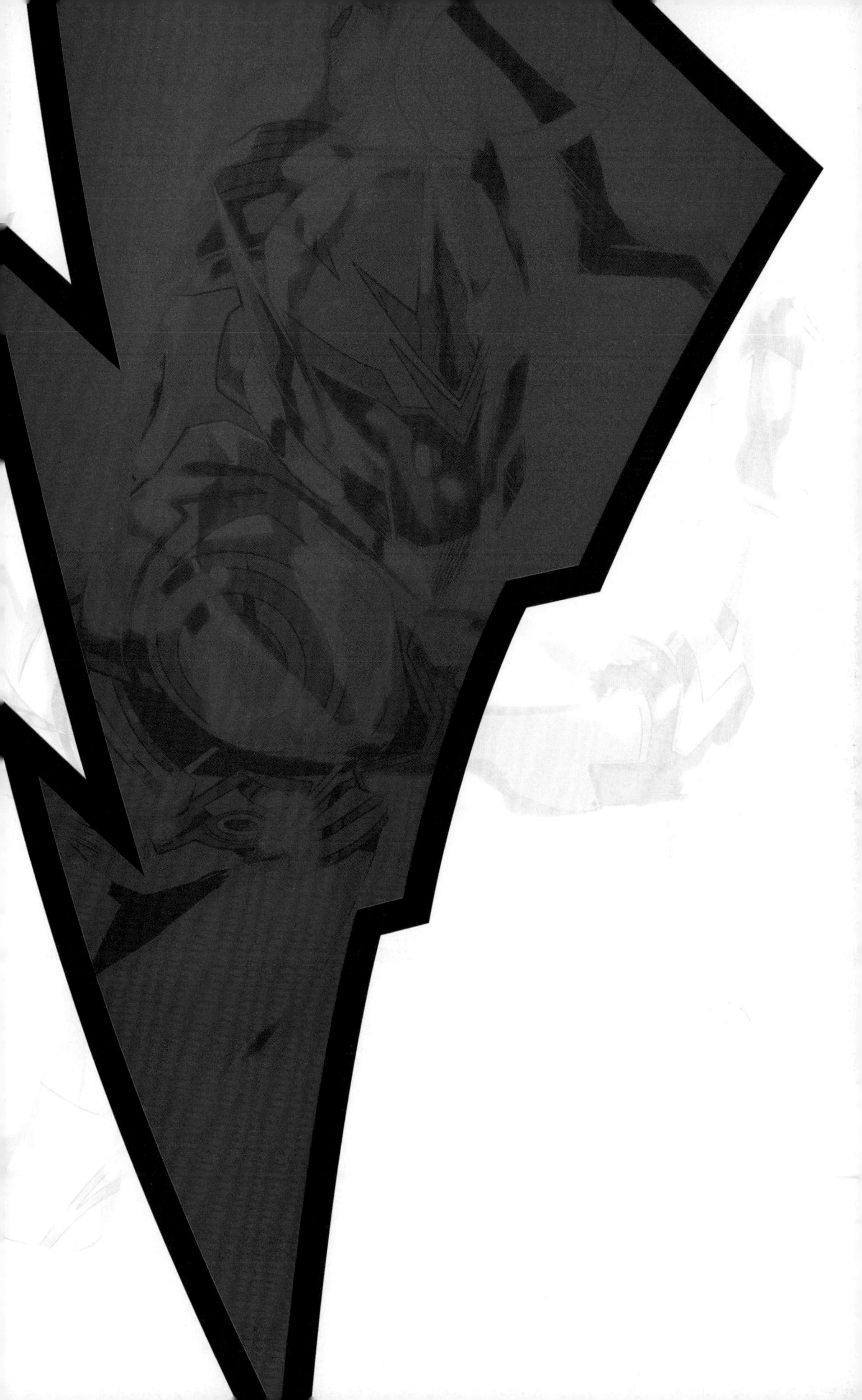

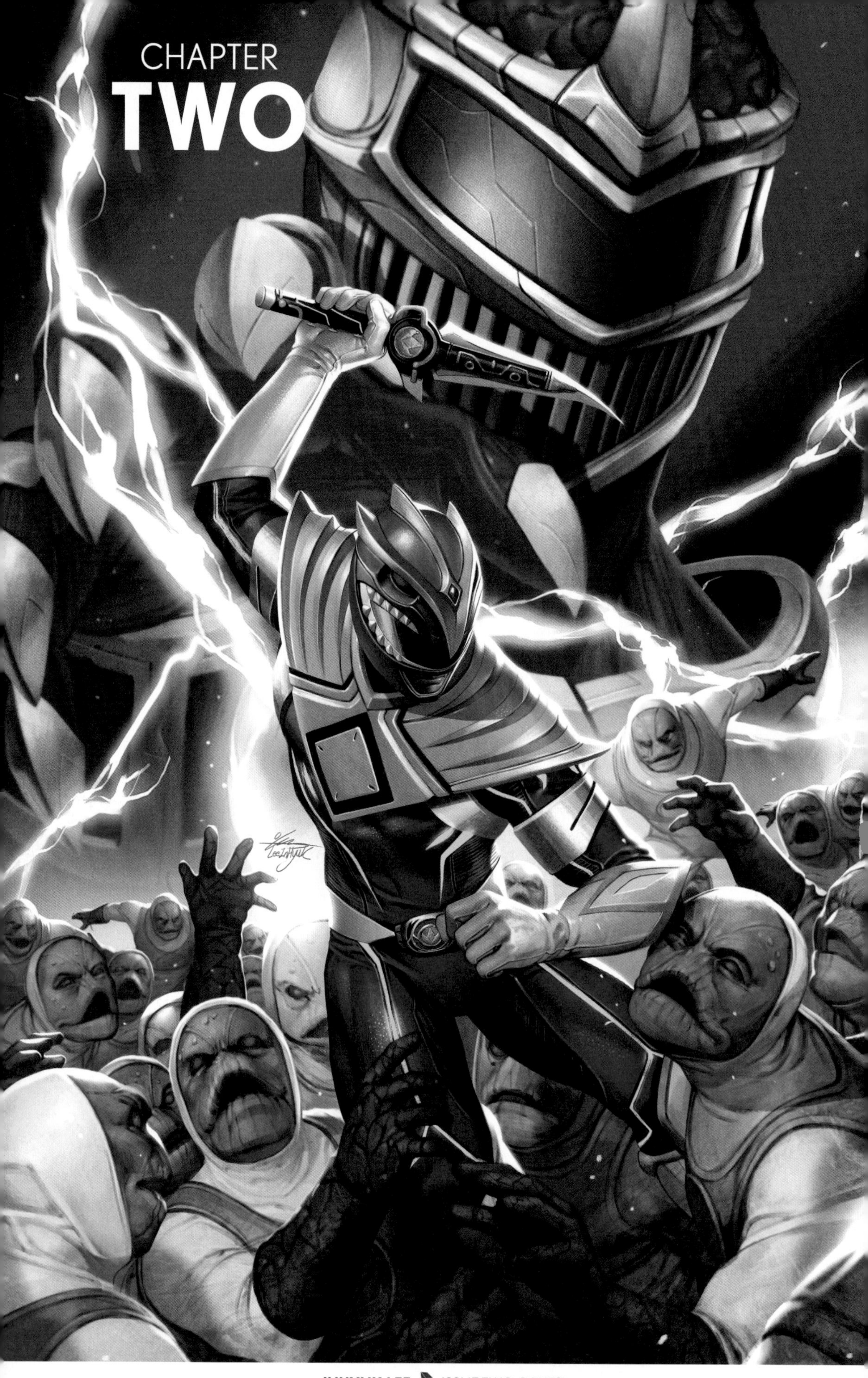
CHAPTER
TWO

INHYUK LEE | ISSUE TWO COVER

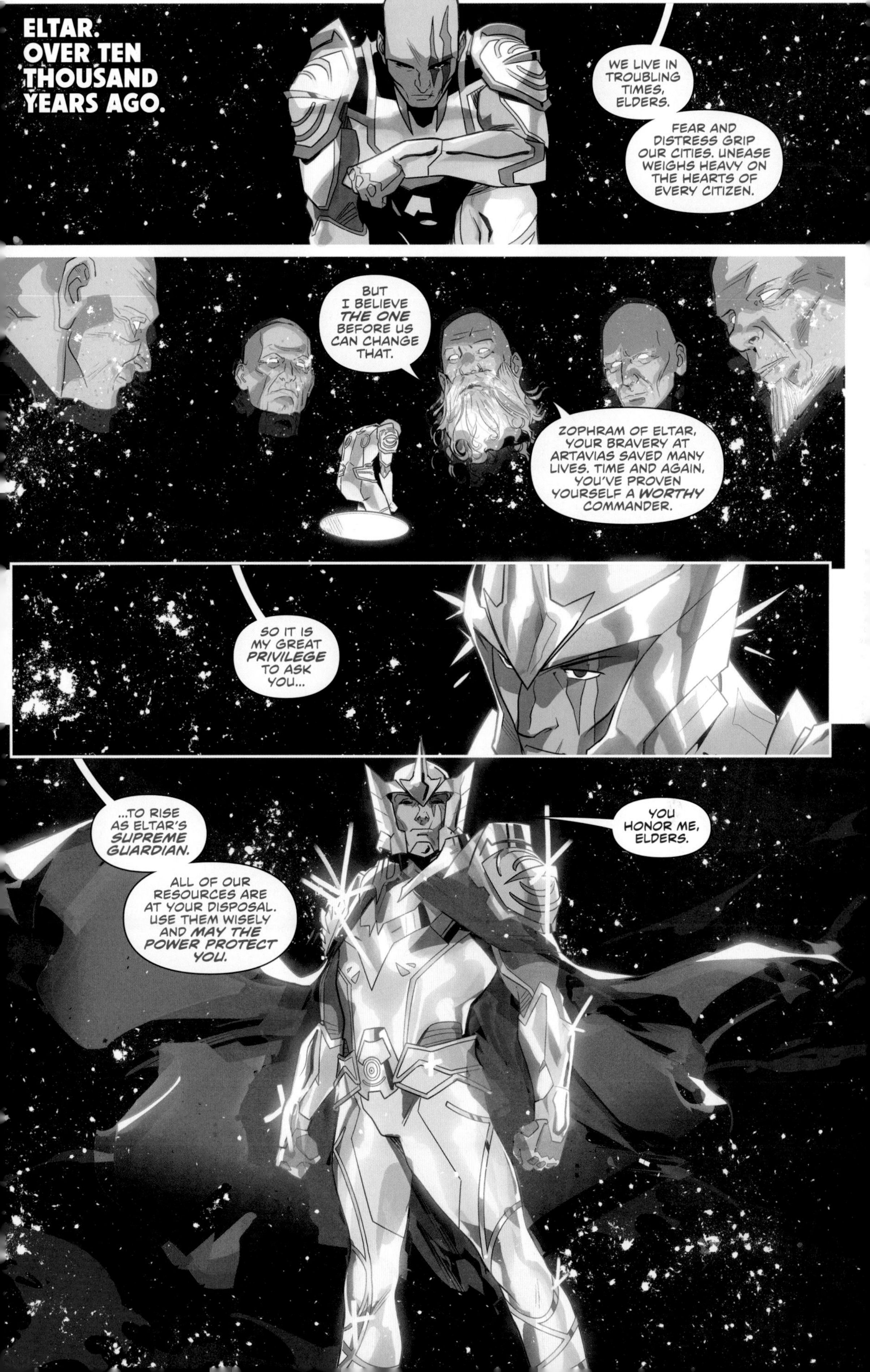
ELTAR. OVER TEN THOUSAND YEARS AGO.
WE LIVE IN TROUBLING TIMES, ELDERS.
FEAR AND DISTRESS GRIP OUR CITIES. UNEASE WEIGHS HEAVY ON THE HEARTS OF EVERY CITIZEN.
BUT I BELIEVE THE ONE BEFORE US CAN CHANGE THAT.
ZOPHRAM OF ELTAR, YOUR BRAVERY AT ARTAVIAS SAVED MANY LIVES. TIME AND AGAIN, YOU'VE PROVEN YOURSELF A WORTHY COMMANDER.
SO IT IS MY GREAT PRIVILEGE TO ASK YOU...
...TO RISE AS ELTAR'S SUPREME GUARDIAN.
ALL OF OUR RESOURCES ARE AT YOUR DISPOSAL. USE THEM WISELY AND MAY THE POWER PROTECT YOU.
YOU HONOR ME, ELDERS.

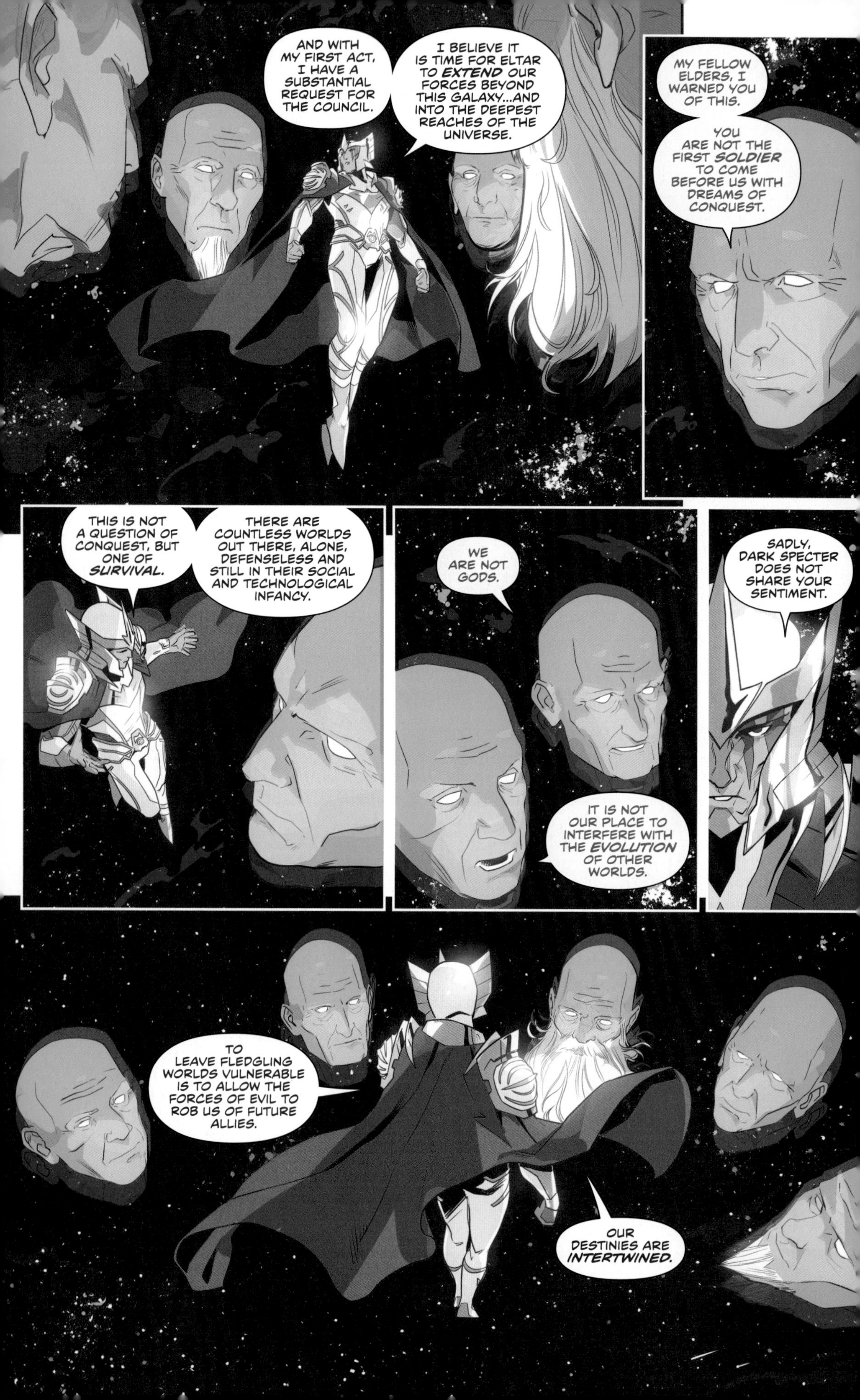
AND WITH MY FIRST ACT, I HAVE A SUBSTANTIAL REQUEST FOR THE COUNCIL.
I BELIEVE IT IS TIME FOR ELTAR TO *EXTEND* OUR FORCES BEYOND THIS GALAXY...AND INTO THE DEEPEST REACHES OF THE UNIVERSE.
MY FELLOW ELDERS, I WARNED YOU OF THIS.
YOU ARE NOT THE FIRST *SOLDIER* TO COME BEFORE US WITH DREAMS OF CONQUEST.
THIS IS NOT A QUESTION OF CONQUEST, BUT ONE OF *SURVIVAL.*
THERE ARE COUNTLESS WORLDS OUT THERE, ALONE, DEFENSELESS AND STILL IN THEIR SOCIAL AND TECHNOLOGICAL INFANCY.
WE ARE NOT GODS.
IT IS NOT OUR PLACE TO INTERFERE WITH THE *EVOLUTION* OF OTHER WORLDS.
SADLY, DARK SPECTER DOES NOT SHARE YOUR SENTIMENT.
TO LEAVE FLEDGLING WORLDS VULNERABLE IS TO ALLOW THE FORCES OF EVIL TO ROB US OF FUTURE ALLIES.
OUR DESTINIES ARE *INTERTWINED.*

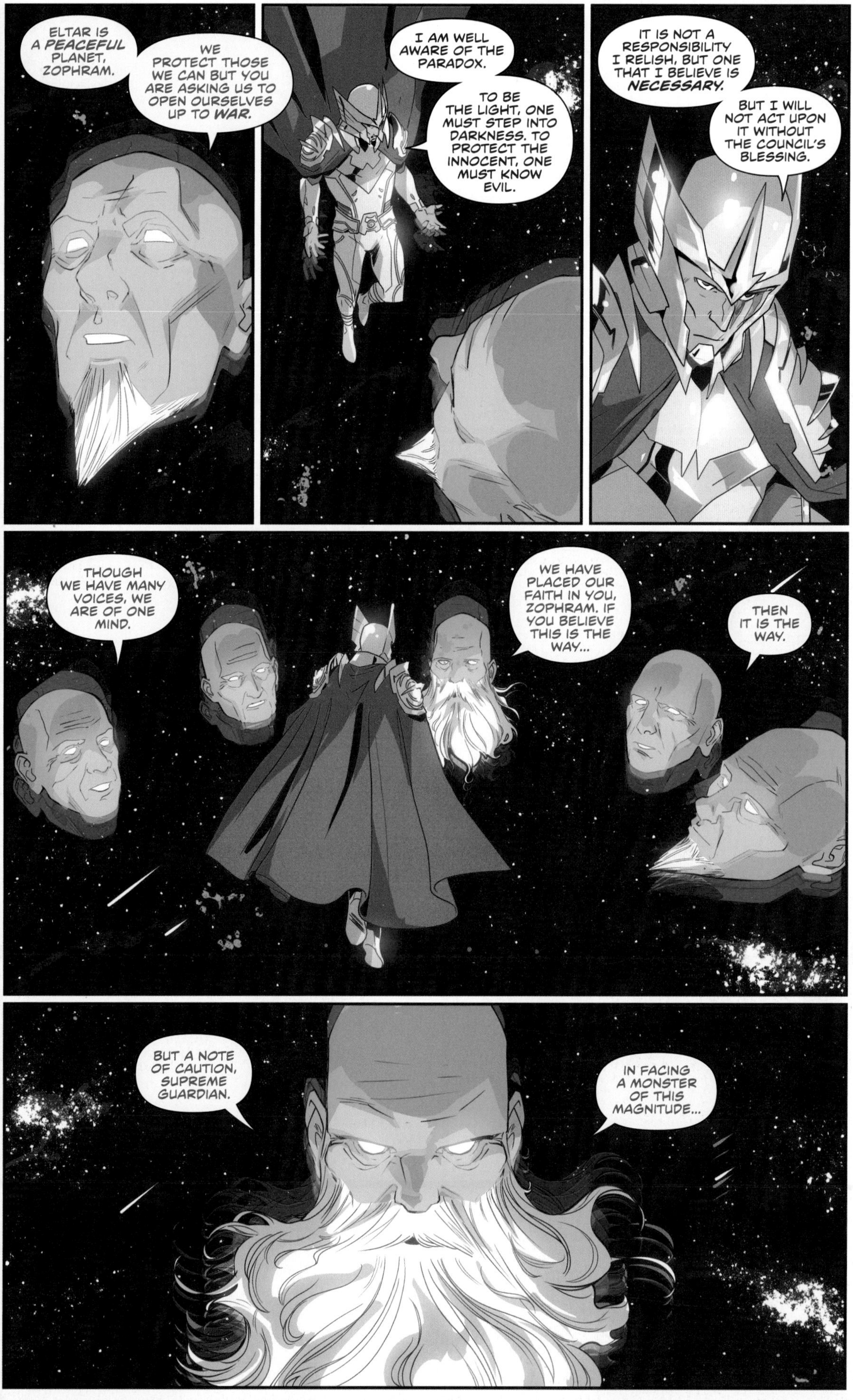
ELTAR IS A *PEACEFUL* PLANET, ZOPHRAM.
WE PROTECT THOSE WE CAN BUT YOU ARE ASKING US TO OPEN OURSELVES UP TO *WAR.*
I AM WELL AWARE OF THE PARADOX.
TO BE THE LIGHT, ONE MUST STEP INTO DARKNESS. TO PROTECT THE INNOCENT, ONE MUST KNOW EVIL.
IT IS NOT A RESPONSIBILITY I RELISH, BUT ONE THAT I BELIEVE IS *NECESSARY.*
BUT I WILL NOT ACT UPON IT WITHOUT THE COUNCIL'S BLESSING.
THOUGH WE HAVE MANY VOICES, WE ARE OF ONE MIND.
WE HAVE PLACED OUR FAITH IN YOU, ZOPHRAM. IF YOU BELIEVE THIS IS THE WAY...
THEN IT IS THE WAY.
BUT A NOTE OF CAUTION, SUPREME GUARDIAN.
IN FACING A MONSTER OF THIS MAGNITUDE...

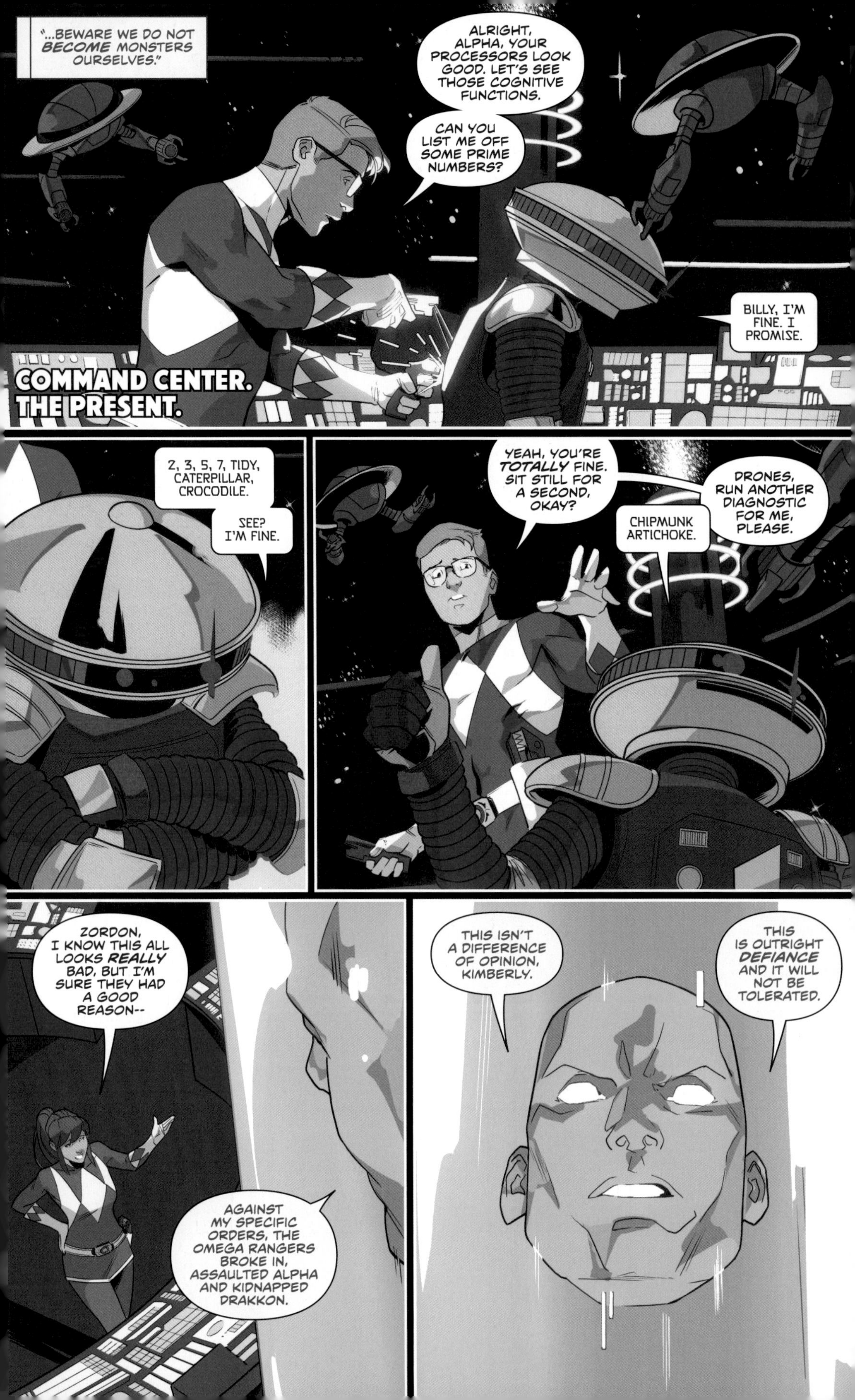
"...BEWARE WE DO NOT *BECOME* MONSTERS OURSELVES."
ALRIGHT, ALPHA, YOUR PROCESSORS LOOK GOOD. LET'S SEE THOSE COGNITIVE FUNCTIONS.
CAN YOU LIST ME OFF SOME PRIME NUMBERS?
BILLY, I'M FINE. I PROMISE.
COMMAND CENTER. THE PRESENT.
2, 3, 5, 7, TIDY, CATERPILLAR, CROCODILE.
SEE? I'M FINE.
YEAH, YOU'RE *TOTALLY* FINE. SIT STILL FOR A SECOND, OKAY?
DRONES, RUN ANOTHER DIAGNOSTIC FOR ME, PLEASE.
CHIPMUNK ARTICHOKE.
ZORDON, I KNOW THIS ALL LOOKS *REALLY* BAD, BUT I'M SURE THEY HAD A GOOD REASON--
AGAINST MY SPECIFIC ORDERS, THE OMEGA RANGERS BROKE IN, ASSAULTED ALPHA AND KIDNAPPED DRAKKON.
THIS ISN'T A DIFFERENCE OF OPINION, KIMBERLY.
THIS IS OUTRIGHT *DEFIANCE* AND IT WILL NOT BE TOLERATED.

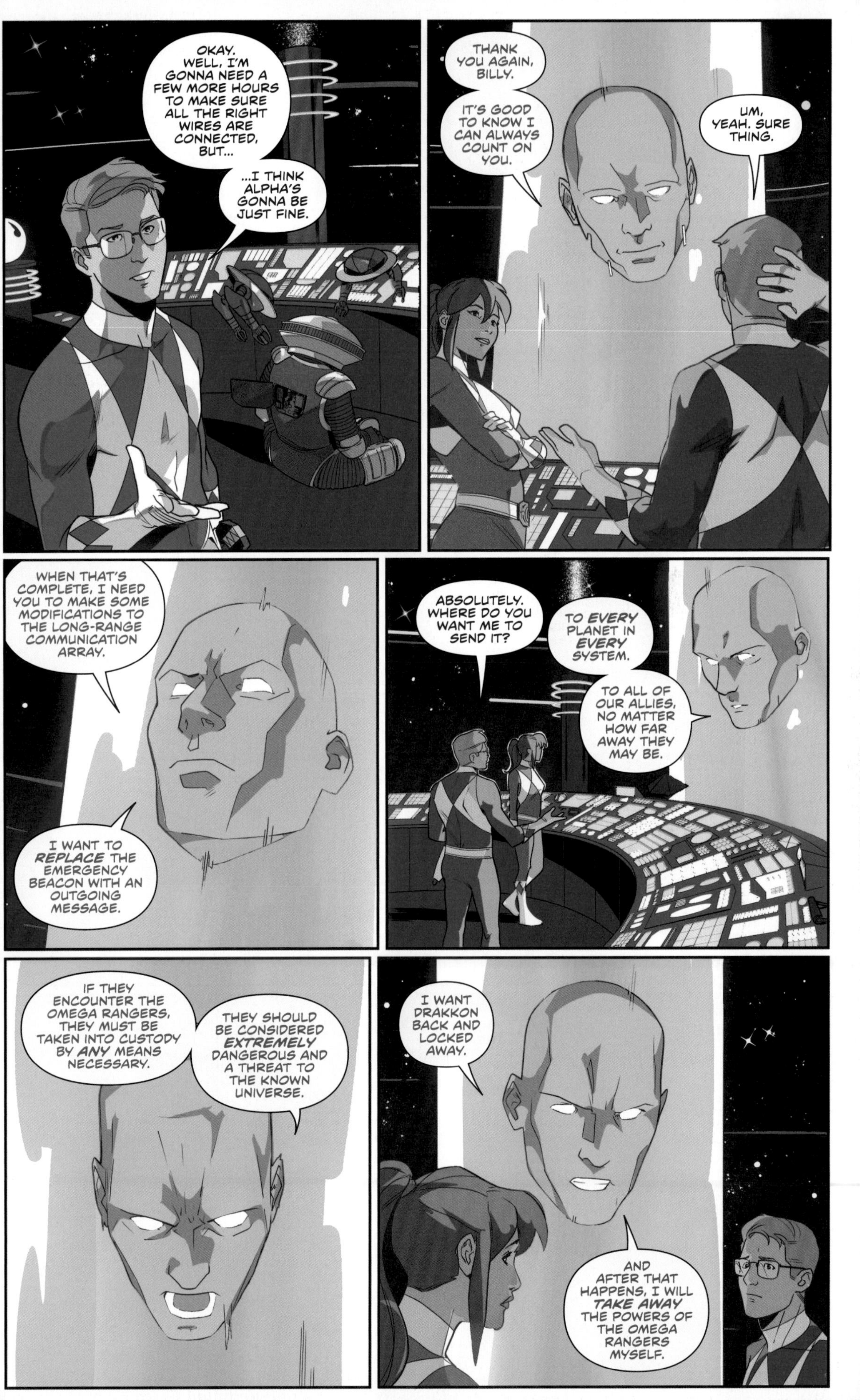
OKAY. WELL, I'M GONNA NEED A FEW MORE HOURS TO MAKE SURE ALL THE RIGHT WIRES ARE CONNECTED, BUT...
...I THINK ALPHA'S GONNA BE JUST FINE.
THANK YOU AGAIN, BILLY.
IT'S GOOD TO KNOW I CAN ALWAYS COUNT ON YOU.
UM, YEAH. SURE THING.
WHEN THAT'S COMPLETE, I NEED YOU TO MAKE SOME MODIFICATIONS TO THE LONG-RANGE COMMUNICATION ARRAY.
I WANT TO *REPLACE* THE EMERGENCY BEACON WITH AN OUTGOING MESSAGE.
ABSOLUTELY. WHERE DO YOU WANT ME TO SEND IT?
TO *EVERY* PLANET IN *EVERY* SYSTEM.
TO ALL OF OUR ALLIES, NO MATTER HOW FAR AWAY THEY MAY BE.
IF THEY ENCOUNTER THE OMEGA RANGERS, THEY MUST BE TAKEN INTO CUSTODY BY *ANY* MEANS NECESSARY.
THEY SHOULD BE CONSIDERED *EXTREMELY* DANGEROUS AND A THREAT TO THE KNOWN UNIVERSE.
I WANT DRAKKON BACK AND LOCKED AWAY.
AND AFTER THAT HAPPENS, I WILL *TAKE AWAY* THE POWERS OF THE OMEGA RANGERS MYSELF.

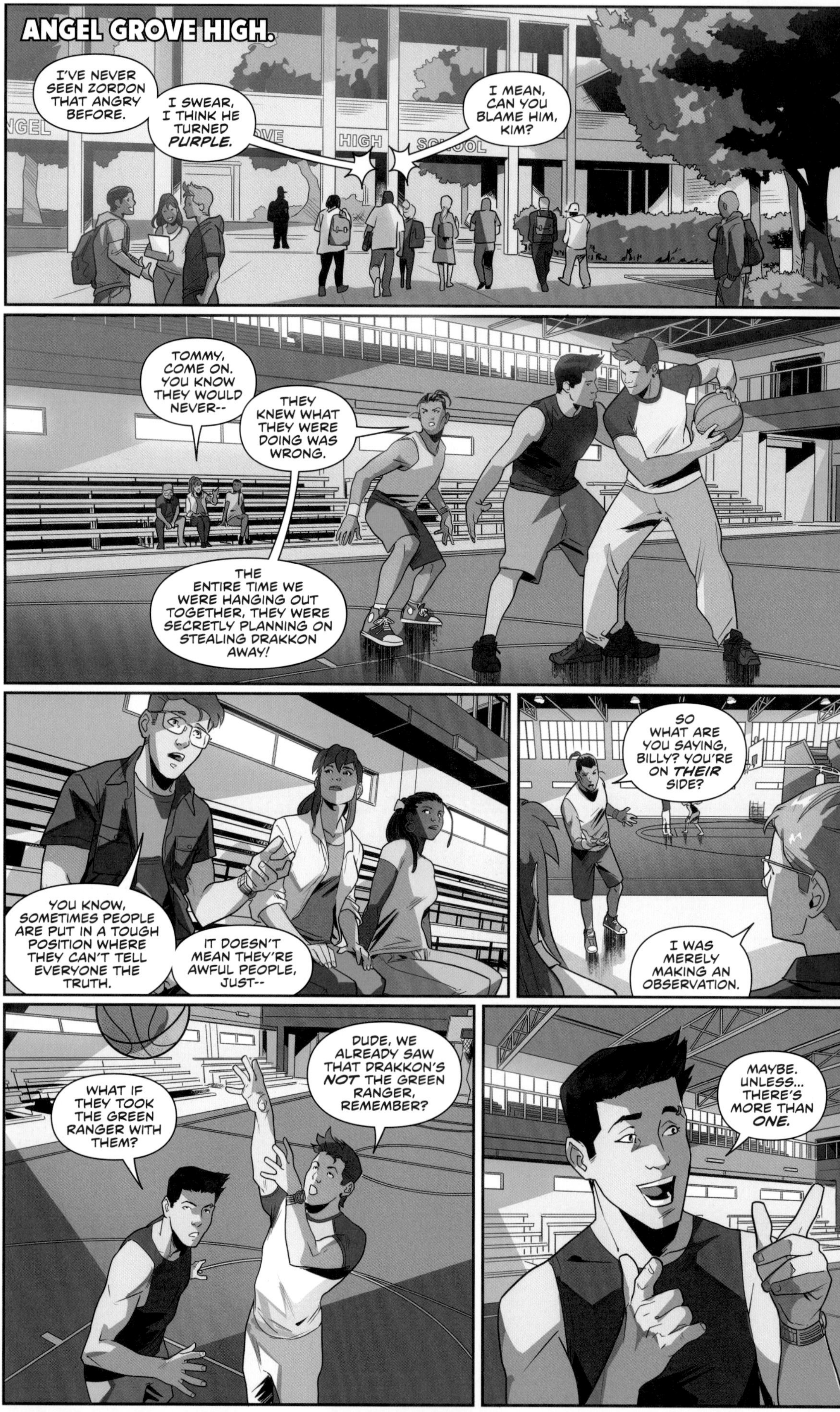
ANGEL GROVE HIGH.
I'VE NEVER SEEN ZORDON THAT ANGRY BEFORE.
I SWEAR, I THINK HE TURNED PURPLE.
I MEAN, CAN YOU BLAME HIM, KIM?
ANGEL GROVE HIGH SCHOOL
TOMMY, COME ON. YOU KNOW THEY WOULD NEVER--
THEY KNEW WHAT THEY WERE DOING WAS WRONG.
THE ENTIRE TIME WE WERE HANGING OUT TOGETHER, THEY WERE SECRETLY PLANNING ON STEALING DRAKKON AWAY!
YOU KNOW, SOMETIMES PEOPLE ARE PUT IN A TOUGH POSITION WHERE THEY CAN'T TELL EVERYONE THE TRUTH.
IT DOESN'T MEAN THEY'RE AWFUL PEOPLE, JUST--
SO WHAT ARE YOU SAYING, BILLY? YOU'RE ON THEIR SIDE?
I WAS MERELY MAKING AN OBSERVATION.
WHAT IF THEY TOOK THE GREEN RANGER WITH THEM?
DUDE, WE ALREADY SAW THAT DRAKKON'S NOT THE GREEN RANGER, REMEMBER?
MAYBE. UNLESS... THERE'S MORE THAN ONE.

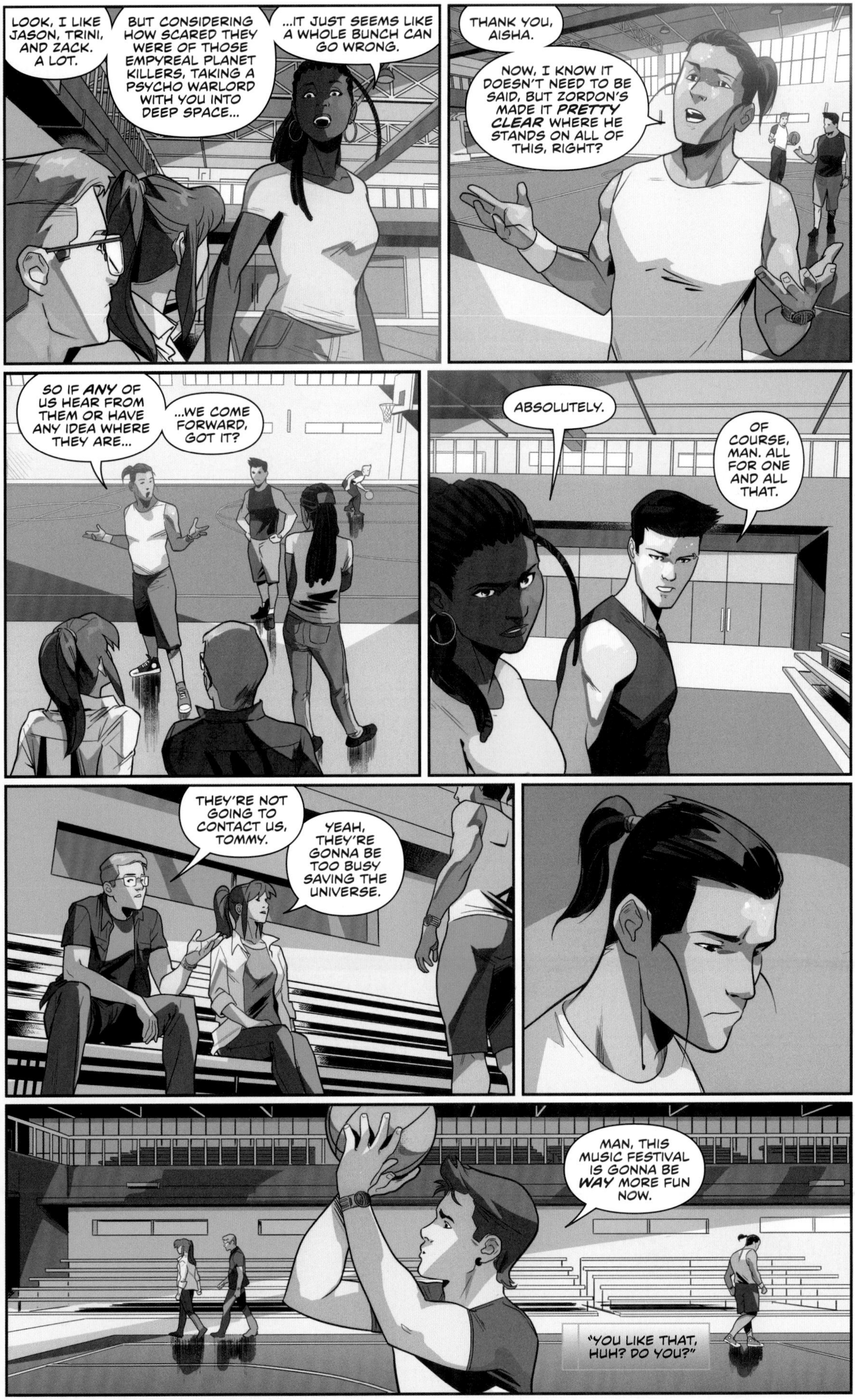
LOOK, I LIKE JASON, TRINI, AND ZACK. A LOT.
BUT CONSIDERING HOW SCARED THEY WERE OF THOSE EMPYREAL PLANET KILLERS, TAKING A PSYCHO WARLORD WITH YOU INTO DEEP SPACE...
...IT JUST SEEMS LIKE A WHOLE BUNCH CAN GO WRONG.
THANK YOU, AISHA.
NOW, I KNOW IT DOESN'T NEED TO BE SAID, BUT ZORDON'S MADE IT PRETTY CLEAR WHERE HE STANDS ON ALL OF THIS, RIGHT?
SO IF ANY OF US HEAR FROM THEM OR HAVE ANY IDEA WHERE THEY ARE...
...WE COME FORWARD, GOT IT?
ABSOLUTELY.
OF COURSE, MAN. ALL FOR ONE AND ALL THAT.
THEY'RE NOT GOING TO CONTACT US, TOMMY.
YEAH, THEY'RE GONNA BE TOO BUSY SAVING THE UNIVERSE.
MAN, THIS MUSIC FESTIVAL IS GONNA BE WAY MORE FUN NOW.
"YOU LIKE THAT, HUH? DO YOU?"

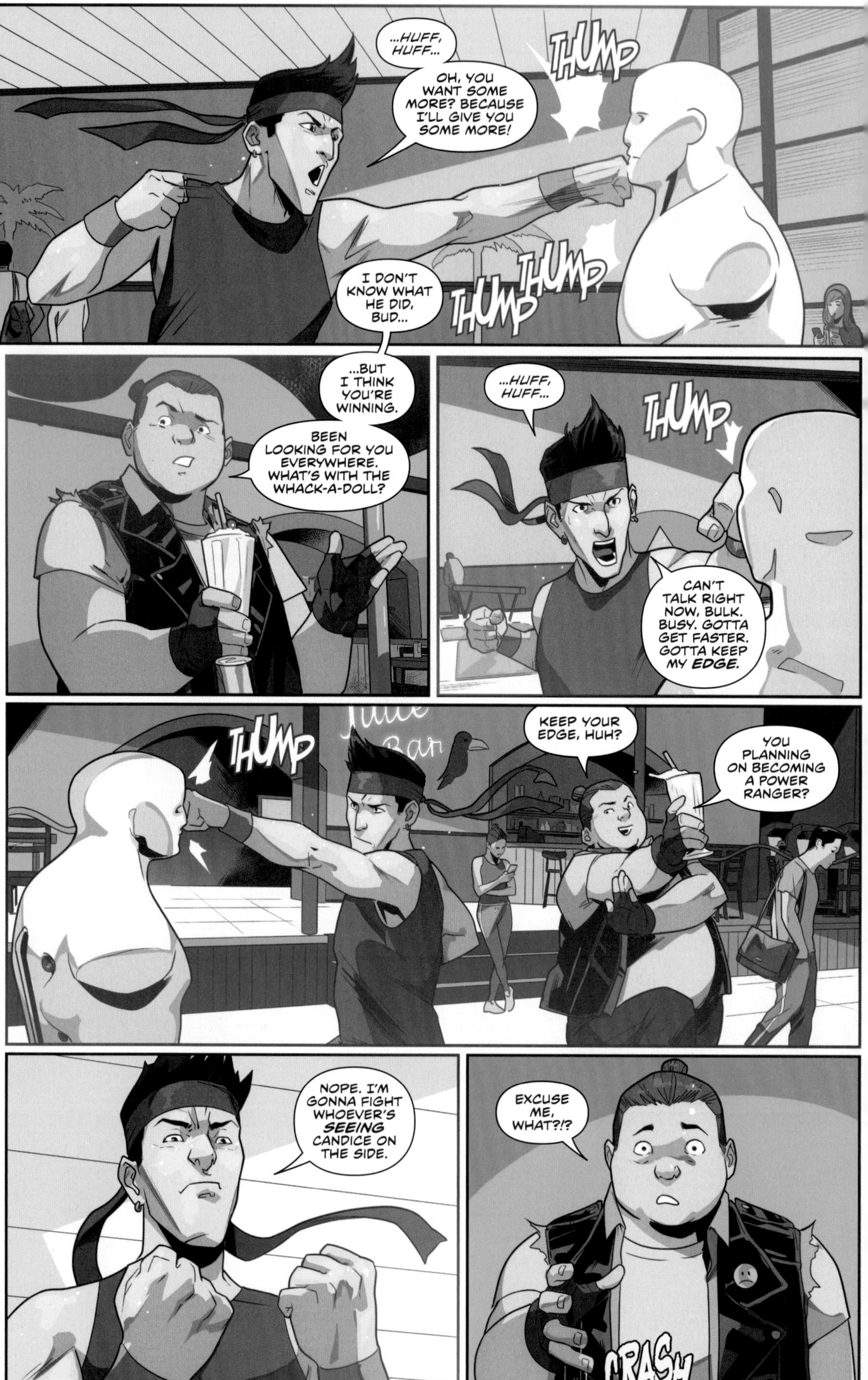
...HUFF, HUFF...
OH, YOU WANT SOME MORE? BECAUSE I'LL GIVE YOU SOME MORE!
THUMP
THUMP
THUMP
I DON'T KNOW WHAT HE DID, BUD...
...BUT I THINK YOU'RE WINNING.
BEEN LOOKING FOR YOU EVERYWHERE. WHAT'S WITH THE WHACK-A-DOLL?
...HUFF, HUFF...
THUMP
CAN'T TALK RIGHT NOW, BULK. BUSY. GOTTA GET FASTER. GOTTA KEEP MY *EDGE*.
THUMP
KEEP YOUR EDGE, HUH?
YOU PLANNING ON BECOMING A POWER RANGER?
NOPE. I'M GONNA FIGHT WHOEVER'S *SEEING* CANDICE ON THE SIDE.
EXCUSE ME, WHAT?!?
CRASH

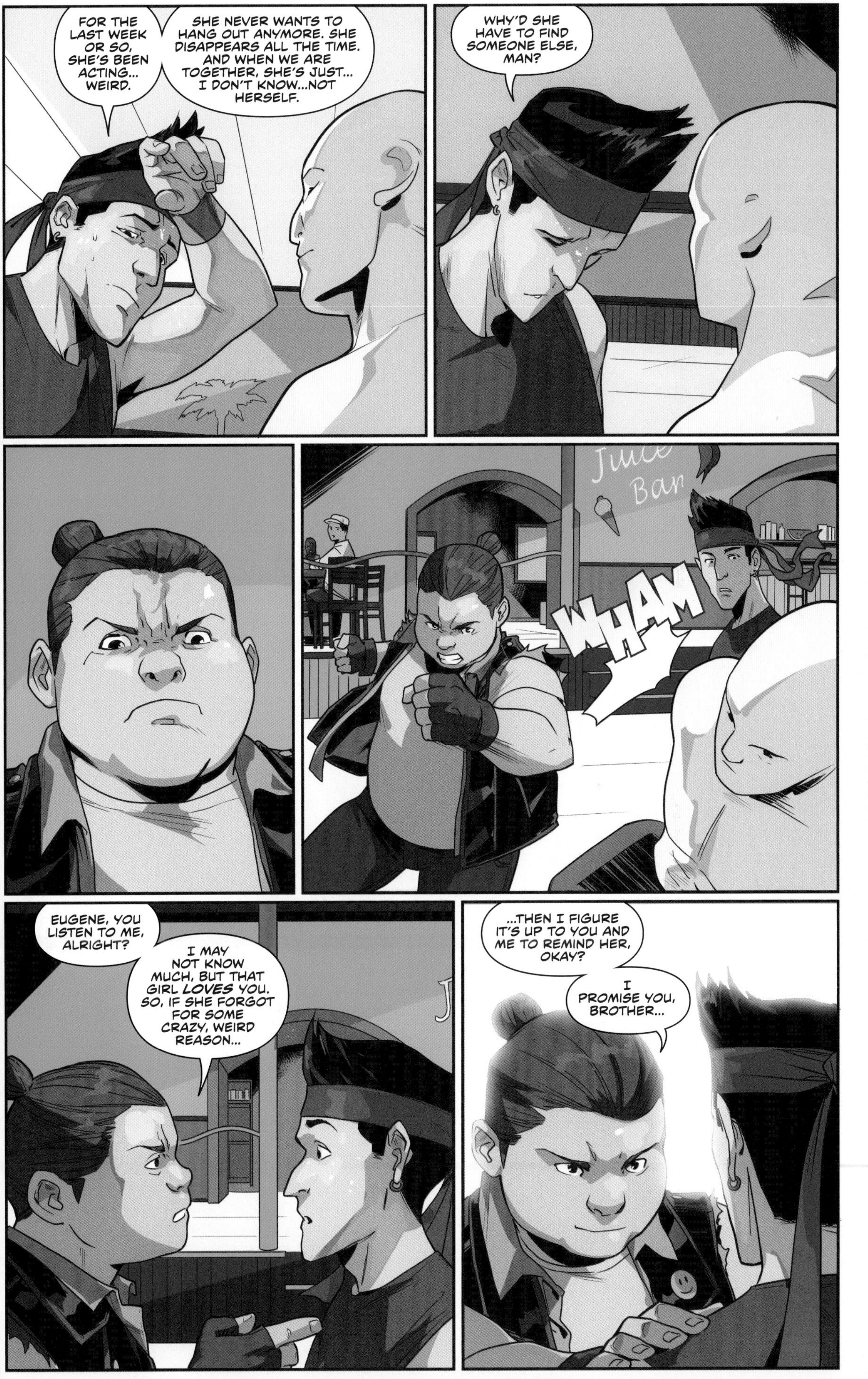
FOR THE LAST WEEK OR SO, SHE'S BEEN ACTING... WEIRD.
SHE NEVER WANTS TO HANG OUT ANYMORE. SHE DISAPPEARS ALL THE TIME. AND WHEN WE ARE TOGETHER, SHE'S JUST... I DON'T KNOW...NOT HERSELF.
WHY'D SHE HAVE TO FIND SOMEONE ELSE, MAN?
Juice Bar
WHAM
EUGENE, YOU LISTEN TO ME, ALRIGHT?
I MAY NOT KNOW MUCH, BUT THAT GIRL *LOVES* YOU. SO, IF SHE FORGOT FOR SOME CRAZY, WEIRD REASON...
...THEN I FIGURE IT'S UP TO YOU AND ME TO REMIND HER, OKAY?
I PROMISE YOU, BROTHER...

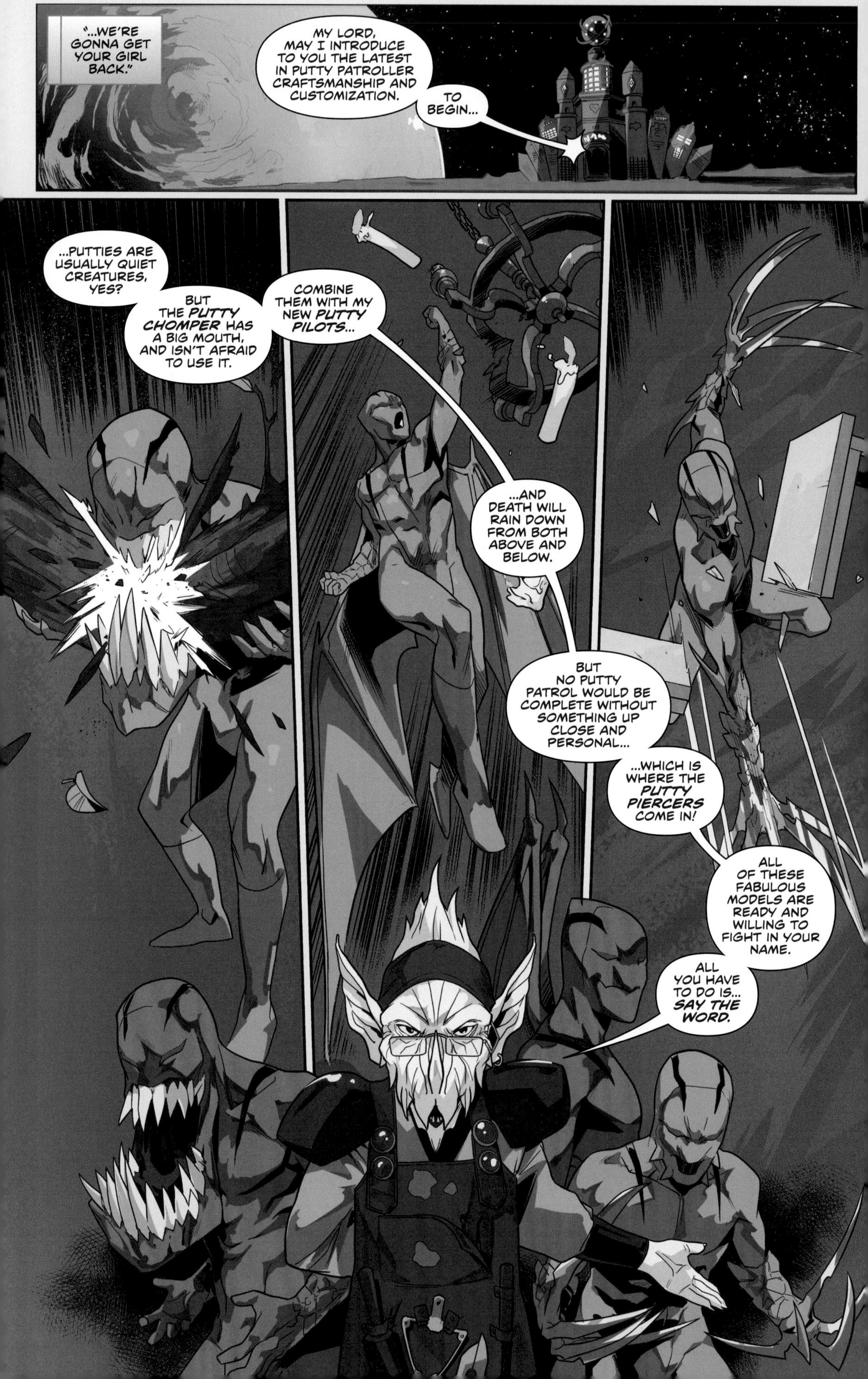
"...WE'RE GONNA GET YOUR GIRL BACK."
MY LORD, MAY I INTRODUCE TO YOU THE LATEST IN PUTTY PATROLLER CRAFTSMANSHIP AND CUSTOMIZATION.
TO BEGIN...
...PUTTIES ARE USUALLY QUIET CREATURES, YES?
BUT THE PUTTY CHOMPER HAS A BIG MOUTH, AND ISN'T AFRAID TO USE IT.
COMBINE THEM WITH MY NEW PUTTY PILOTS...
...AND DEATH WILL RAIN DOWN FROM BOTH ABOVE AND BELOW.
BUT NO PUTTY PATROL WOULD BE COMPLETE WITHOUT SOMETHING UP CLOSE AND PERSONAL...
...WHICH IS WHERE THE PUTTY PIERCERS COME IN!
ALL OF THESE FABULOUS MODELS ARE READY AND WILLING TO FIGHT IN YOUR NAME.
ALL YOU HAVE TO DO IS... SAY THE WORD.

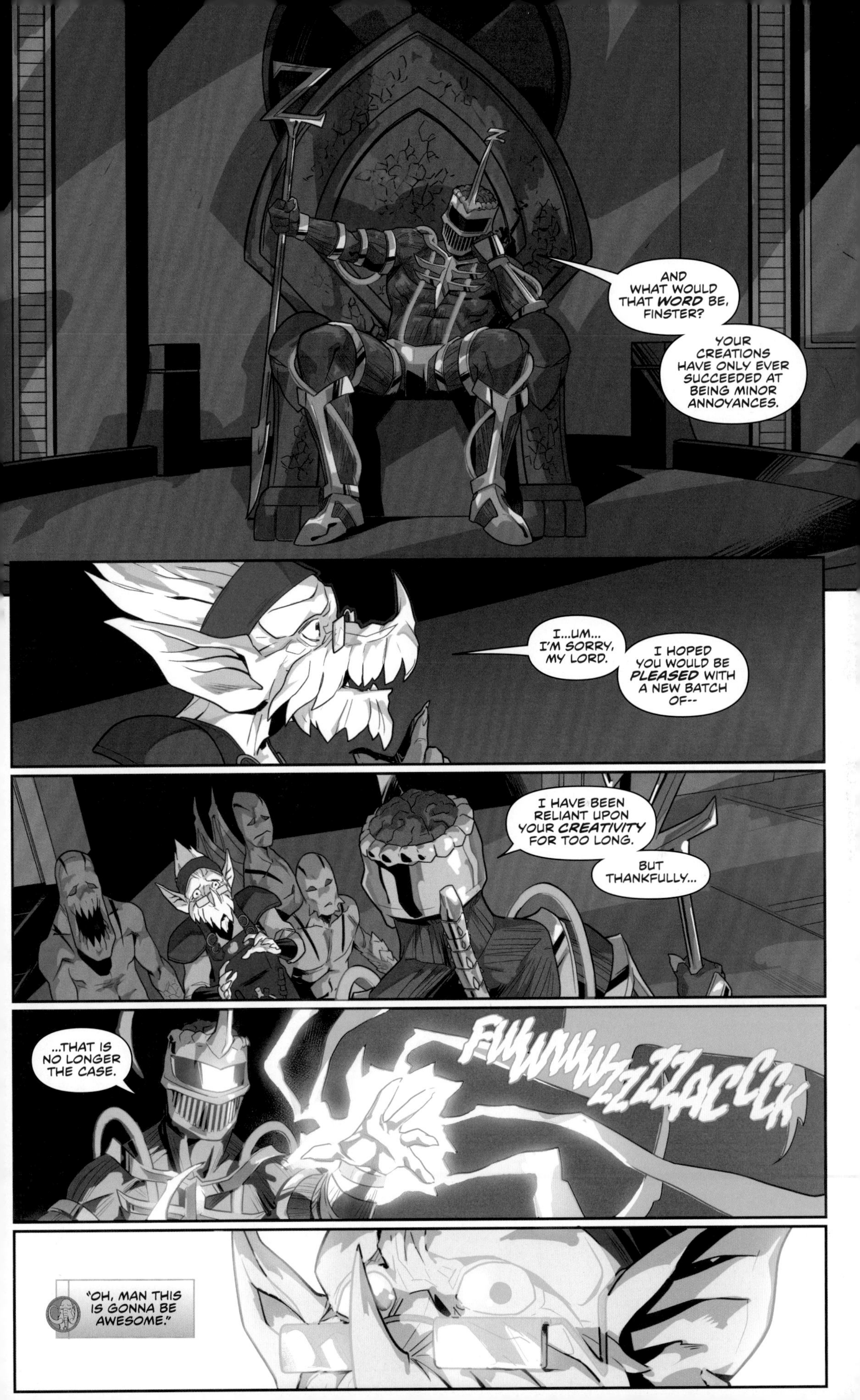
AND WHAT WOULD THAT WORD BE, FINSTER?
YOUR CREATIONS HAVE ONLY EVER SUCCEEDED AT BEING MINOR ANNOYANCES.
I...UM... I'M SORRY, MY LORD.
I HOPED YOU WOULD BE PLEASED WITH A NEW BATCH OF--
I HAVE BEEN RELIANT UPON YOUR CREATIVITY FOR TOO LONG.
BUT THANKFULLY...
...THAT IS NO LONGER THE CASE.
FWWWWZZZZACCCK
"OH, MAN THIS IS GONNA BE AWESOME."

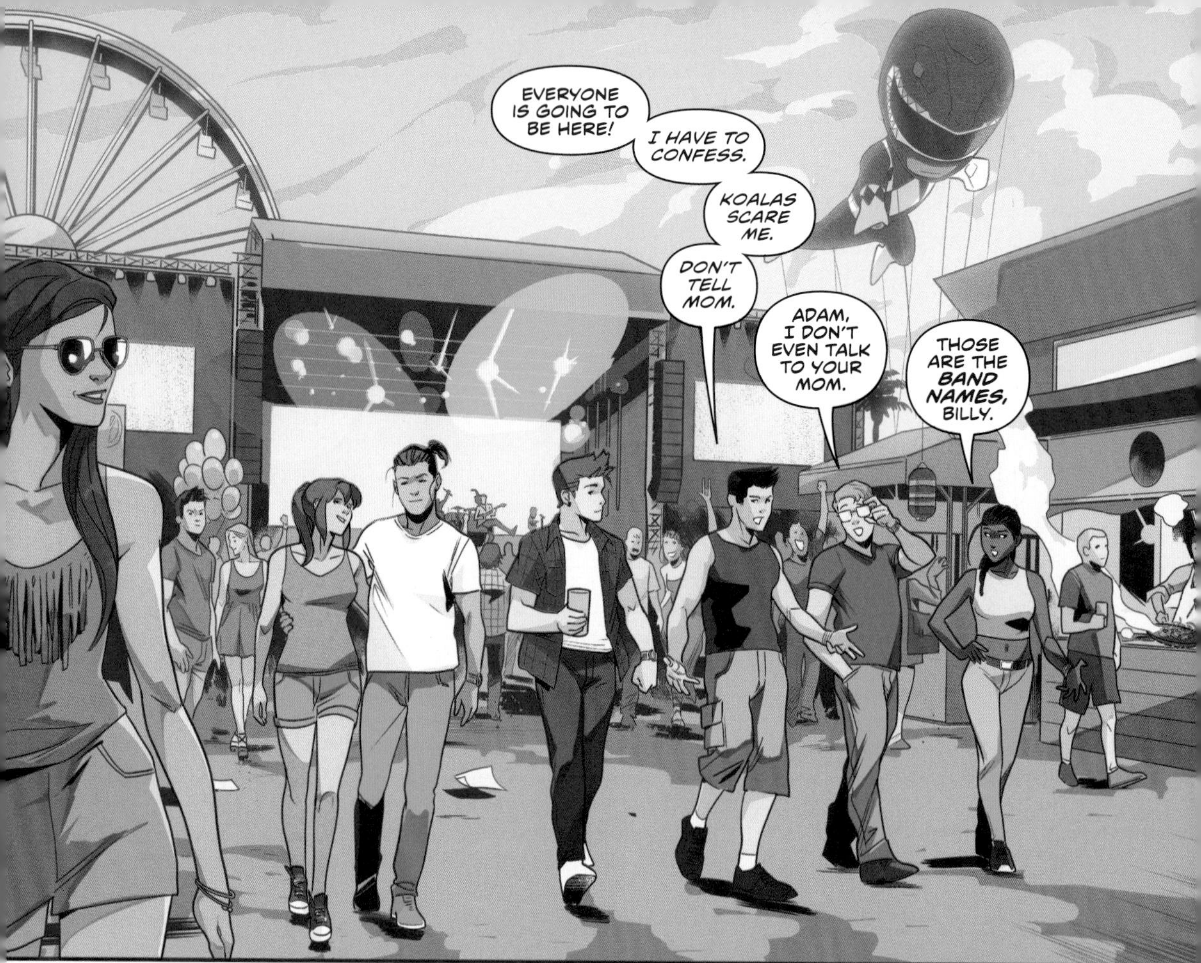
EVERYONE IS GOING TO BE HERE!
I HAVE TO CONFESS.
KOALAS SCARE ME.
DON'T TELL MOM.
ADAM, I DON'T EVEN TALK TO YOUR MOM.
THOSE ARE THE **BAND NAMES,** BILLY.

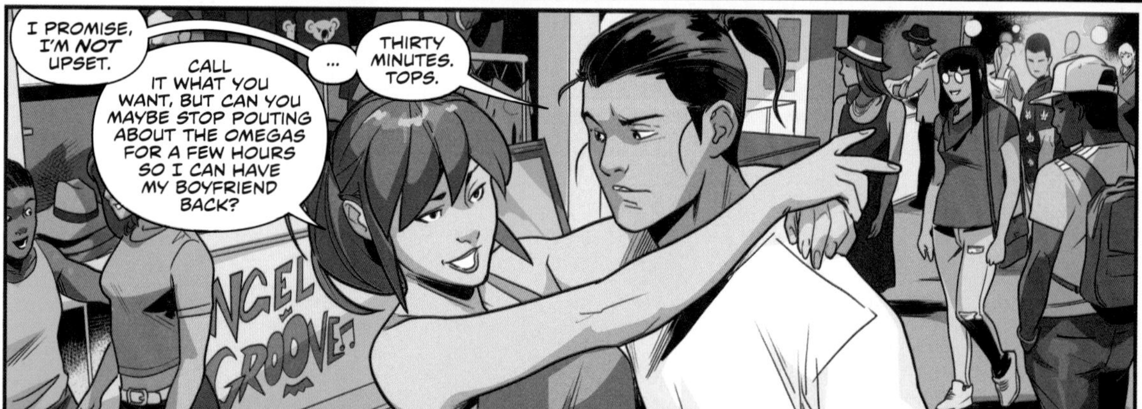
I PROMISE, I'M **NOT** UPSET.
...
THIRTY MINUTES. TOPS.
CALL IT WHAT YOU WANT, BUT CAN YOU MAYBE STOP POUTING ABOUT THE OMEGAS FOR A FEW HOURS SO I CAN HAVE MY BOYFRIEND BACK?
NGEL GROOVE!

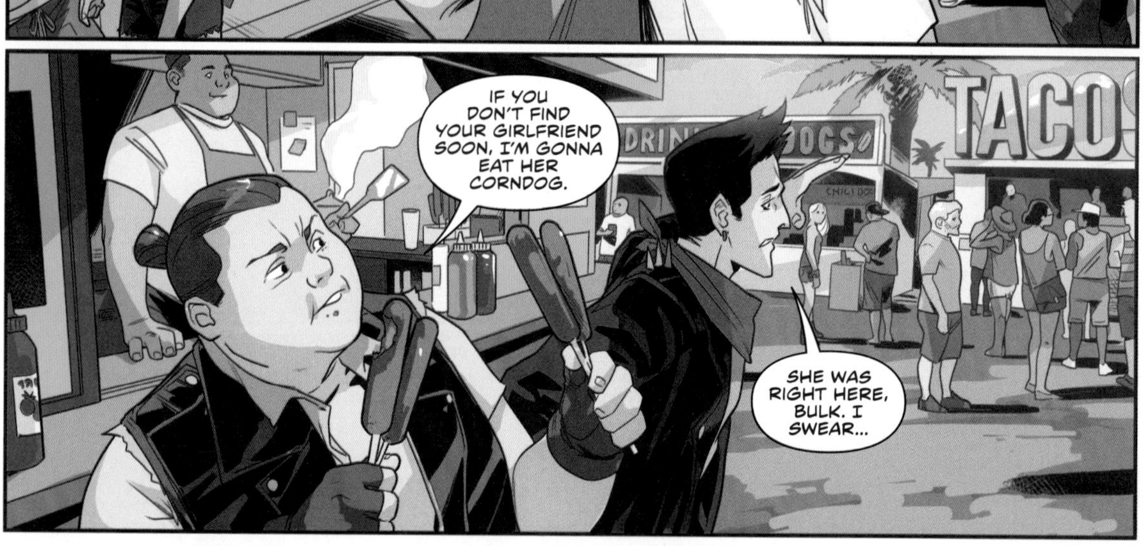
TACOS
IF YOU DON'T FIND YOUR GIRLFRIEND SOON, I'M GONNA EAT HER CORNDOG.
SHE WAS RIGHT HERE, BULK. I SWEAR...

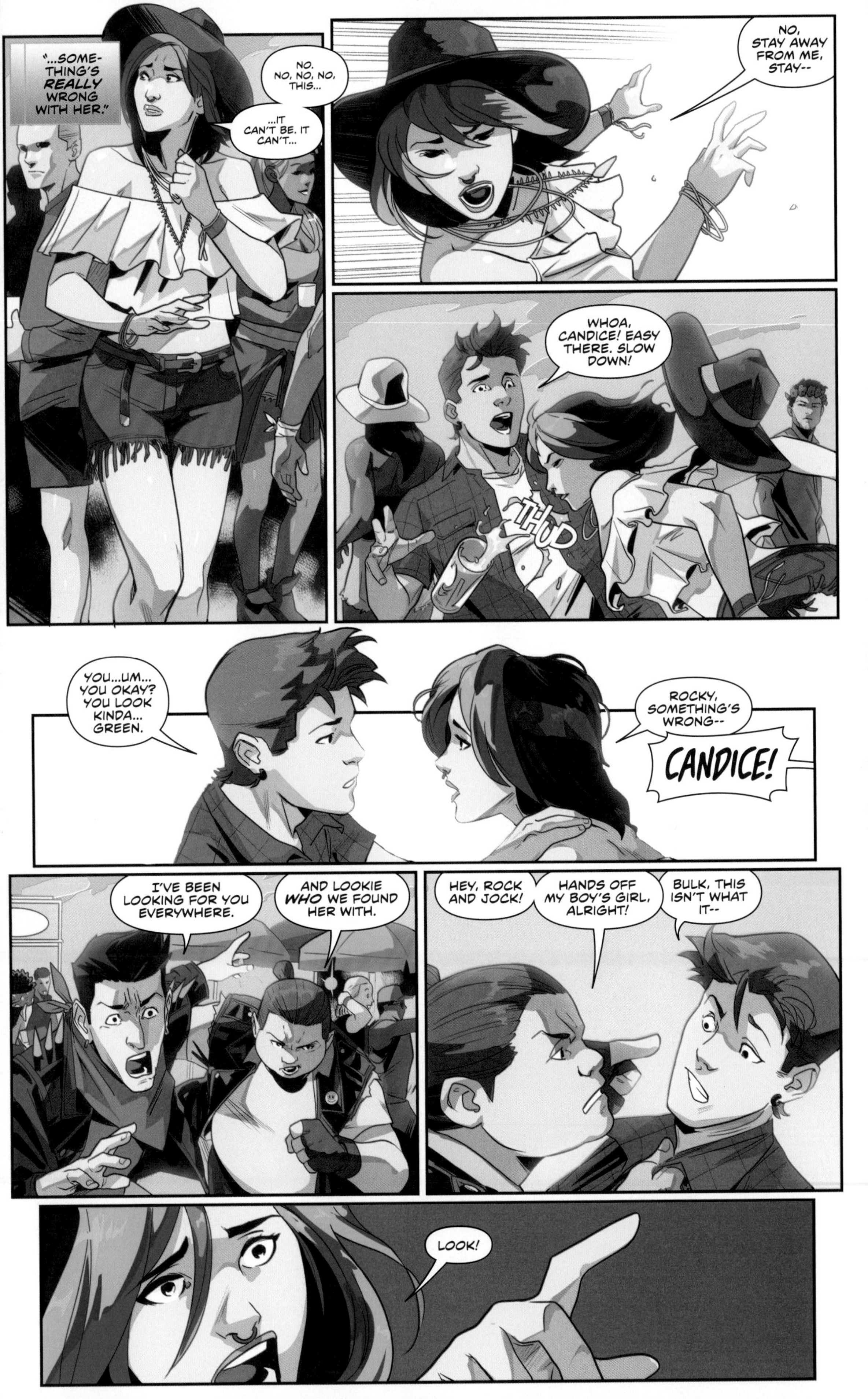
"...SOME-THING'S *REALLY* WRONG WITH HER."
NO. NO, NO, NO, THIS...
...IT CAN'T BE. IT CAN'T...
NO, STAY AWAY FROM ME, STAY--
WHOA, CANDICE! EASY THERE. SLOW DOWN!
THUD
YOU...UM... YOU OKAY? YOU LOOK KINDA... GREEN.
ROCKY, SOMETHING'S WRONG--
CANDICE!
I'VE BEEN LOOKING FOR YOU EVERYWHERE.
AND LOOKIE *WHO* WE FOUND HER WITH.
HEY, ROCK AND JOCK!
HANDS OFF MY BOY'S GIRL, ALRIGHT!
BULK, THIS ISN'T WHAT IT--
LOOK!

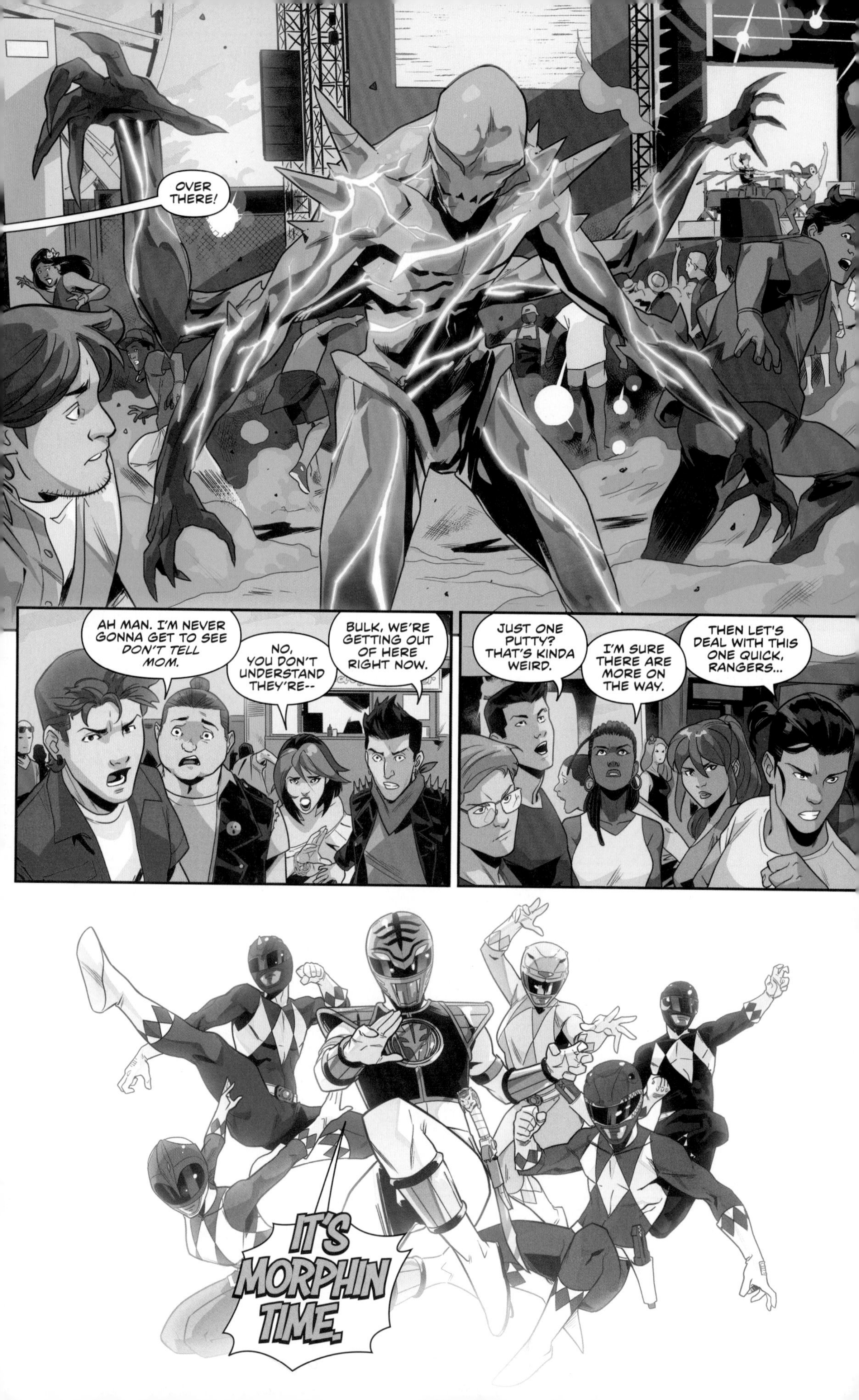
OVER THERE!
AH MAN. I'M NEVER GONNA GET TO SEE DON'T TELL MOM.
NO, YOU DON'T UNDERSTAND THEY'RE--
BULK, WE'RE GETTING OUT OF HERE RIGHT NOW.
JUST ONE PUTTY? THAT'S KINDA WEIRD.
I'M SURE THERE ARE MORE ON THE WAY.
THEN LET'S DEAL WITH THIS ONE QUICK, RANGERS...
IT'S MORPHIN TIME.

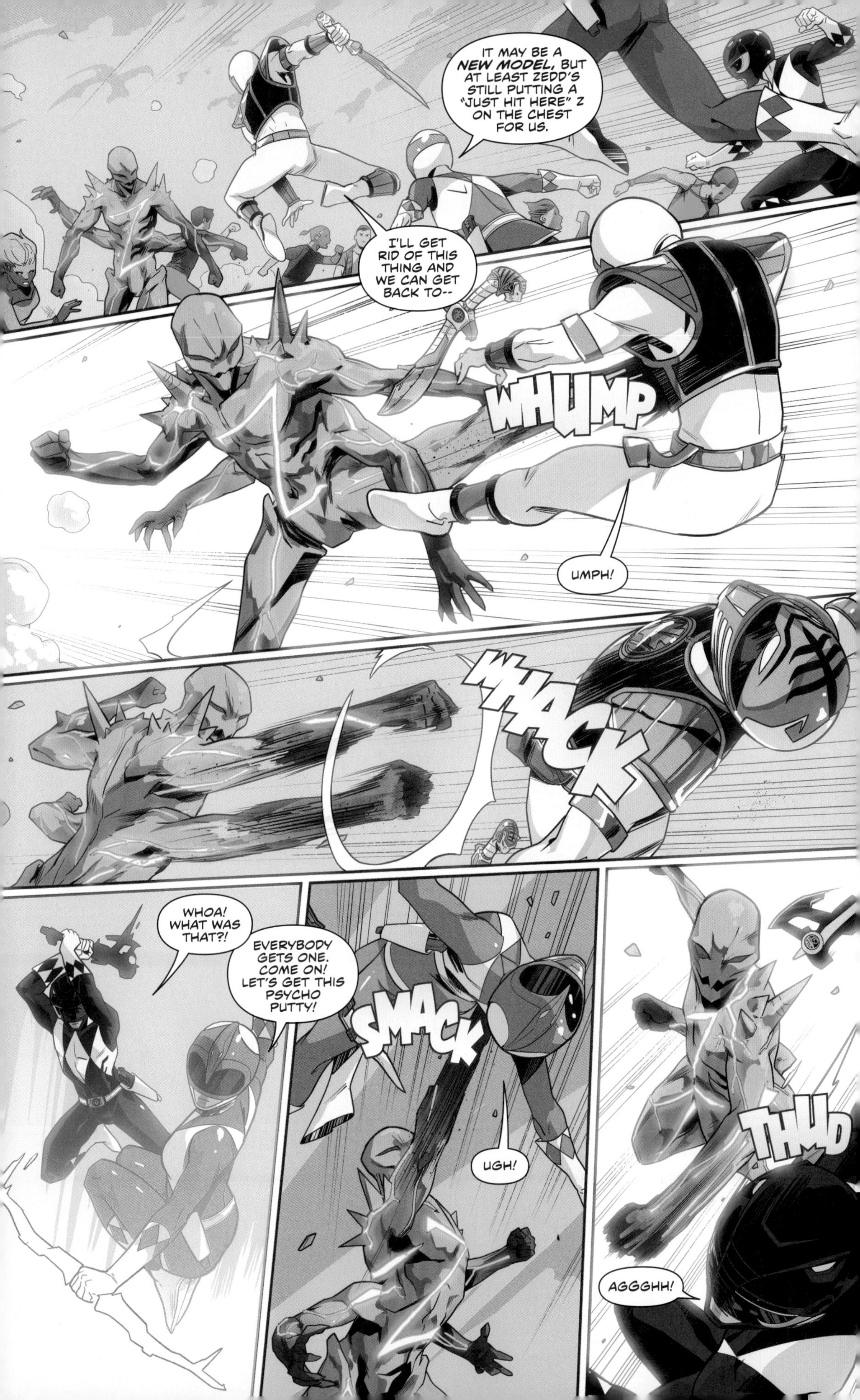
IT MAY BE A NEW MODEL, BUT AT LEAST ZEDD'S STILL PUTTING A "JUST HIT HERE" Z ON THE CHEST FOR US.
I'LL GET RID OF THIS THING AND WE CAN GET BACK TO--
WHUMP
UMPH!
WHACK
WHOA! WHAT WAS THAT?!
EVERYBODY GETS ONE. COME ON! LET'S GET THIS PSYCHO PUTTY!
SMACK
UGH!
THUD
AGGGHH!

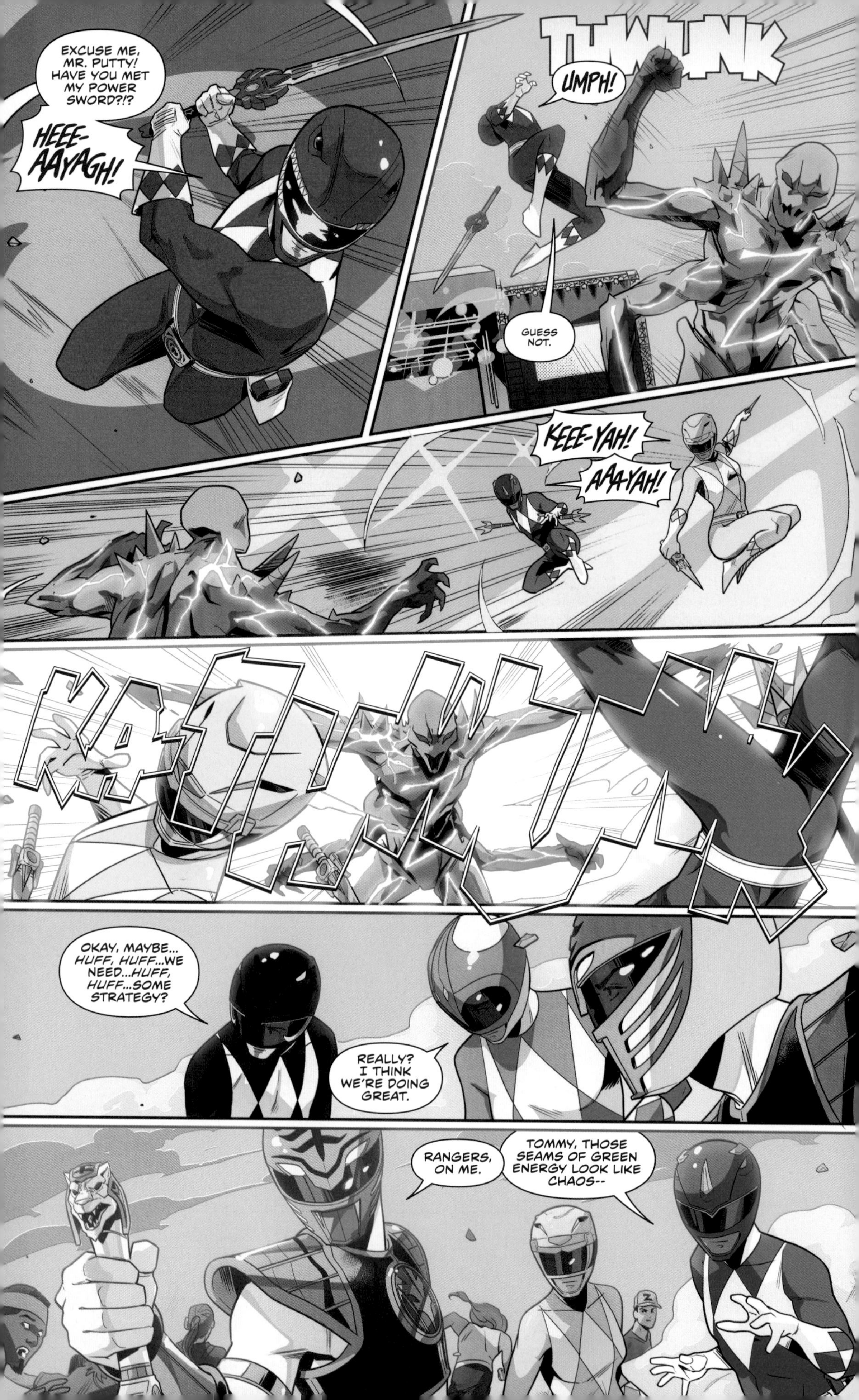
EXCUSE ME, MR. PUTTY! HAVE YOU MET MY POWER SWORD?!?
HEEE-AAYAGH!
THWUNK
UMPH!
GUESS NOT.
KEEE-YAH!
AAA-YAH!
OKAY, MAYBE... HUFF, HUFF...WE NEED...HUFF, HUFF...SOME STRATEGY?
REALLY? I THINK WE'RE DOING GREAT.
RANGERS, ON ME.
TOMMY, THOSE SEAMS OF GREEN ENERGY LOOK LIKE CHAOS--

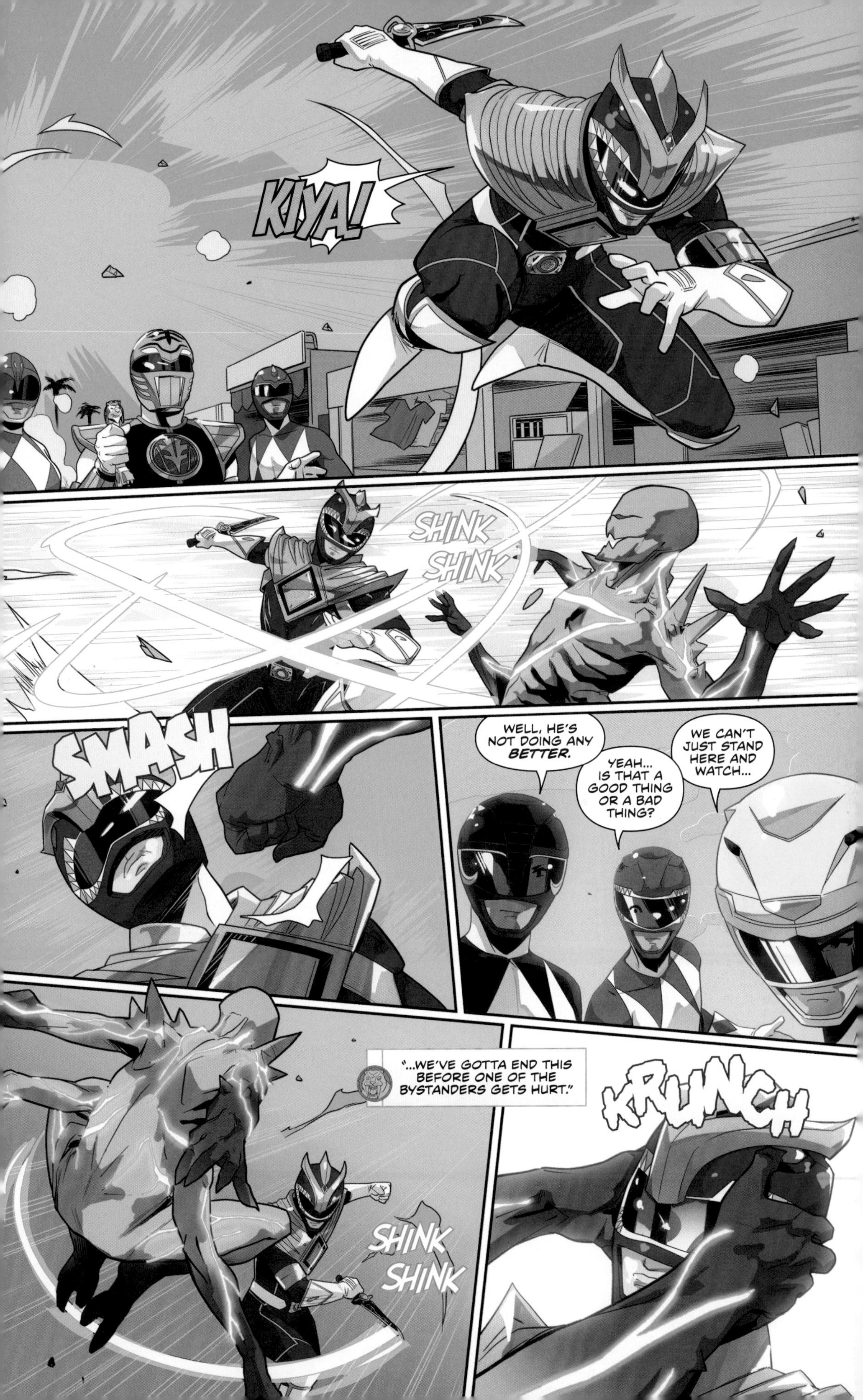
KIYA!
SHINK
SHINK
SMASH
WELL, HE'S NOT DOING ANY *BETTER*.
YEAH... IS THAT A GOOD THING OR A BAD THING?
WE CAN'T JUST STAND HERE AND WATCH...
"...WE'VE GOTTA END THIS BEFORE ONE OF THE BYSTANDERS GETS HURT."
SHINK
SHINK
KRUNCH

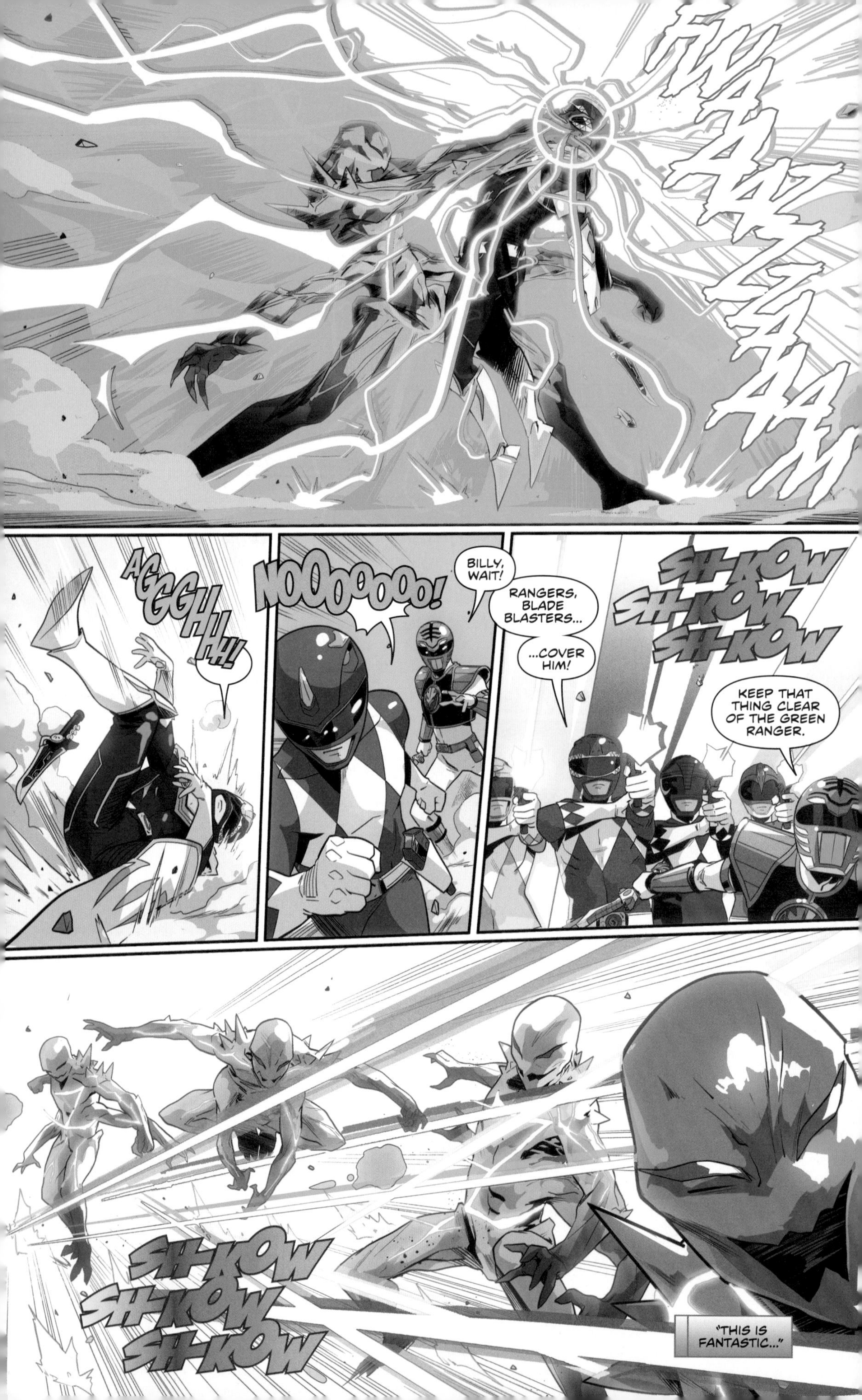
FWAAAZZAAAAM
AGGGHHH!
NOOOOOOOO!
BILLY, WAIT!
RANGERS, BLADE BLASTERS...
...COVER HIM!
SH-KOW SH-KOW SH-KOW
KEEP THAT THING CLEAR OF THE GREEN RANGER.
SH-KOW SH-KOW SH-KOW
"THIS IS FANTASTIC..."

...HAVE IT ELECTROCUTE THE WHITE ONE NEXT!

WAIT, NO! THE RED ONE!

SQUATT, STOP HOGGING THE TELESCOPE! I WANT TO LOOK TOO!

YOU'VE NEARLY TAKEN DOWN THE RANGERS WITH ONE CHAOS PUTTY, MY LORD.

YES.

BUT WE CAN DO SO MUCH BETTER.

KA-THWOOOM

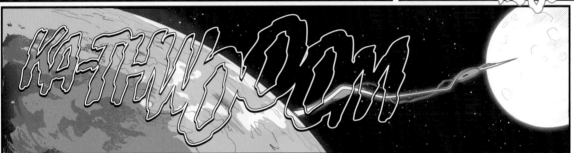

KA-THWOOOM

"REMOVE YOUR DISGUISES AND COME OUT OF HIDING, MY CHILDREN.

"IT'S TIME TO FULFILL YOUR TRUE DESTINY."

UM, IS THAT EVERYBODY?!

OH, NO. NO WAY...

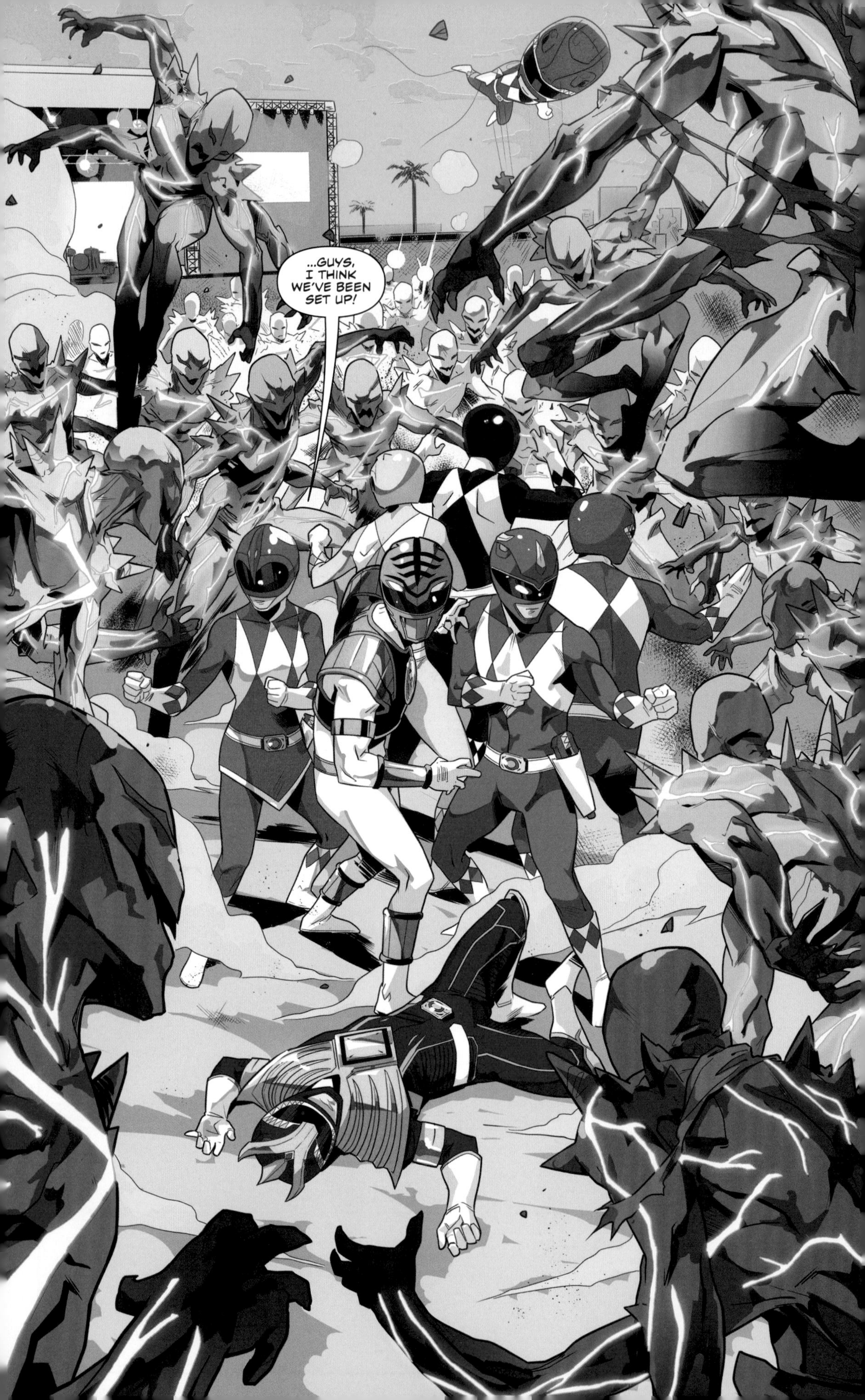
...GUYS, I THINK WE'VE BEEN SET UP!

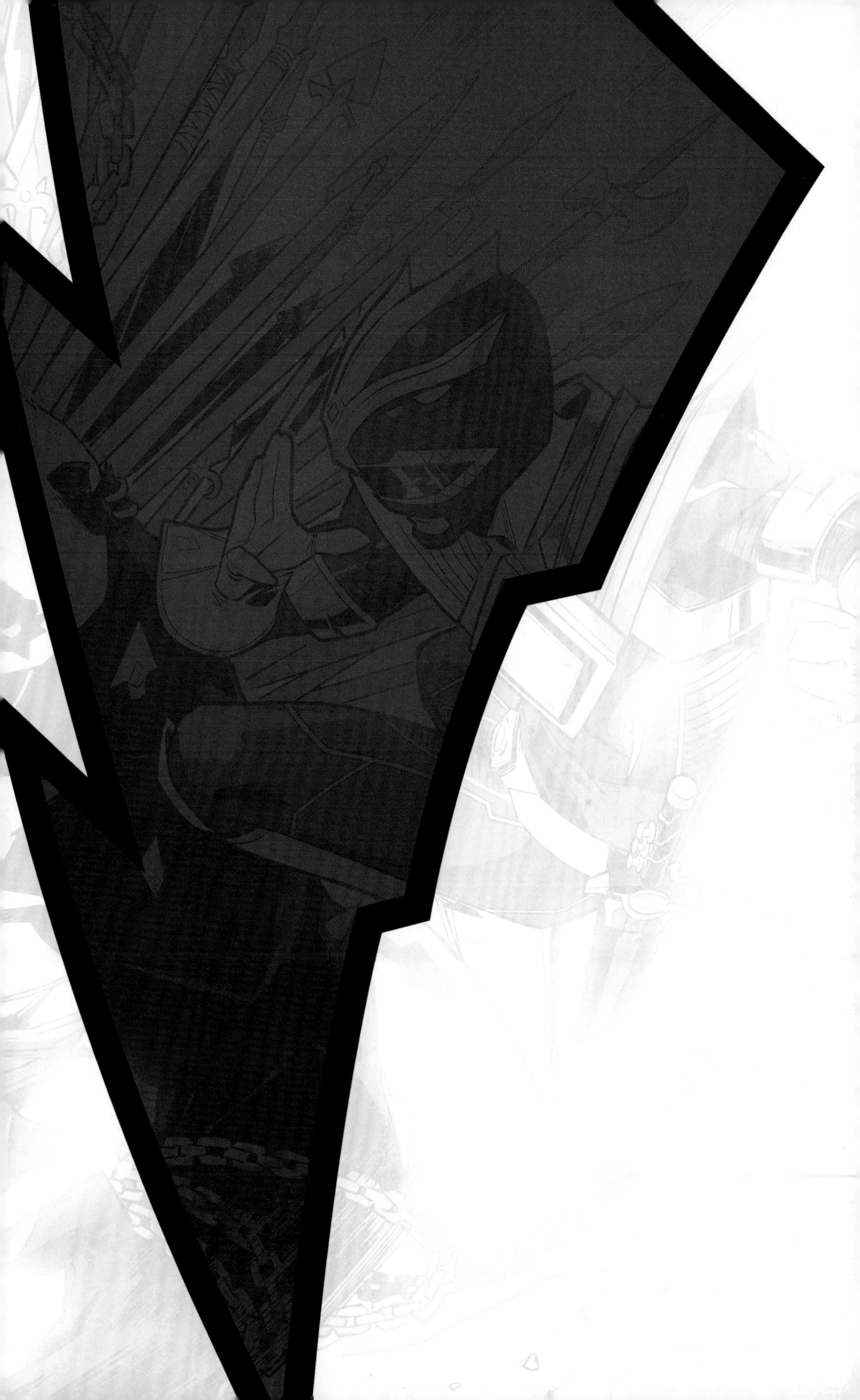

# CHAPTER THREE

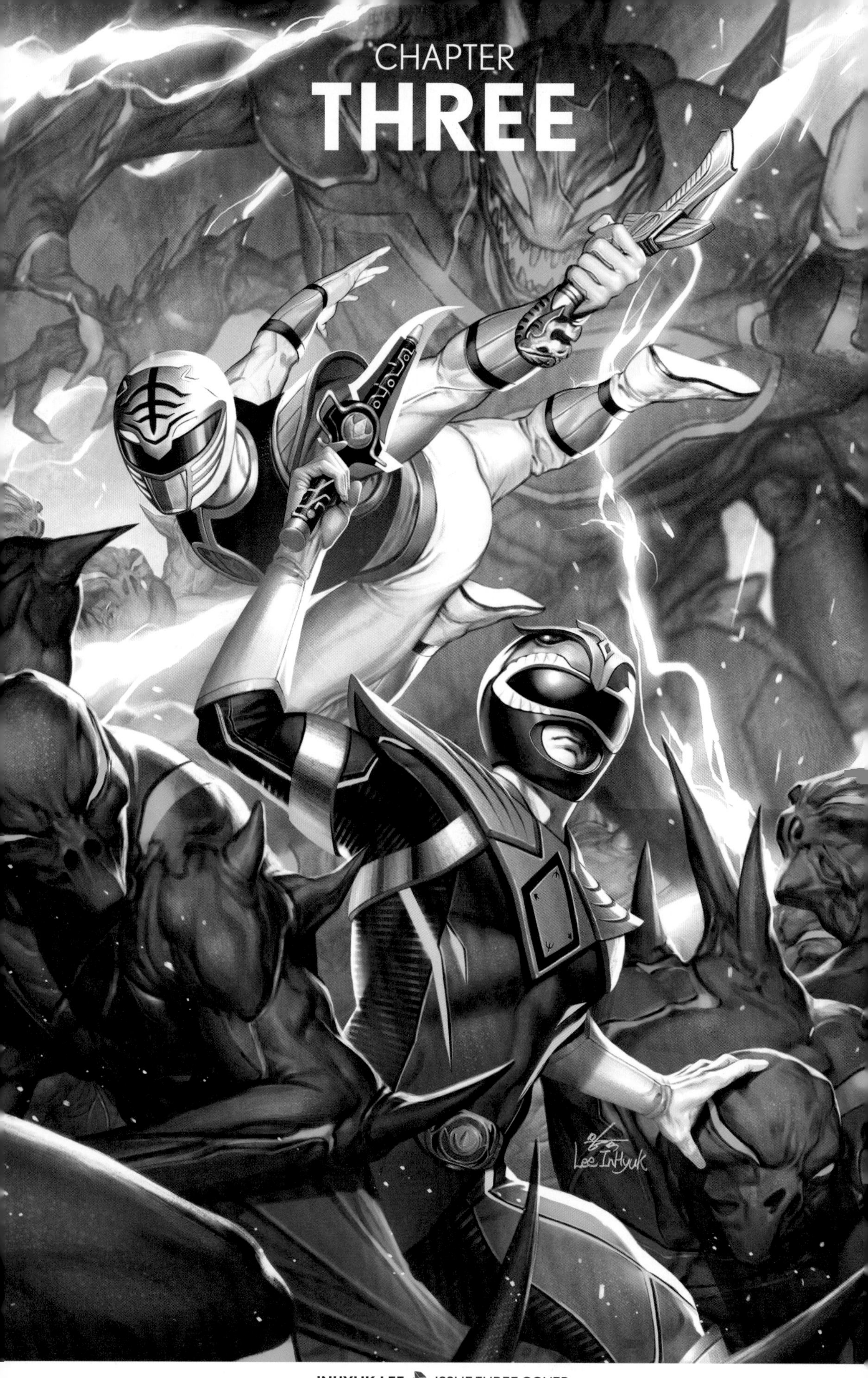
Lee InHyuK

**INHYUK LEE** ISSUE THREE COVER

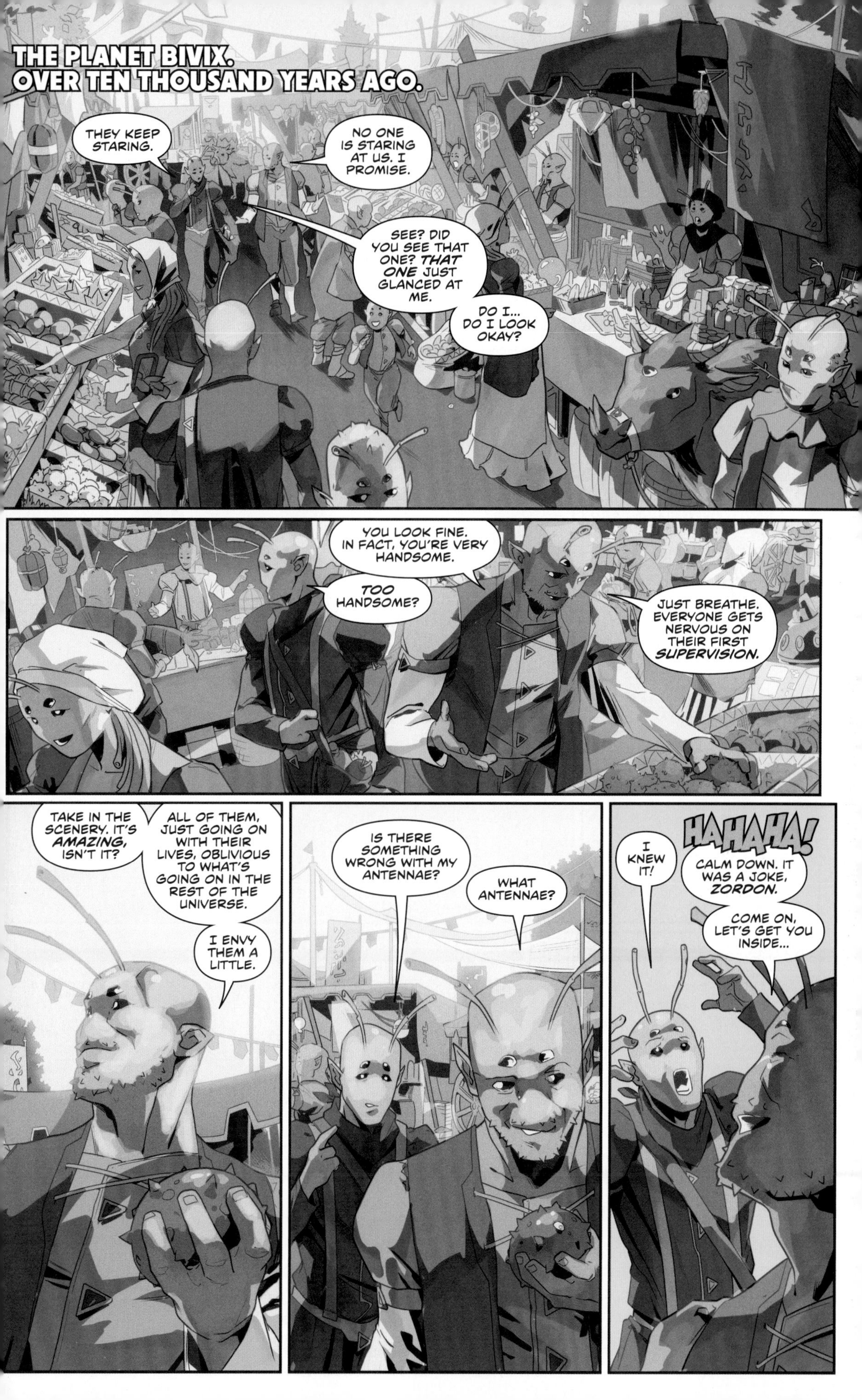
THE PLANET BIVIX.
OVER TEN THOUSAND YEARS AGO.
THEY KEEP STARING.
NO ONE IS STARING AT US. I PROMISE.
SEE? DID YOU SEE THAT ONE? THAT ONE JUST GLANCED AT ME.
DO I... DO I LOOK OKAY?
YOU LOOK FINE. IN FACT, YOU'RE VERY HANDSOME.
TOO HANDSOME?
JUST BREATHE. EVERYONE GETS NERVOUS ON THEIR FIRST SUPERVISION.
TAKE IN THE SCENERY. IT'S AMAZING, ISN'T IT?
ALL OF THEM, JUST GOING ON WITH THEIR LIVES, OBLIVIOUS TO WHAT'S GOING ON IN THE REST OF THE UNIVERSE.
I ENVY THEM A LITTLE.
IS THERE SOMETHING WRONG WITH MY ANTENNAE?
WHAT ANTENNAE?
HAHAHA!
I KNEW IT!
CALM DOWN. IT WAS A JOKE, ZORDON.
COME ON, LET'S GET YOU INSIDE...

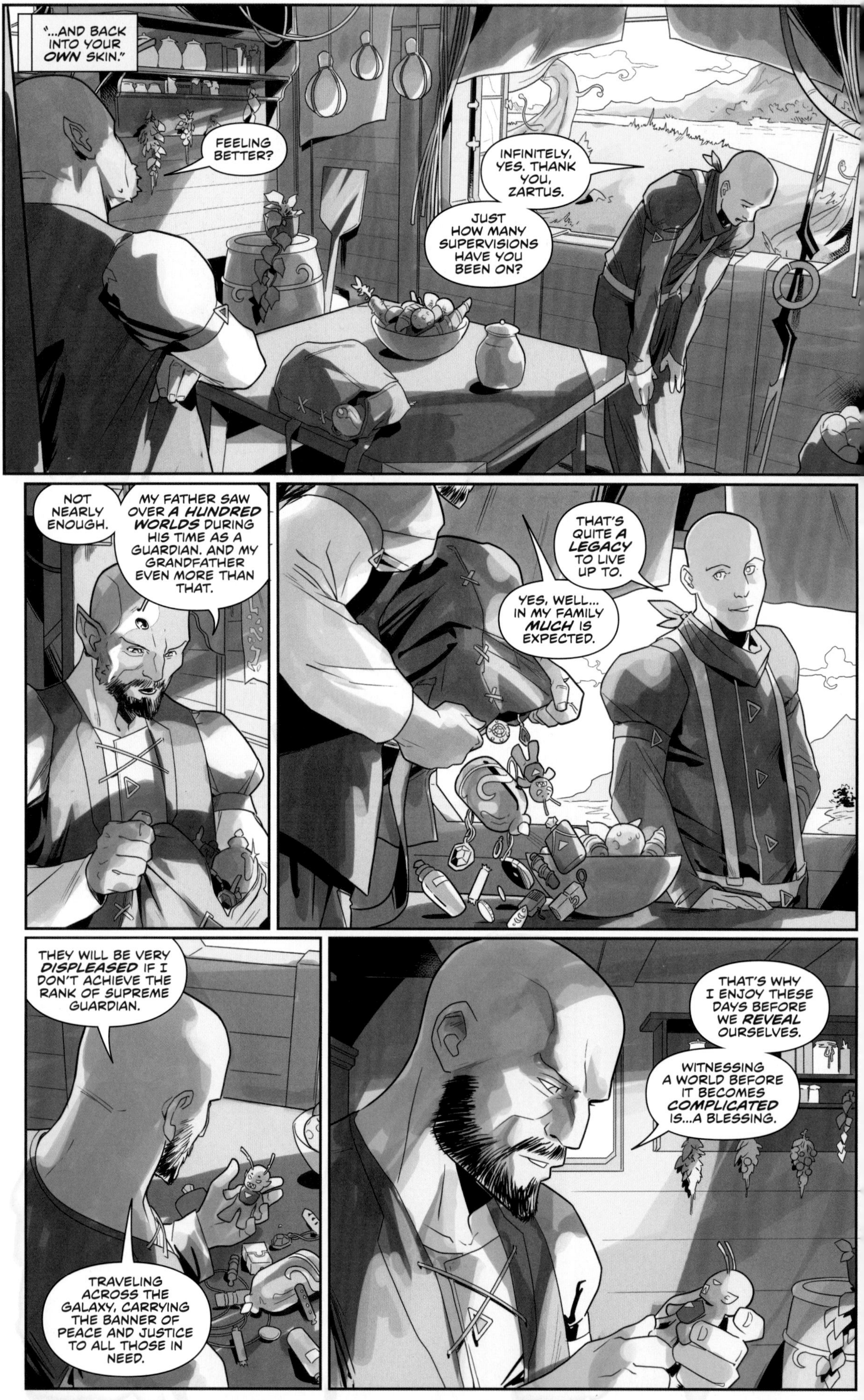
"...AND BACK INTO YOUR OWN SKIN."
FEELING BETTER?
INFINITELY, YES. THANK YOU, ZARTUS.
JUST HOW MANY SUPERVISIONS HAVE YOU BEEN ON?
NOT NEARLY ENOUGH.
MY FATHER SAW OVER A HUNDRED WORLDS DURING HIS TIME AS A GUARDIAN. AND MY GRANDFATHER EVEN MORE THAN THAT.
THAT'S QUITE A LEGACY TO LIVE UP TO.
YES, WELL... IN MY FAMILY MUCH IS EXPECTED.
THEY WILL BE VERY DISPLEASED IF I DON'T ACHIEVE THE RANK OF SUPREME GUARDIAN.
TRAVELING ACROSS THE GALAXY, CARRYING THE BANNER OF PEACE AND JUSTICE TO ALL THOSE IN NEED.
THAT'S WHY I ENJOY THESE DAYS BEFORE WE REVEAL OURSELVES.
WITNESSING A WORLD BEFORE IT BECOMES COMPLICATED IS...A BLESSING.

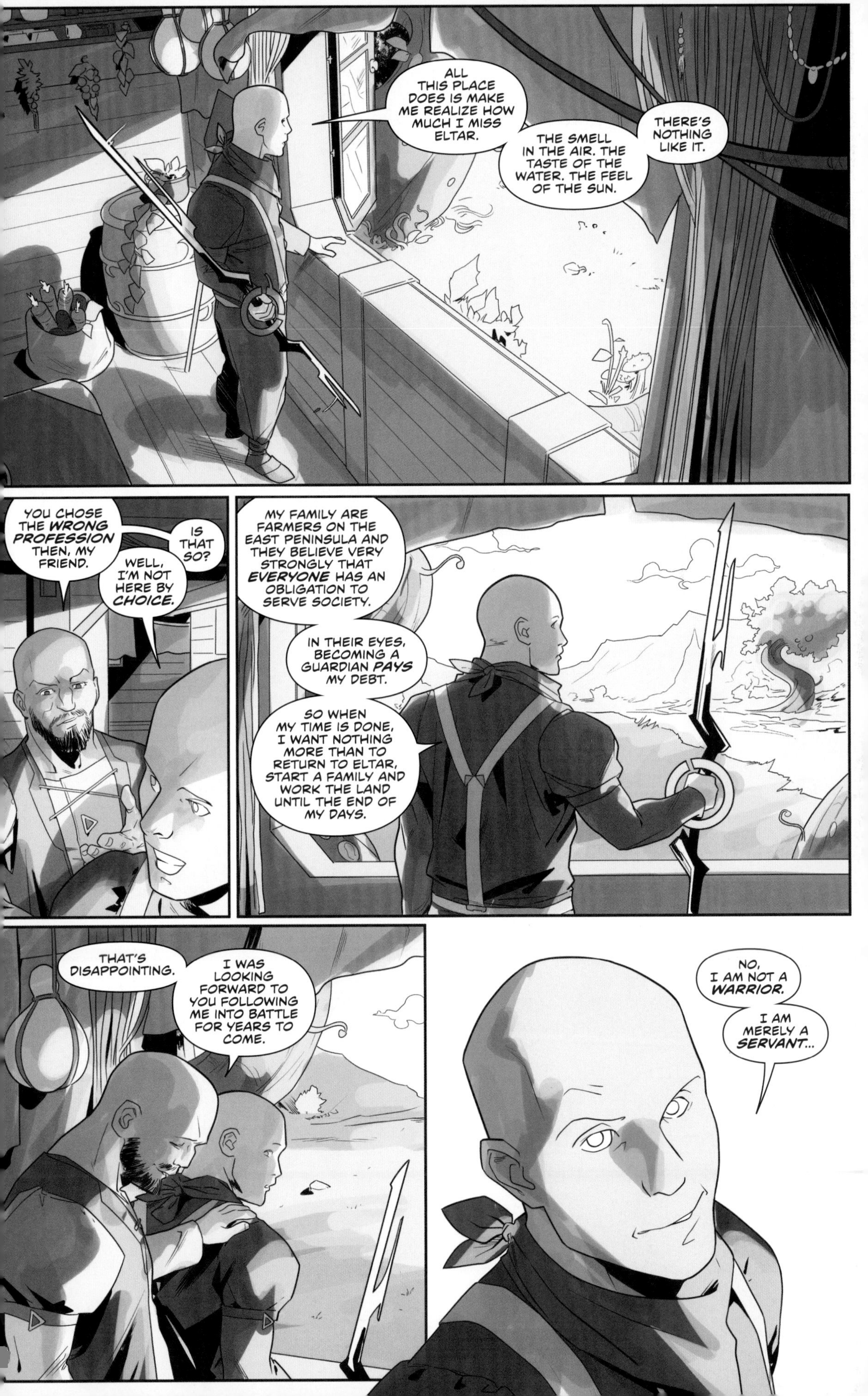
ALL THIS PLACE DOES IS MAKE ME REALIZE HOW MUCH I MISS ELTAR.
THE SMELL IN THE AIR. THE TASTE OF THE WATER. THE FEEL OF THE SUN.
THERE'S NOTHING LIKE IT.
YOU CHOSE THE WRONG PROFESSION THEN, MY FRIEND.
IS THAT SO?
WELL, I'M NOT HERE BY CHOICE.
MY FAMILY ARE FARMERS ON THE EAST PENINSULA AND THEY BELIEVE VERY STRONGLY THAT EVERYONE HAS AN OBLIGATION TO SERVE SOCIETY.
IN THEIR EYES, BECOMING A GUARDIAN PAYS MY DEBT.
SO WHEN MY TIME IS DONE, I WANT NOTHING MORE THAN TO RETURN TO ELTAR, START A FAMILY AND WORK THE LAND UNTIL THE END OF MY DAYS.
THAT'S DISAPPOINTING.
I WAS LOOKING FORWARD TO YOU FOLLOWING ME INTO BATTLE FOR YEARS TO COME.
NO, I AM NOT A WARRIOR.
I AM MERELY A SERVANT...

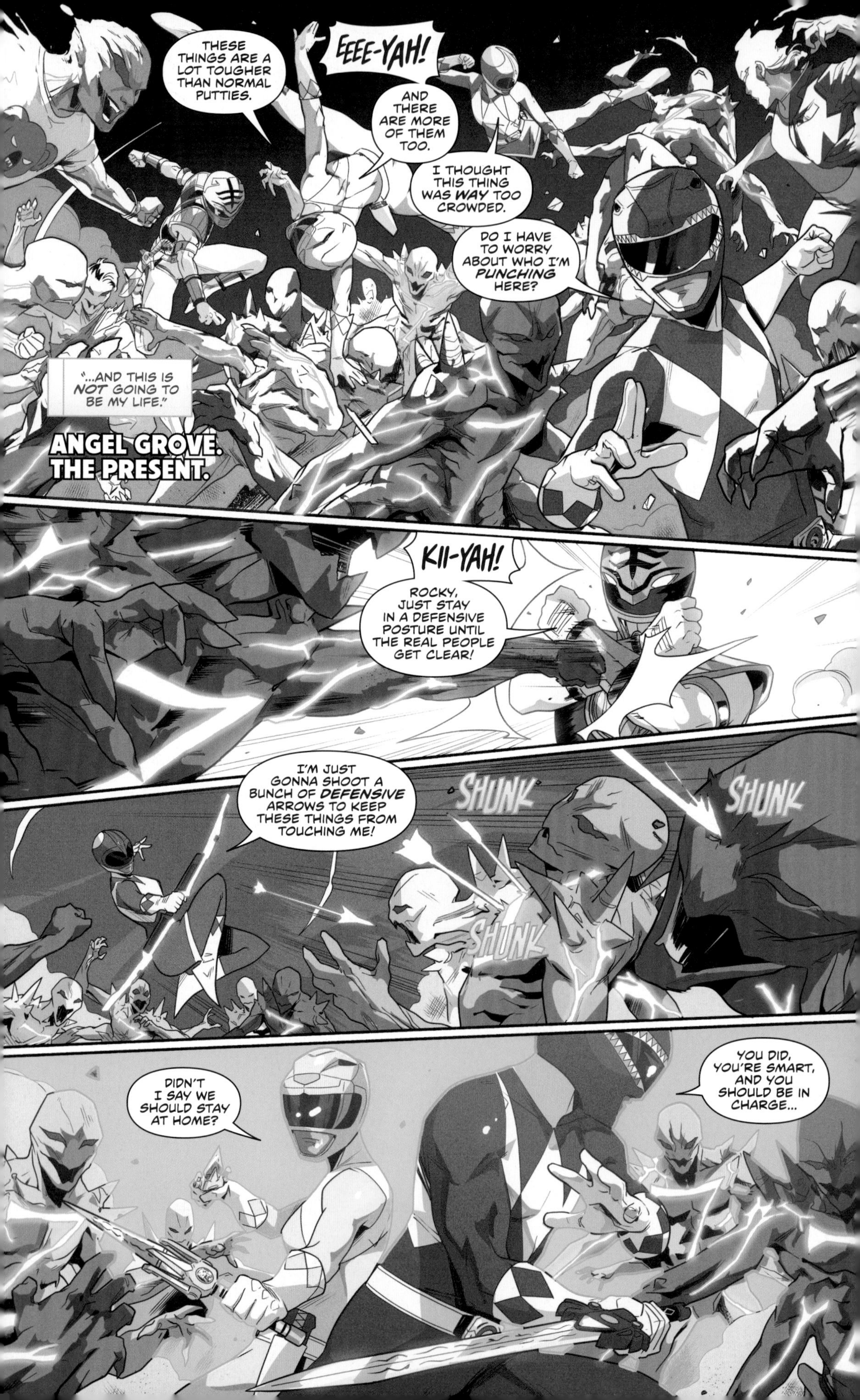

THESE THINGS ARE A LOT TOUGHER THAN NORMAL PUTTIES.
EEEE-YAH!
AND THERE ARE MORE OF THEM TOO.
I THOUGHT THIS THING WAS *WAY* TOO CROWDED.
DO I HAVE TO WORRY ABOUT WHO I'M *PUNCHING* HERE?
"...AND THIS IS *NOT* GOING TO BE MY LIFE."
ANGEL GROVE. THE PRESENT.
KII-YAH!
ROCKY, JUST STAY IN A DEFENSIVE POSTURE UNTIL THE REAL PEOPLE GET CLEAR!
I'M JUST GONNA SHOOT A BUNCH OF *DEFENSIVE* ARROWS TO KEEP THESE THINGS FROM TOUCHING ME!
SHUNK
SHUNK
SHUNK
DIDN'T I SAY WE SHOULD STAY AT HOME?
YOU DID, YOU'RE SMART, AND YOU SHOULD BE IN CHARGE...

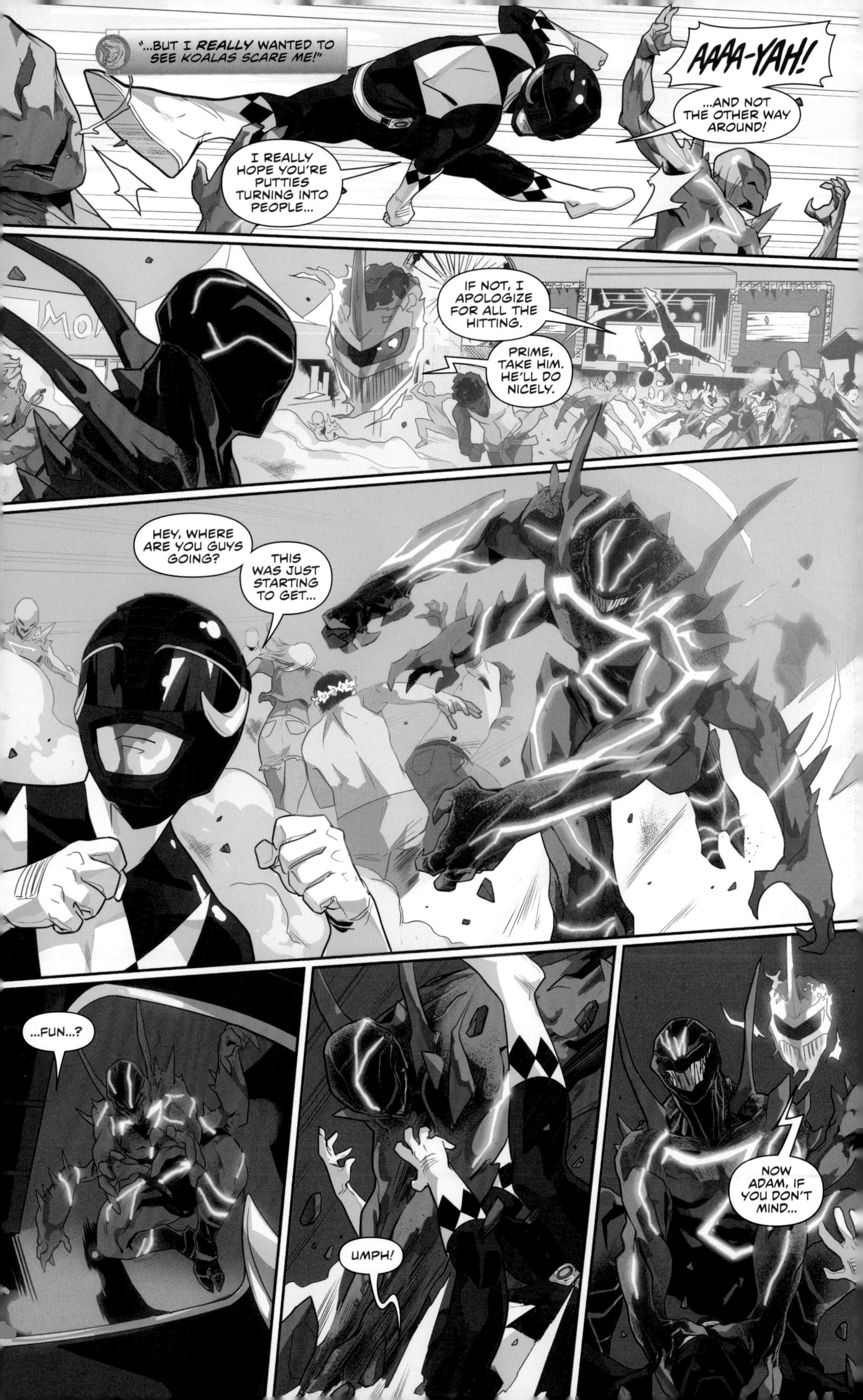
"...BUT I REALLY WANTED TO SEE KOALAS SCARE ME!"
AAAA-YAH!
...AND NOT THE OTHER WAY AROUND!
I REALLY HOPE YOU'RE PUTTIES TURNING INTO PEOPLE...
IF NOT, I APOLOGIZE FOR ALL THE HITTING.
PRIME, TAKE HIM. HE'LL DO NICELY.
HEY, WHERE ARE YOU GUYS GOING?
THIS WAS JUST STARTING TO GET...
...FUN...?
UMPH!
NOW ADAM, IF YOU DON'T MIND...

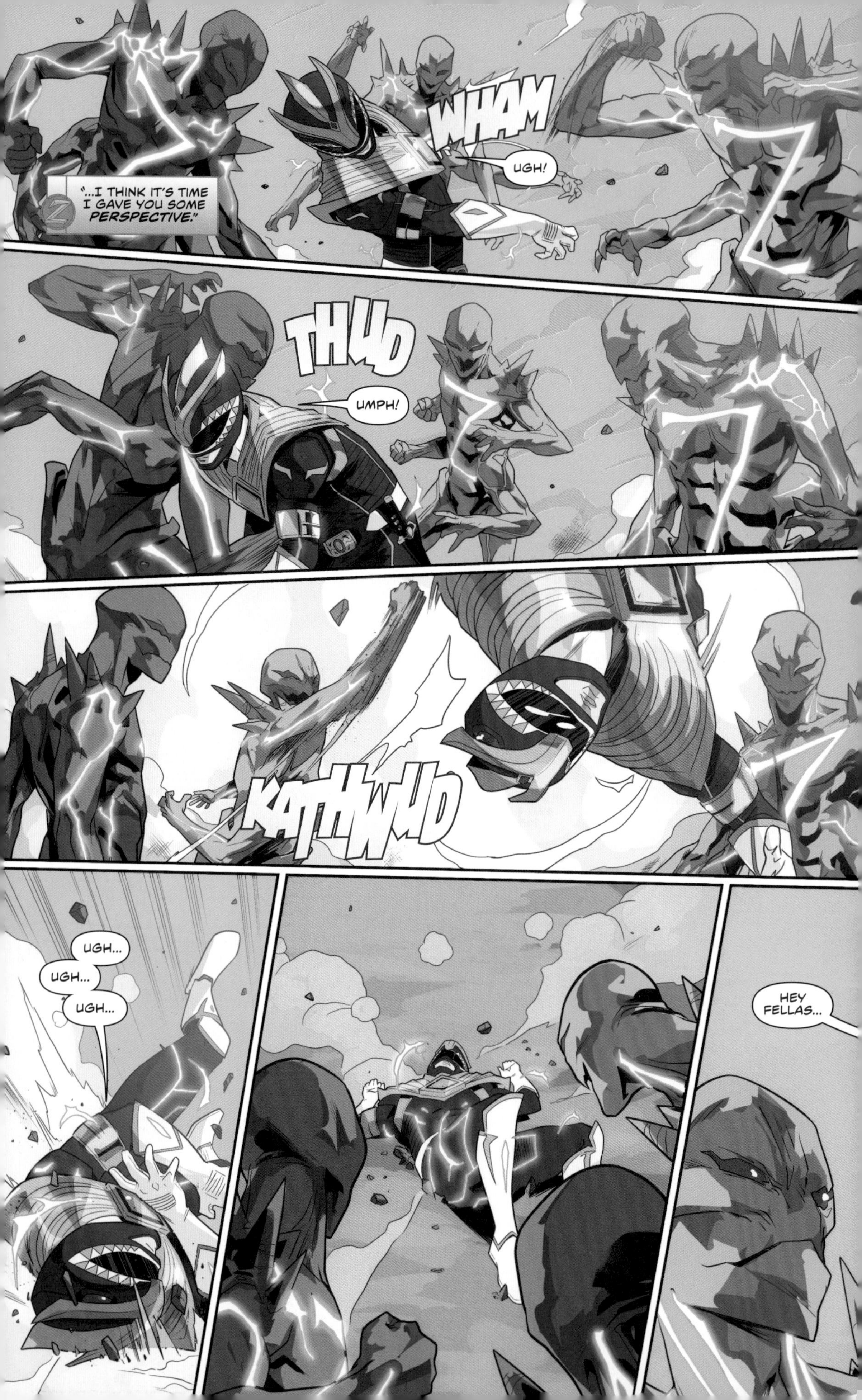
"...I THINK IT'S TIME I GAVE YOU SOME PERSPECTIVE."
WHAM
UGH!
THUD
UMPH!
KATHWUD
UGH...
UGH...
UGH...
HEY FELLAS...

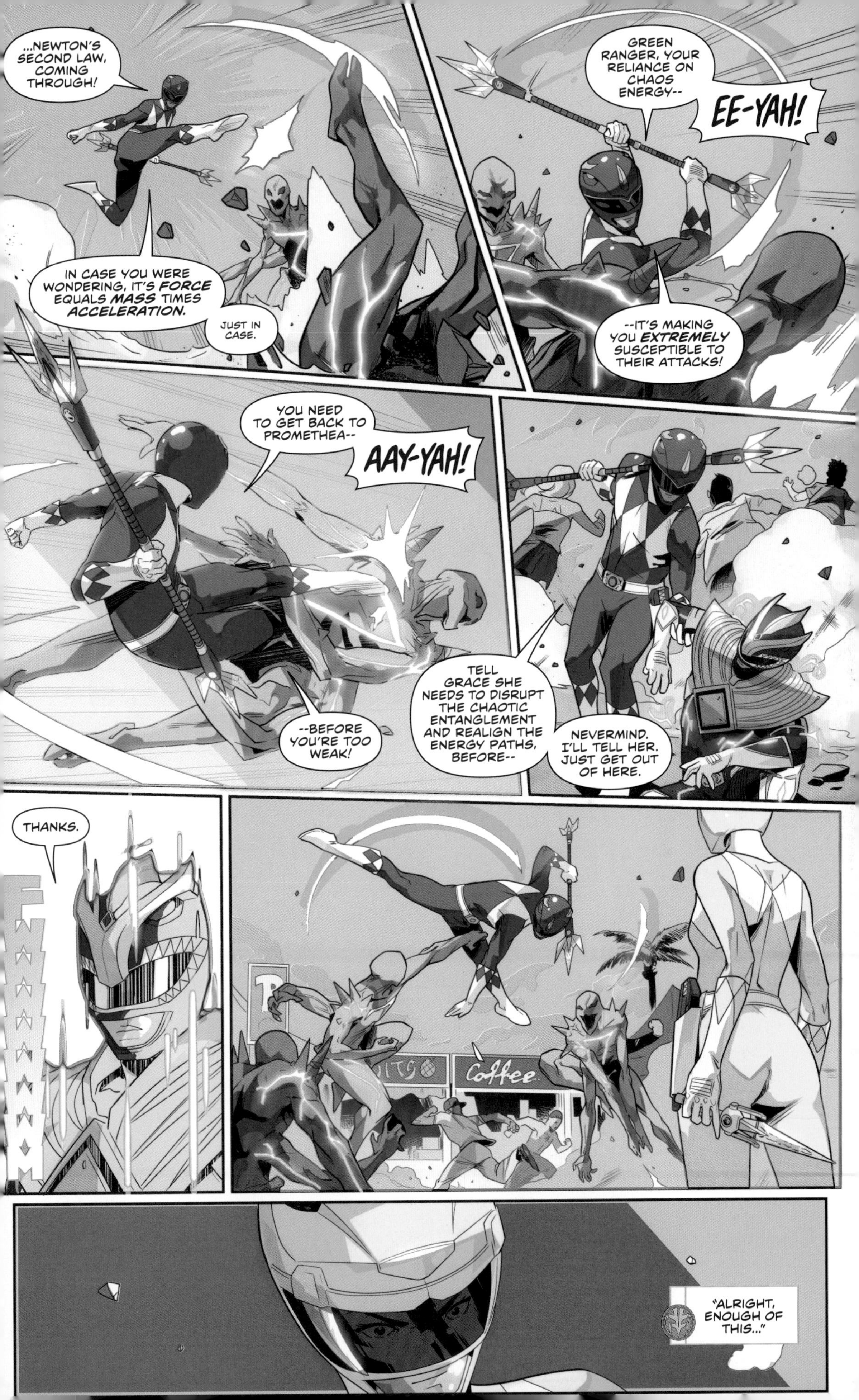
...NEWTON'S SECOND LAW, COMING THROUGH!
IN CASE YOU WERE WONDERING, IT'S FORCE EQUALS MASS TIMES ACCELERATION.
JUST IN CASE.
GREEN RANGER, YOUR RELIANCE ON CHAOS ENERGY--
EE-YAH!
--IT'S MAKING YOU EXTREMELY SUSCEPTIBLE TO THEIR ATTACKS!
YOU NEED TO GET BACK TO PROMETHEA--
AAY-YAH!
--BEFORE YOU'RE TOO WEAK!
TELL GRACE SHE NEEDS TO DISRUPT THE CHAOTIC ENTANGLEMENT AND REALIGN THE ENERGY PATHS, BEFORE--
NEVERMIND. I'LL TELL HER. JUST GET OUT OF HERE.
THANKS.
FWAAAAAAAM
Coffee
"ALRIGHT, ENOUGH OF THIS..."

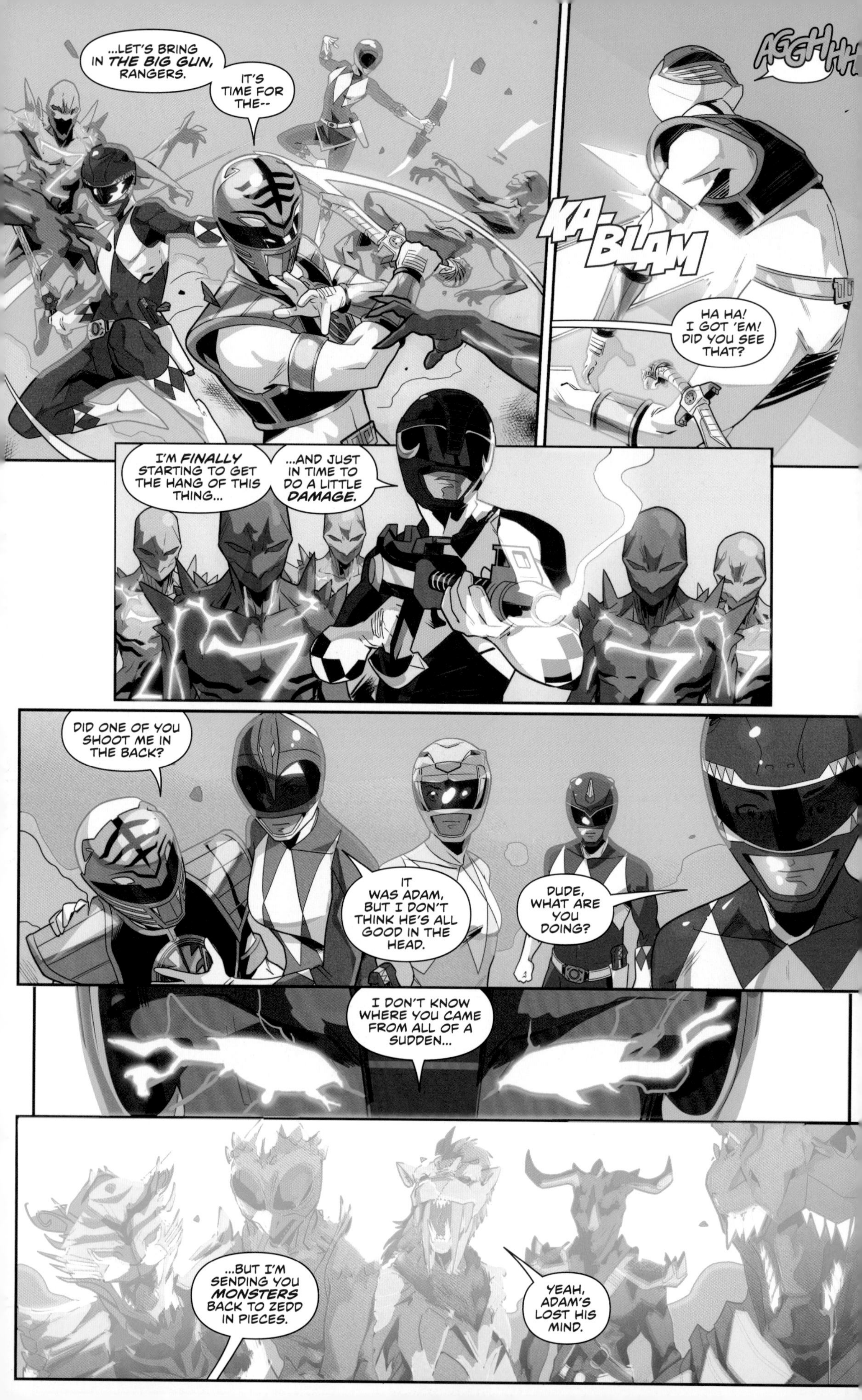
...LET'S BRING IN THE BIG GUN, RANGERS.
IT'S TIME FOR THE--
AGGHHH
KA-BLAM
HA HA! I GOT 'EM! DID YOU SEE THAT?
I'M FINALLY STARTING TO GET THE HANG OF THIS THING...
...AND JUST IN TIME TO DO A LITTLE DAMAGE.
DID ONE OF YOU SHOOT ME IN THE BACK?
IT WAS ADAM, BUT I DON'T THINK HE'S ALL GOOD IN THE HEAD.
DUDE, WHAT ARE YOU DOING?
I DON'T KNOW WHERE YOU CAME FROM ALL OF A SUDDEN...
...BUT I'M SENDING YOU MONSTERS BACK TO ZEDD IN PIECES.
YEAH, ADAM'S LOST HIS MIND.

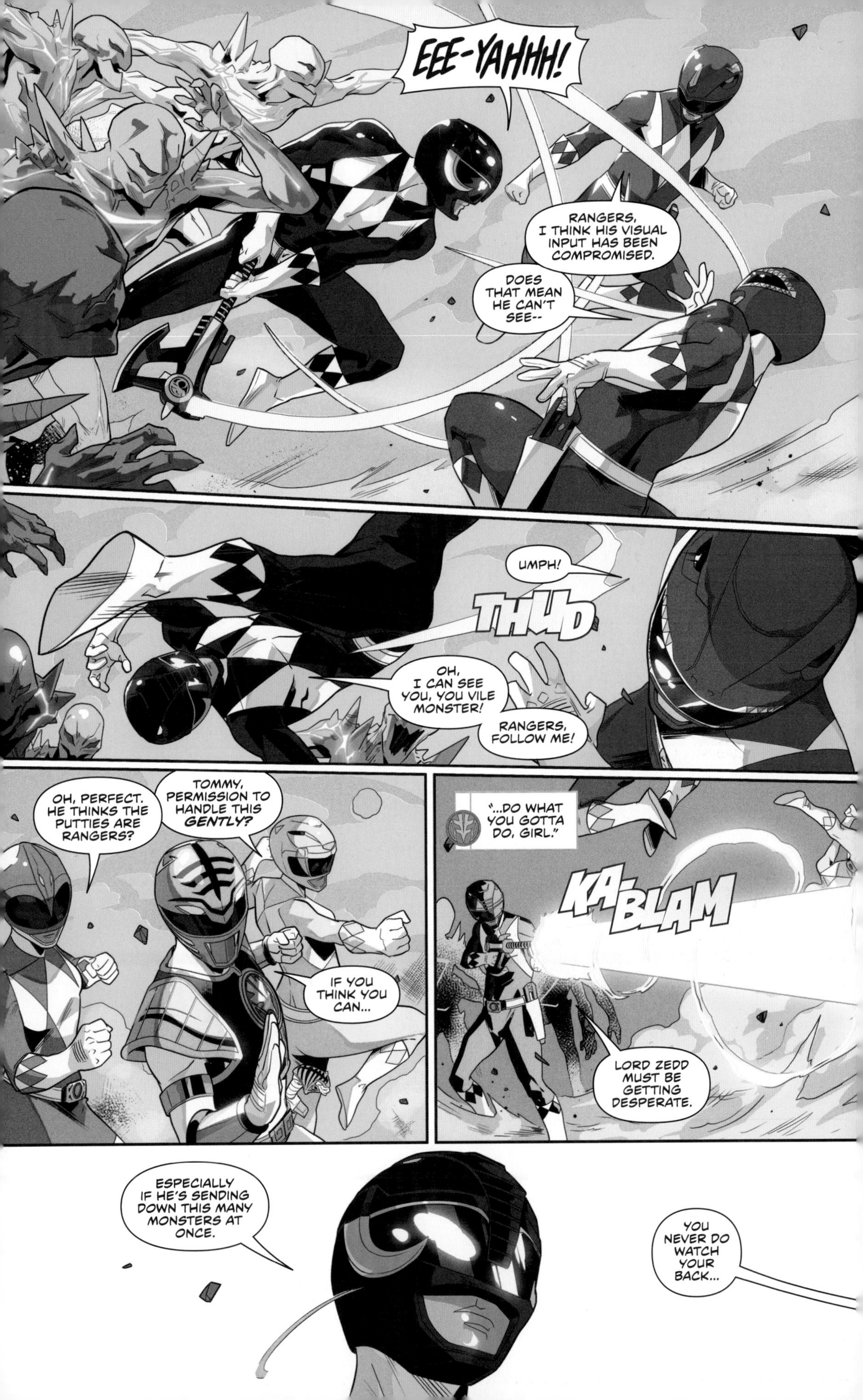
EEE-YAHHH!
RANGERS, I THINK HIS VISUAL INPUT HAS BEEN COMPROMISED.
DOES THAT MEAN HE CAN'T SEE--
UMPH!
THUD
OH, I CAN SEE YOU, YOU VILE MONSTER!
RANGERS, FOLLOW ME!
OH, PERFECT. HE THINKS THE PUTTIES ARE RANGERS?
TOMMY, PERMISSION TO HANDLE THIS *GENTLY*?
IF YOU THINK YOU CAN...
"...DO WHAT YOU GOTTA DO, GIRL."
KA-BLAM
LORD ZEDD MUST BE GETTING DESPERATE.
ESPECIALLY IF HE'S SENDING DOWN THIS MANY MONSTERS AT ONCE.
YOU NEVER DO WATCH YOUR BACK...

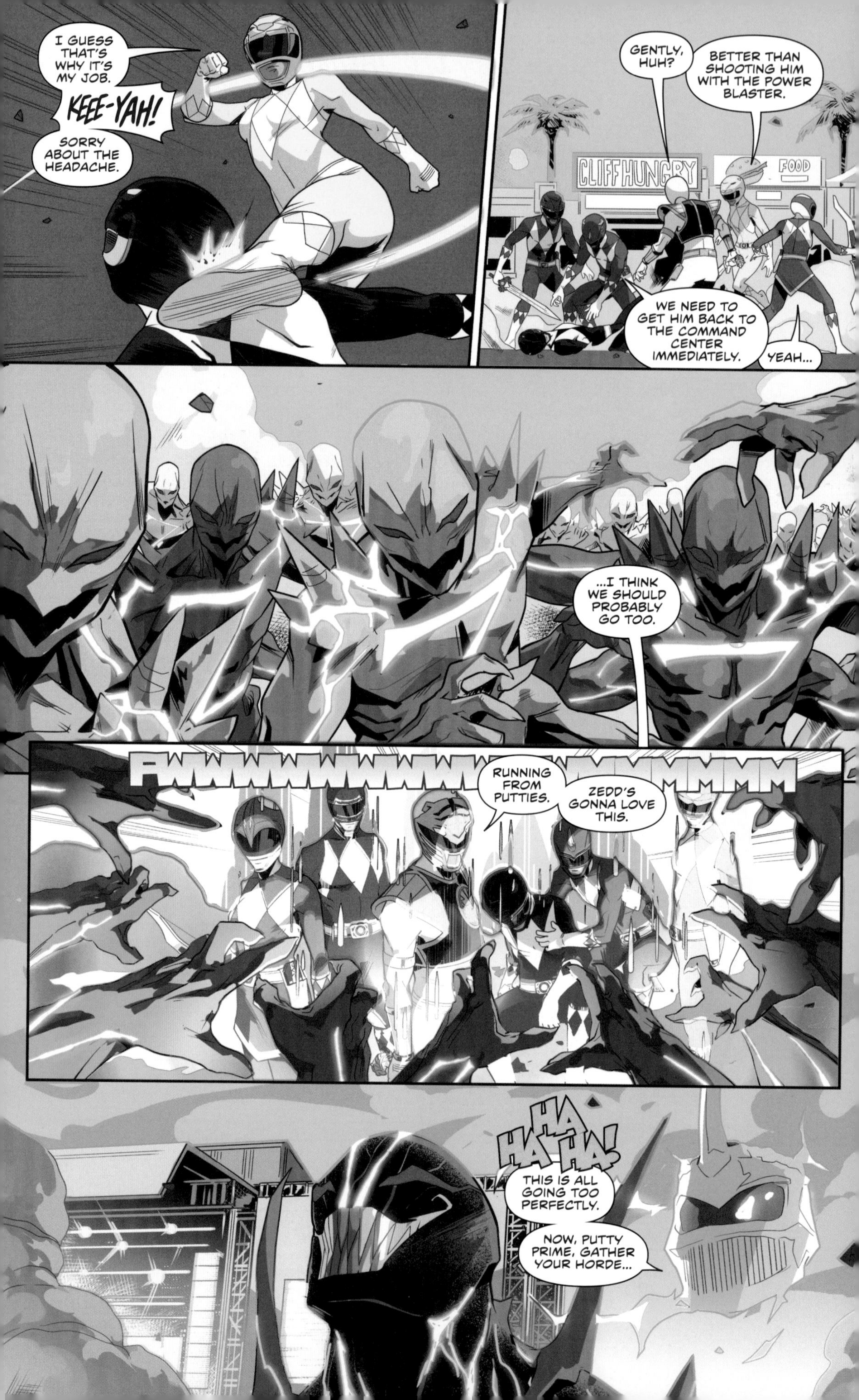
I GUESS THAT'S WHY IT'S MY JOB.
KEEE-YAH!
SORRY ABOUT THE HEADACHE.
GENTLY, HUH?
BETTER THAN SHOOTING HIM WITH THE POWER BLASTER.
CLIFFHUNGRY
FOOD
WE NEED TO GET HIM BACK TO THE COMMAND CENTER IMMEDIATELY.
YEAH...
...I THINK WE SHOULD PROBABLY GO TOO.
FWWWWWWWWWWMMMMMMM
RUNNING FROM PUTTIES.
ZEDD'S GONNA LOVE THIS.
HA HA HA!
THIS IS ALL GOING TOO PERFECTLY.
NOW, PUTTY PRIME, GATHER YOUR HORDE...

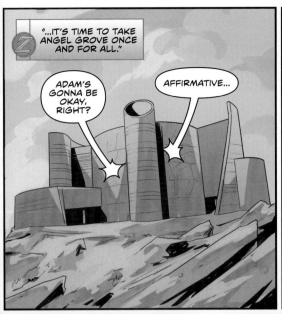

"...IT'S TIME TO TAKE ANGEL GROVE ONCE AND FOR ALL."

ADAM'S GONNA BE OKAY, RIGHT?

AFFIRMATIVE...

...BUT I NEED TO PURGE HIM OF ANY VALENCE ENERGY SIGNATURES.

COOL. IS THAT GONNA HURT?

NOT AS MUCH AS GETTING KICKED IN THE HEAD BY AISHA.

SO THOSE PUTTIES...ARE THEY GETTING *STRONGER* OR ARE WE GETTING *WEAKER*?

JUDGING FROM OUR READINGS, THEY'VE BEEN LACED WITH CHAOS ENERGY.

THEY'RE SIGNIFICANTLY MORE DANGEROUS.

AND RIGHT NOW, THEY'RE PROBABLY SPREADING OUT OVER THE ENTIRE CITY.

WE GOTTA GET BACK IN THE GAME, ZORDON.

WE WILL, TOMMY. AS SOON AS YOU'RE BACK AT FULL STRENGTH.

RIGHT NOW, WE'RE--

ZORDON! ZORDON! I DID IT!

I WAS FINALLY ABLE TO TRACE THE GREEN RANGER'S TELEPORTATION TRAJECTORY...

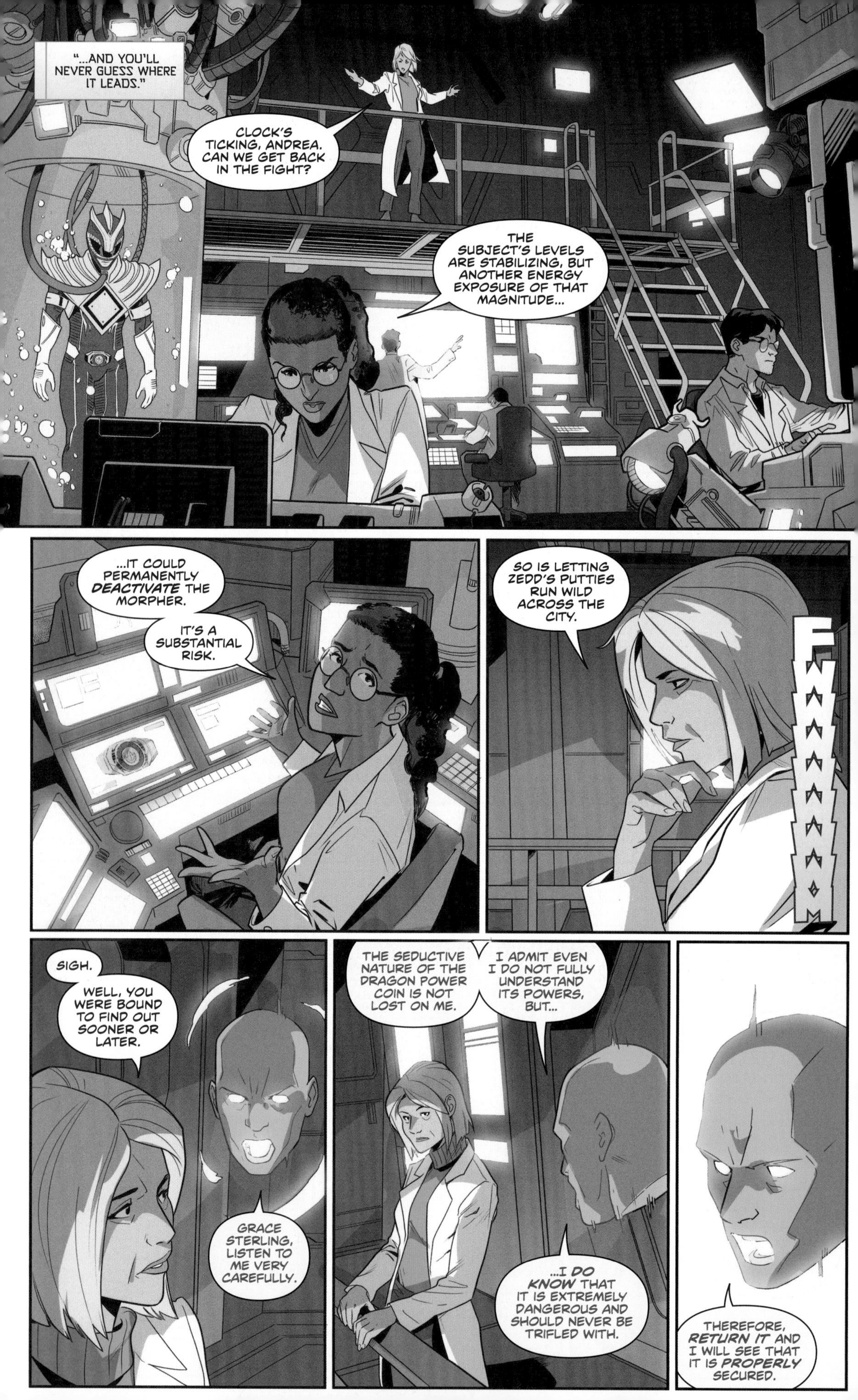
"...AND YOU'LL NEVER GUESS WHERE IT LEADS."
CLOCK'S TICKING, ANDREA. CAN WE GET BACK IN THE FIGHT?
THE SUBJECT'S LEVELS ARE STABILIZING, BUT ANOTHER ENERGY EXPOSURE OF THAT MAGNITUDE...
...IT COULD PERMANENTLY DEACTIVATE THE MORPHER.
IT'S A SUBSTANTIAL RISK.
SO IS LETTING ZEDD'S PUTTIES RUN WILD ACROSS THE CITY.
FWAAAAAAAAAM
SIGH.
WELL, YOU WERE BOUND TO FIND OUT SOONER OR LATER.
GRACE STERLING, LISTEN TO ME VERY CAREFULLY.
THE SEDUCTIVE NATURE OF THE DRAGON POWER COIN IS NOT LOST ON ME.
I ADMIT EVEN I DO NOT FULLY UNDERSTAND ITS POWERS, BUT...
...I DO KNOW THAT IT IS EXTREMELY DANGEROUS AND SHOULD NEVER BE TRIFLED WITH.
THEREFORE, RETURN IT AND I WILL SEE THAT IT IS PROPERLY SECURED.

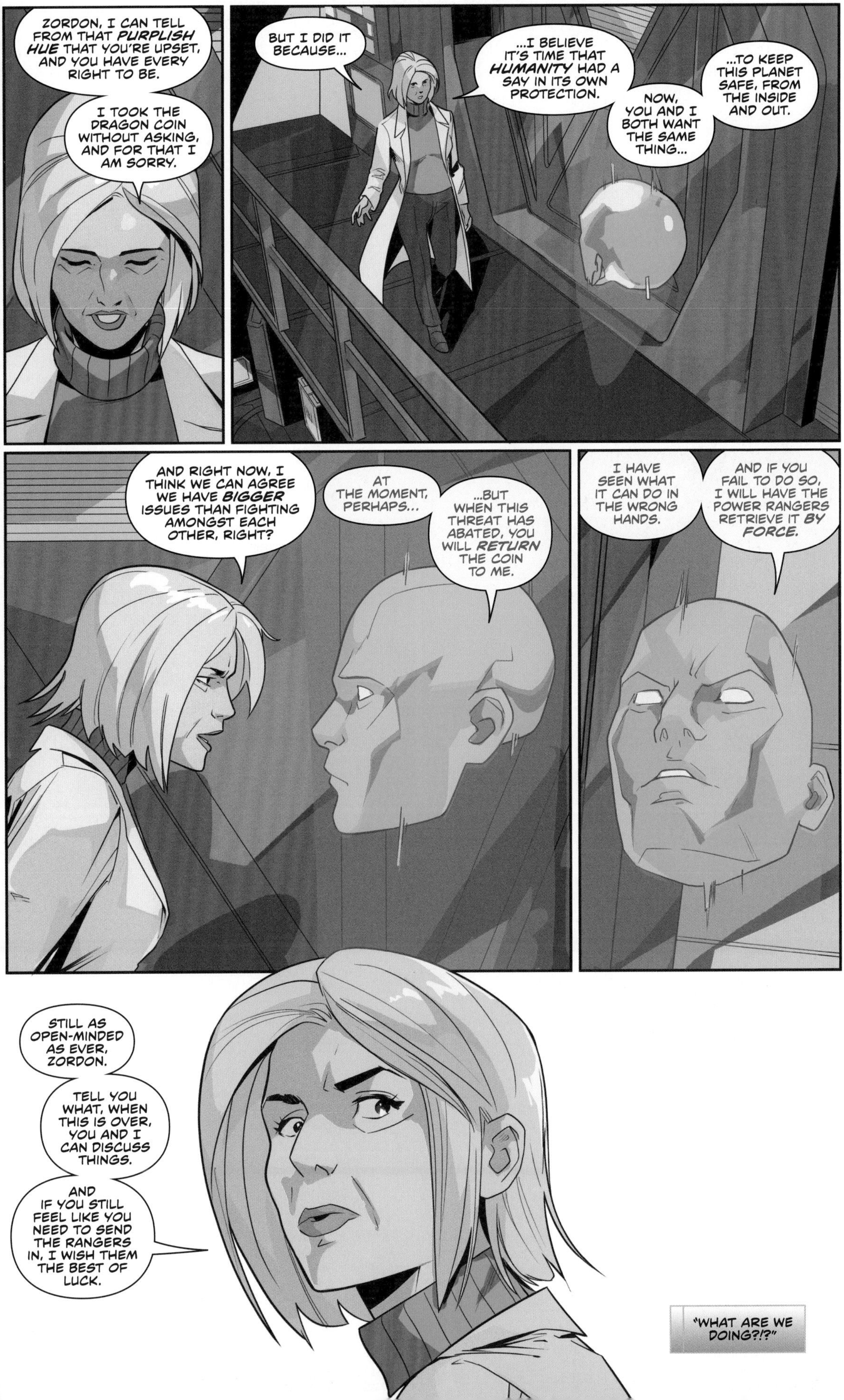
ZORDON, I CAN TELL FROM THAT PURPLISH HUE THAT YOU'RE UPSET, AND YOU HAVE EVERY RIGHT TO BE.
I TOOK THE DRAGON COIN WITHOUT ASKING, AND FOR THAT I AM SORRY.
BUT I DID IT BECAUSE...
...I BELIEVE IT'S TIME THAT HUMANITY HAD A SAY IN ITS OWN PROTECTION.
NOW, YOU AND I BOTH WANT THE SAME THING...
...TO KEEP THIS PLANET SAFE, FROM THE INSIDE AND OUT.
AND RIGHT NOW, I THINK WE CAN AGREE WE HAVE BIGGER ISSUES THAN FIGHTING AMONGST EACH OTHER, RIGHT?
AT THE MOMENT, PERHAPS...
...BUT WHEN THIS THREAT HAS ABATED, YOU WILL RETURN THE COIN TO ME.
I HAVE SEEN WHAT IT CAN DO IN THE WRONG HANDS.
AND IF YOU FAIL TO DO SO, I WILL HAVE THE POWER RANGERS RETRIEVE IT BY FORCE.
STILL AS OPEN-MINDED AS EVER, ZORDON.
TELL YOU WHAT, WHEN THIS IS OVER, YOU AND I CAN DISCUSS THINGS.
AND IF YOU STILL FEEL LIKE YOU NEED TO SEND THE RANGERS IN, I WISH THEM THE BEST OF LUCK.
"WHAT ARE WE DOING?!?"

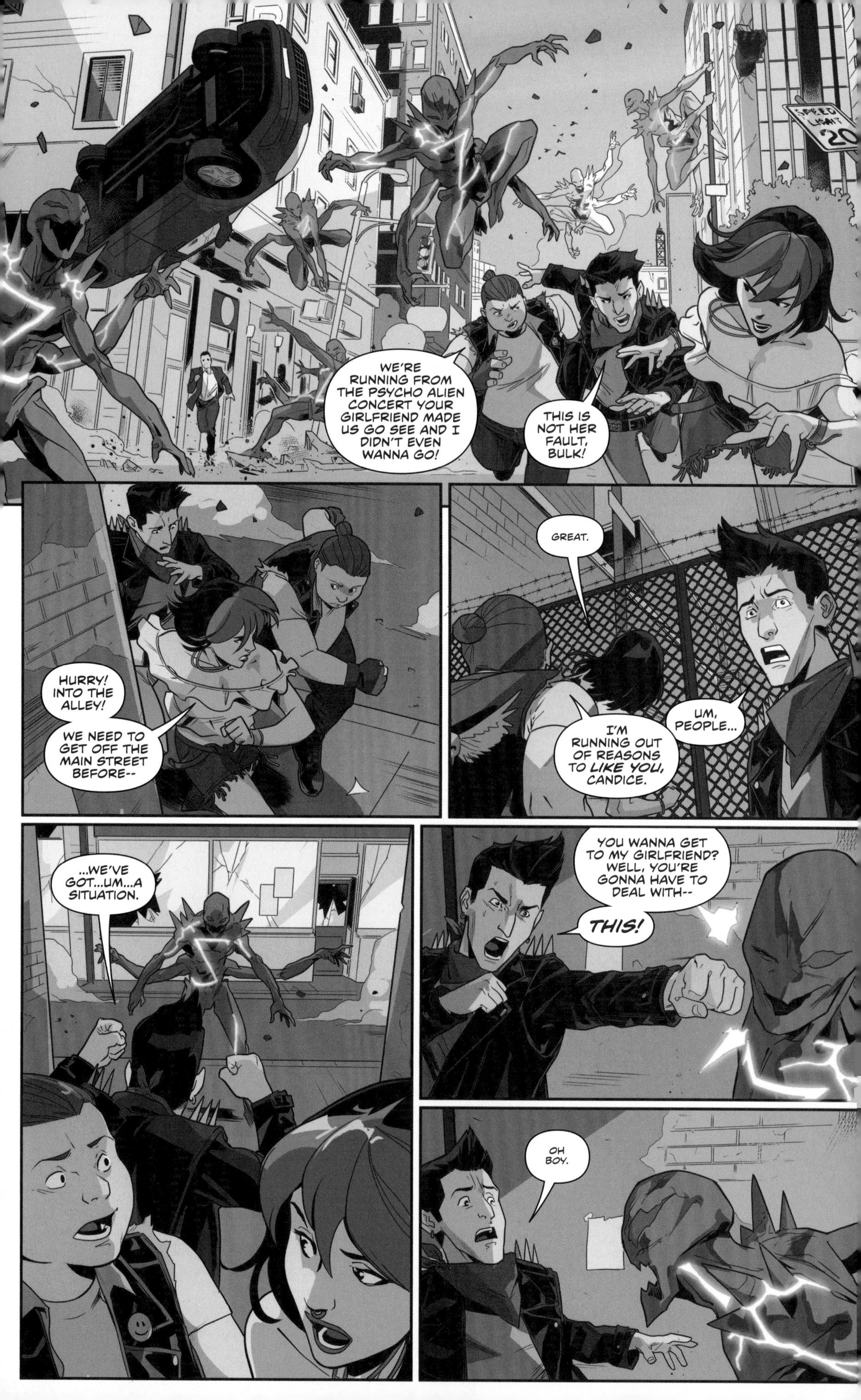
SPEED LIMIT 20
WE'RE RUNNING FROM THE PSYCHO ALIEN CONCERT YOUR GIRLFRIEND MADE US GO SEE AND I DIDN'T EVEN WANNA GO!
THIS IS NOT HER FAULT, BULK!
HURRY! INTO THE ALLEY!
WE NEED TO GET OFF THE MAIN STREET BEFORE--
GREAT.
I'M RUNNING OUT OF REASONS TO LIKE YOU, CANDICE.
UM, PEOPLE...
...WE'VE GOT...UM...A SITUATION.
YOU WANNA GET TO MY GIRLFRIEND? WELL, YOU'RE GONNA HAVE TO DEAL WITH--
THIS!
OH BOY.

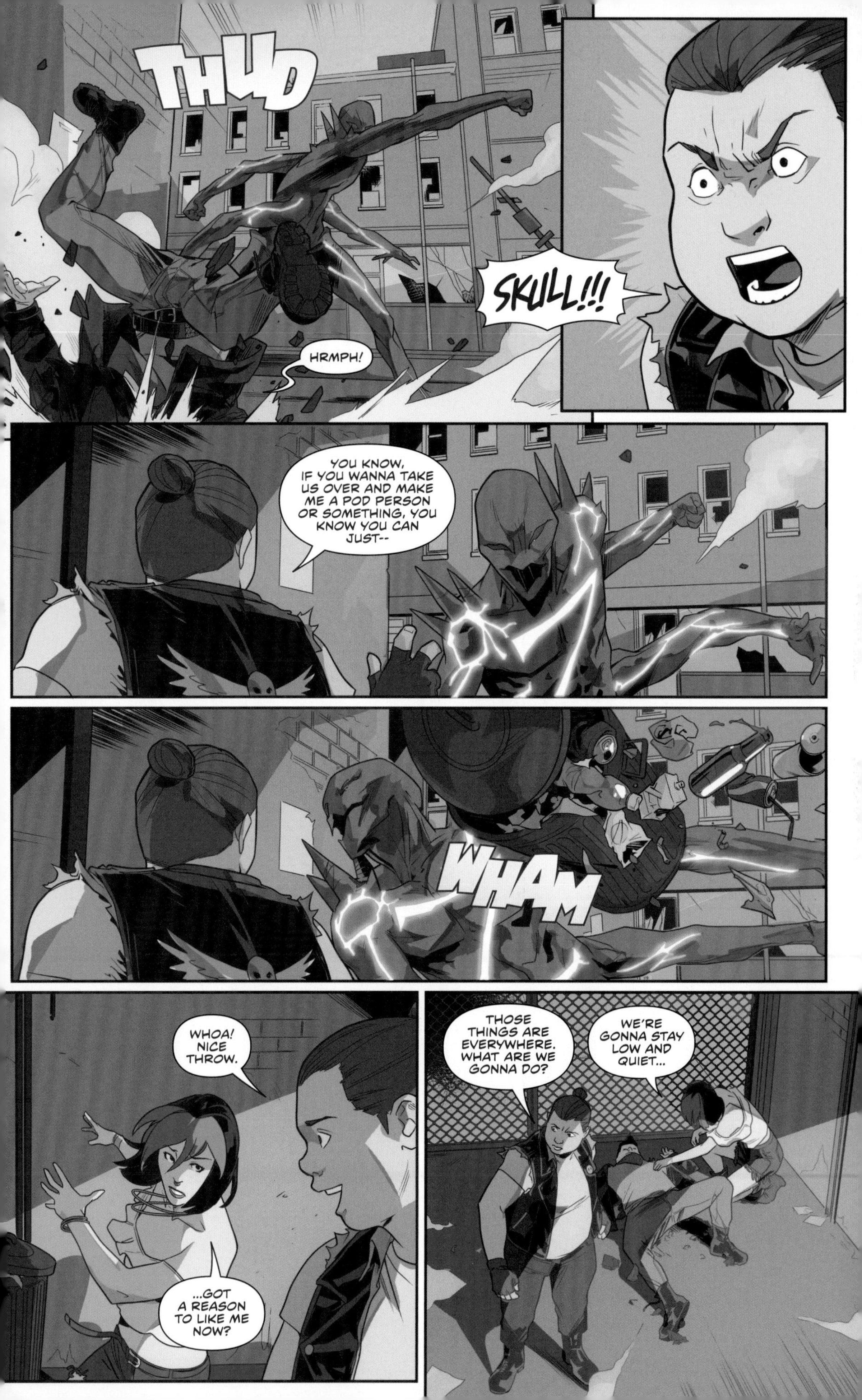
THUD
HRMPH!
SKULL!!!
YOU KNOW, IF YOU WANNA TAKE US OVER AND MAKE ME A POD PERSON OR SOMETHING, YOU KNOW YOU CAN JUST--
WHAM
WHOA! NICE THROW.
...GOT A REASON TO LIKE ME NOW?
THOSE THINGS ARE EVERYWHERE. WHAT ARE WE GONNA DO?
WE'RE GONNA STAY LOW AND QUIET...

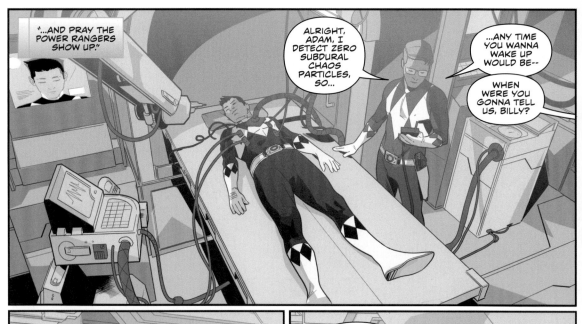

"...AND PRAY THE POWER RANGERS SHOW UP."

ALRIGHT, ADAM, I DETECT ZERO SUBDURAL CHAOS PARTICLES, SO...

...ANY TIME YOU WANNA WAKE UP WOULD BE--

WHEN WERE YOU GONNA TELL US, BILLY?

I'M SORRY? TELL YOU--

I SAW YOU TALKING TO HIM AT THE CONCERT.

THE GREEN RANGER.

OF COURSE I WAS TALKING TO HIM. I WAS TRYING TO GET HIM TO JOIN OUR SIDE.

NO, NO, NO. YOU KNEW EACH OTHER. I HEARD EVERYTHING.

LOOK, I HAVE MORE TESTS TO RUN ON--

THAT'S HOW GRACE GOT THE COIN.

YOU SMUGGLED IT OUT OF THE COMMAND CENTER.

HOW LONG HAVE YOU BEEN LYING TO US, BILLY?

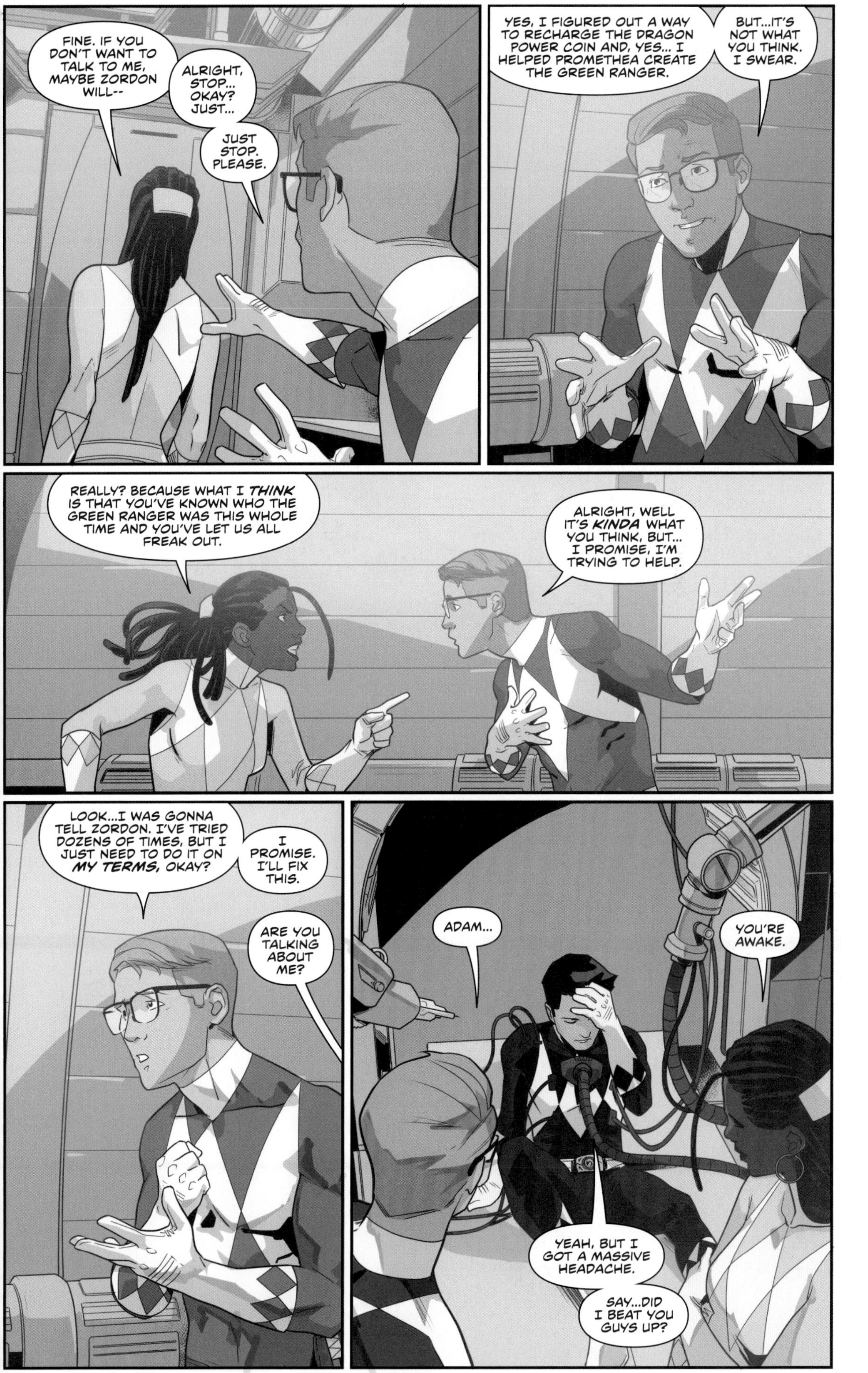
FINE. IF YOU DON'T WANT TO TALK TO ME, MAYBE ZORDON WILL--
ALRIGHT, STOP... OKAY? JUST...
JUST STOP. PLEASE.
YES, I FIGURED OUT A WAY TO RECHARGE THE DRAGON POWER COIN AND, YES... I HELPED PROMETHEA CREATE THE GREEN RANGER.
BUT...IT'S NOT WHAT YOU THINK. I SWEAR.
REALLY? BECAUSE WHAT I *THINK* IS THAT YOU'VE KNOWN WHO THE GREEN RANGER WAS THIS WHOLE TIME AND YOU'VE LET US ALL FREAK OUT.
ALRIGHT, WELL IT'S *KINDA* WHAT YOU THINK, BUT... I PROMISE, I'M TRYING TO HELP.
LOOK...I WAS GONNA TELL ZORDON. I'VE TRIED DOZENS OF TIMES, BUT I JUST NEED TO DO IT ON ***MY TERMS***, OKAY?
I PROMISE. I'LL FIX THIS.
ARE YOU TALKING ABOUT ME?
ADAM...
YOU'RE AWAKE.
YEAH, BUT I GOT A MASSIVE HEADACHE.
SAY...DID I BEAT YOU GUYS UP?

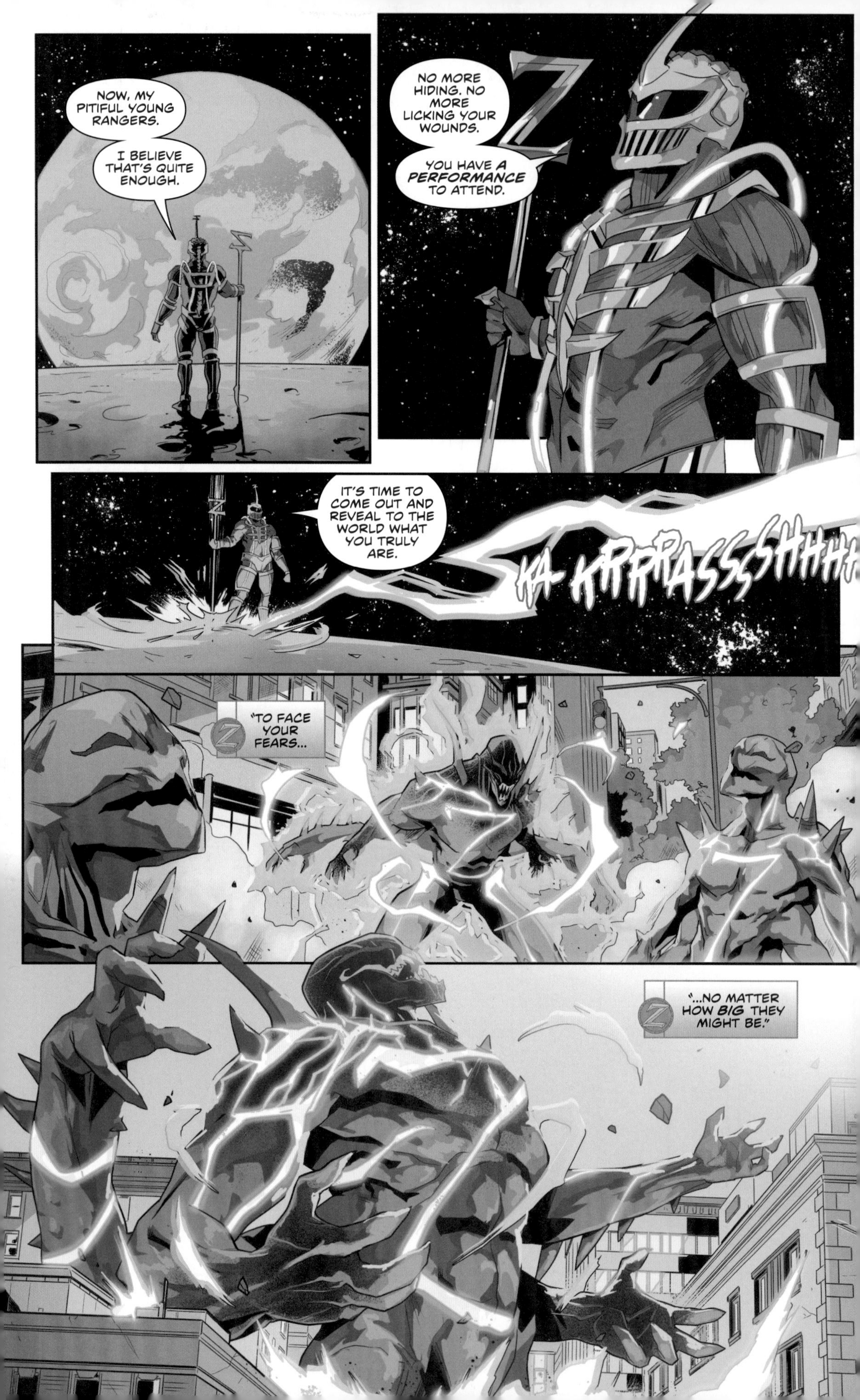
NOW, MY PITIFUL YOUNG RANGERS.
I BELIEVE THAT'S QUITE ENOUGH.
NO MORE HIDING. NO MORE LICKING YOUR WOUNDS.
YOU HAVE A *PERFORMANCE* TO ATTEND.
IT'S TIME TO COME OUT AND REVEAL TO THE WORLD WHAT YOU TRULY ARE.
KA-KRRRASSSSHHH
"TO FACE YOUR FEARS...
"...NO MATTER HOW *BIG* THEY MIGHT BE."

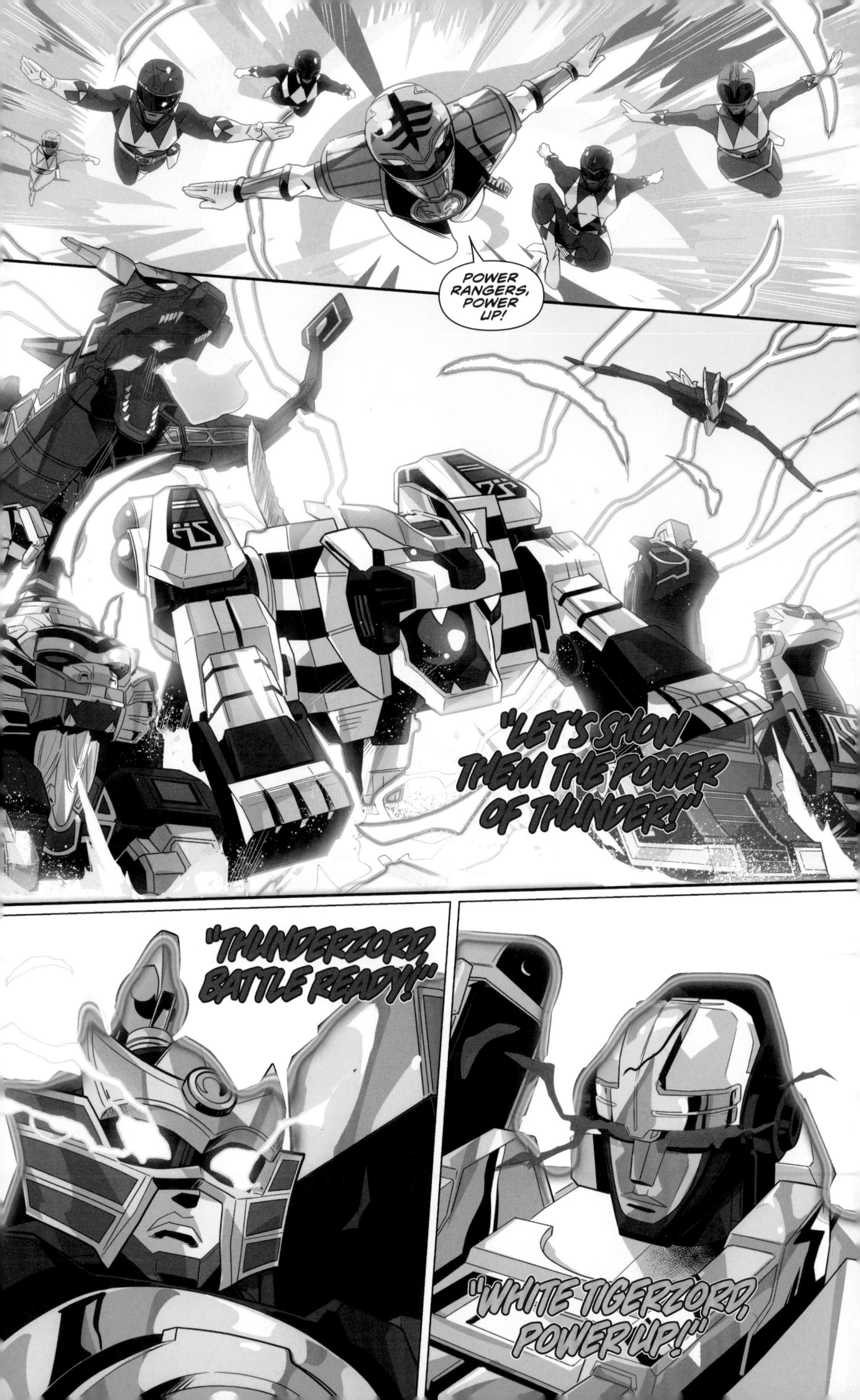
POWER RANGERS, POWER UP!
"LET'S SHOW THEM THE POWER OF THUNDER!"
"THUNDERZORD, BATTLE READY!"
"WHITE TIGERZORD, POWER UP!"

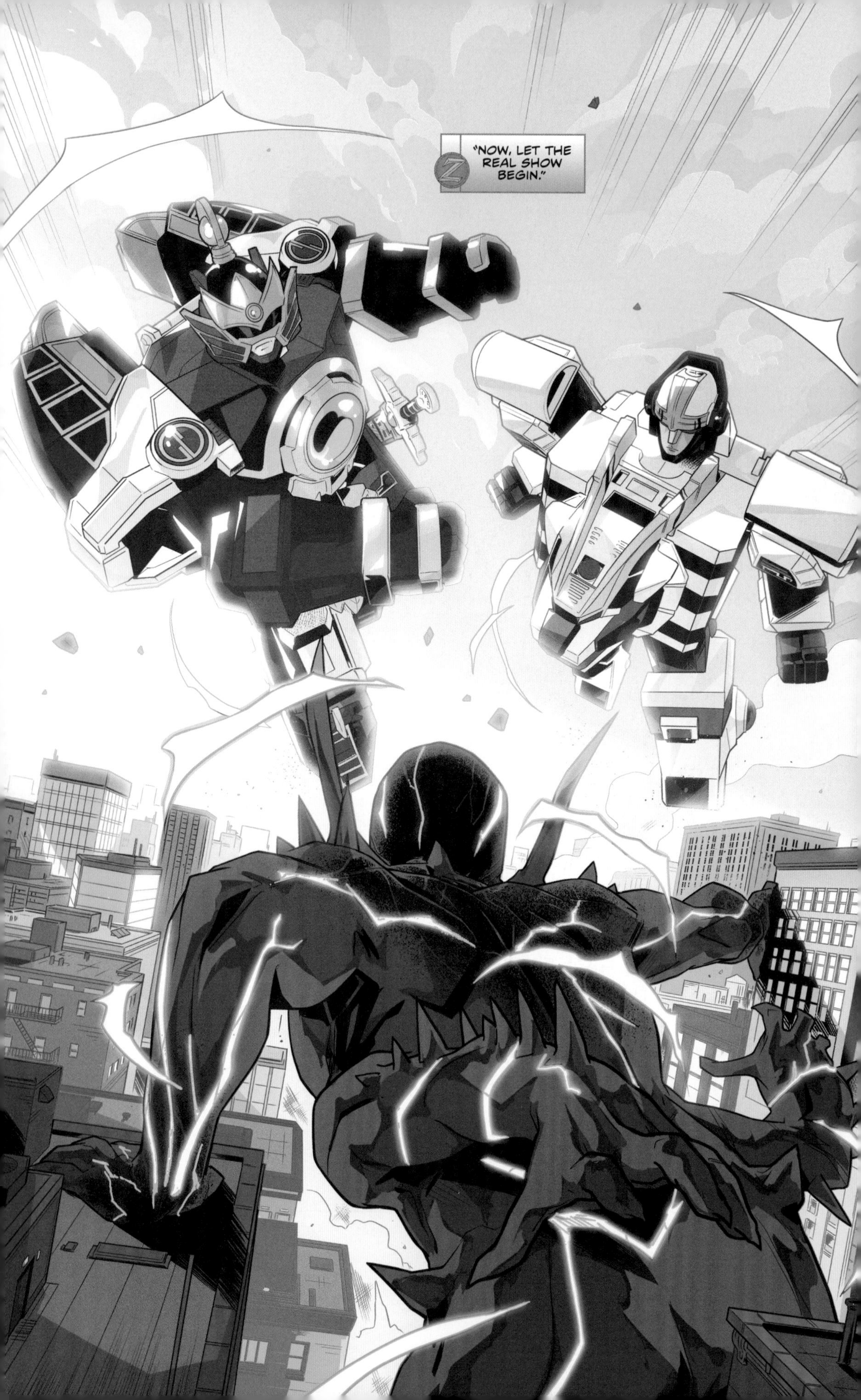
"NOW, LET THE
REAL SHOW
BEGIN."

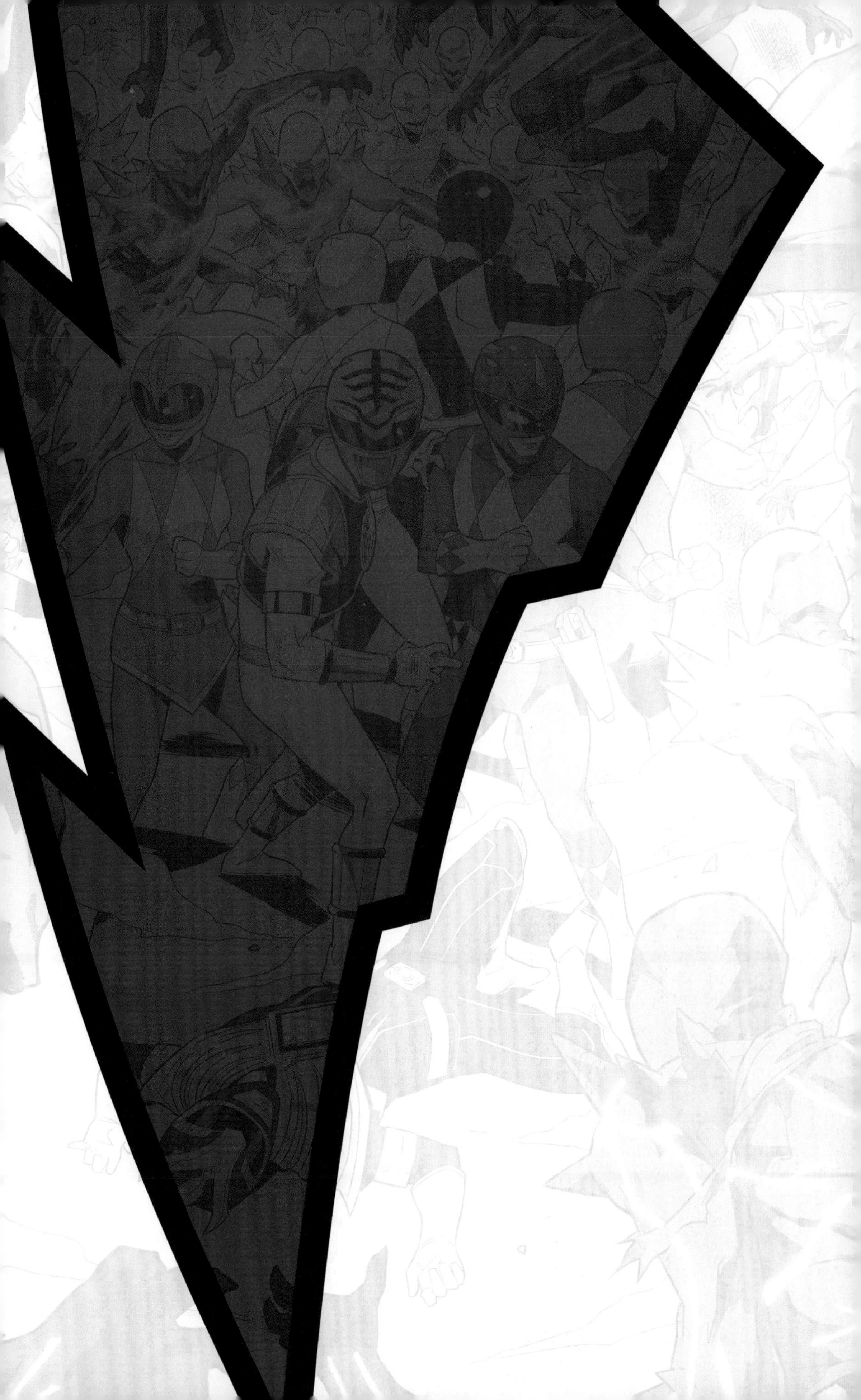

# CHAPTER FOUR

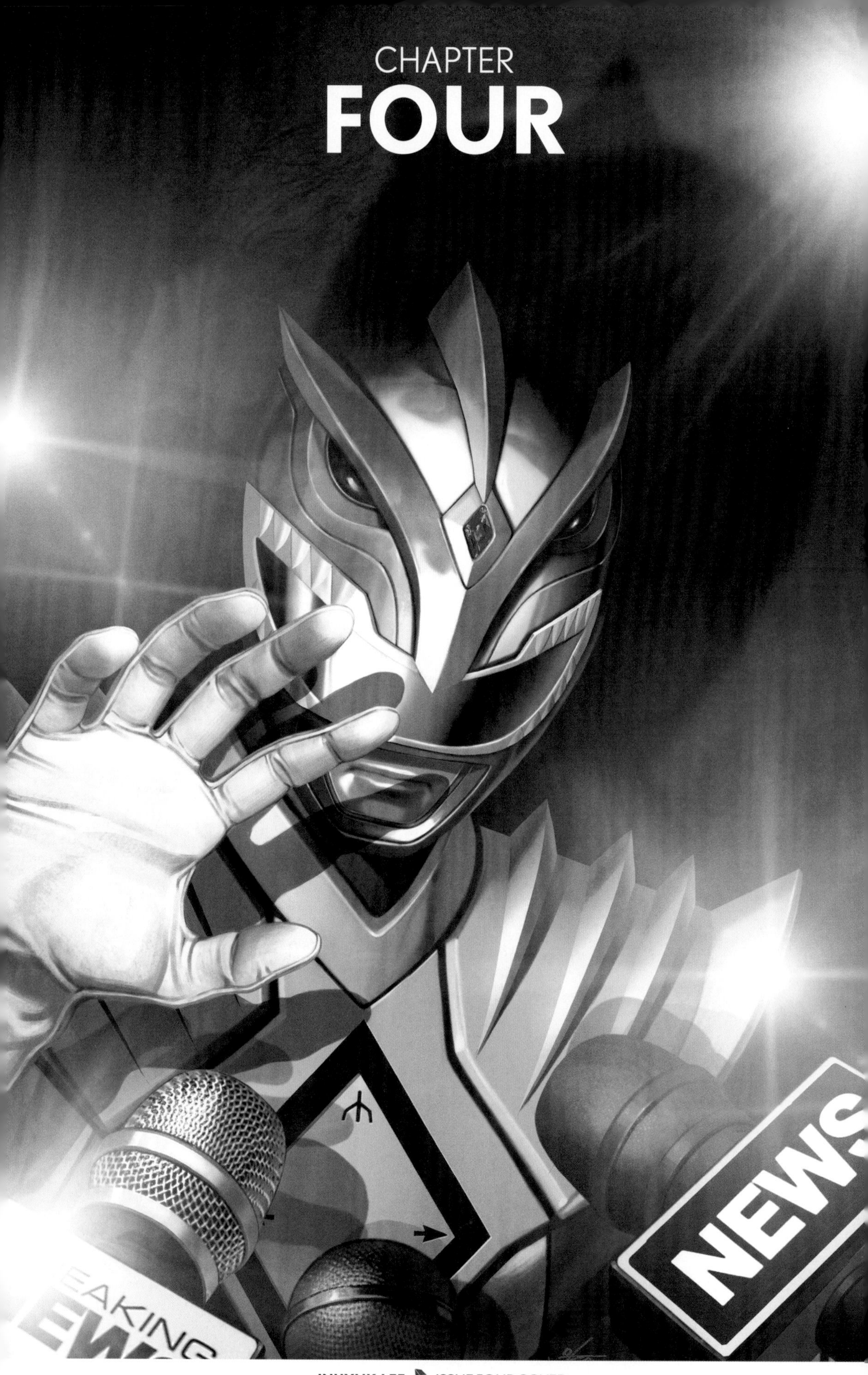
NEWS
EAKING
NEWS

INHYUK LEE ISSUE FOUR COVER

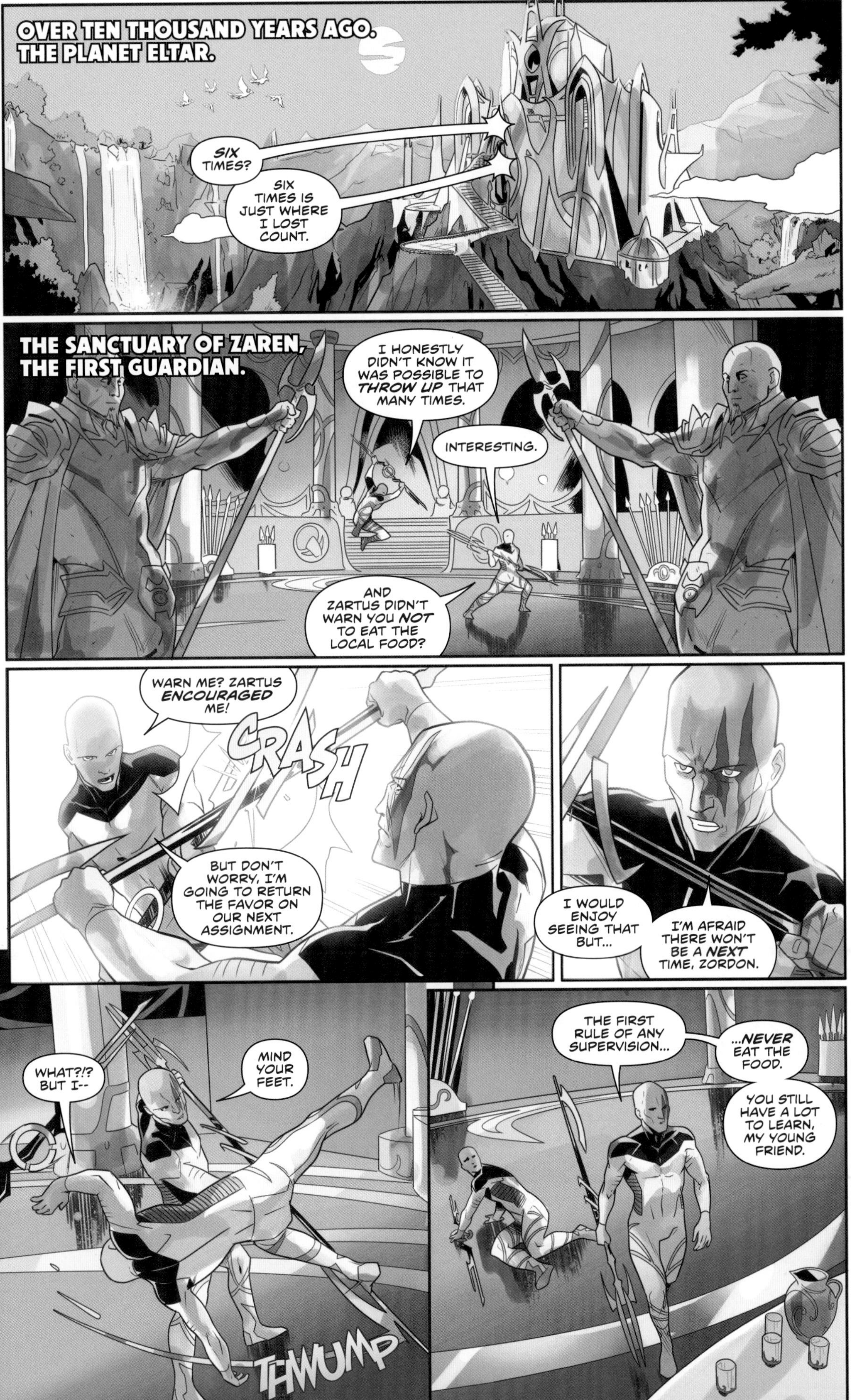
OVER TEN THOUSAND YEARS AGO. THE PLANET ELTAR.
SIX TIMES?
SIX TIMES IS JUST WHERE I LOST COUNT.
THE SANCTUARY OF ZAREN, THE FIRST GUARDIAN.
I HONESTLY DIDN'T KNOW IT WAS POSSIBLE TO THROW UP THAT MANY TIMES.
INTERESTING.
AND ZARTUS DIDN'T WARN YOU NOT TO EAT THE LOCAL FOOD?
WARN ME? ZARTUS ENCOURAGED ME!
CRASH
BUT DON'T WORRY, I'M GOING TO RETURN THE FAVOR ON OUR NEXT ASSIGNMENT.
I WOULD ENJOY SEEING THAT BUT...
I'M AFRAID THERE WON'T BE A NEXT TIME, ZORDON.
WHAT?!? BUT I--
MIND YOUR FEET.
THWUMP
THE FIRST RULE OF ANY SUPERVISION...
...NEVER EAT THE FOOD.
YOU STILL HAVE A LOT TO LEARN, MY YOUNG FRIEND.

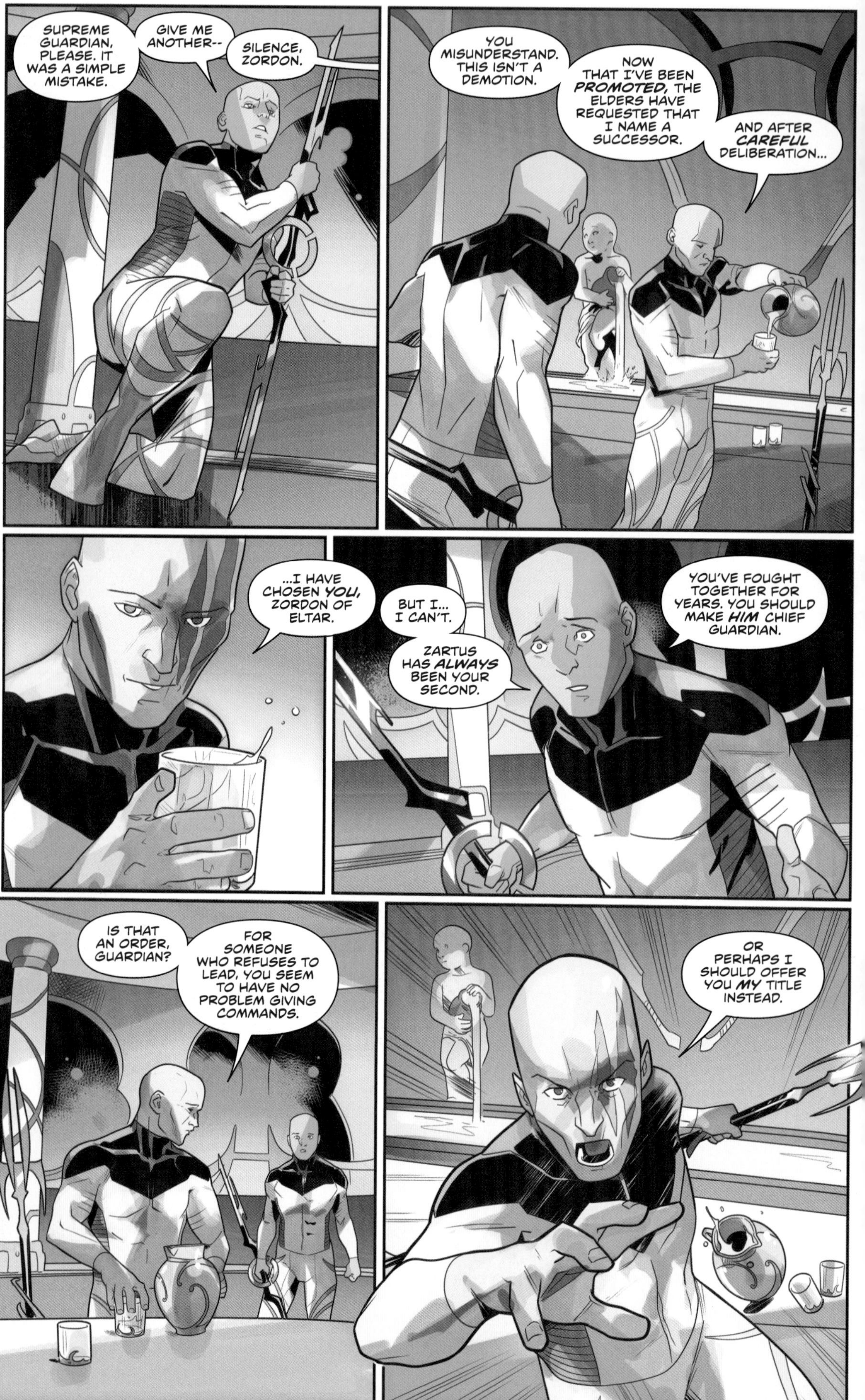
SUPREME GUARDIAN, PLEASE. IT WAS A SIMPLE MISTAKE.
GIVE ME ANOTHER--
SILENCE, ZORDON.
YOU MISUNDERSTAND. THIS ISN'T A DEMOTION.
NOW THAT I'VE BEEN PROMOTED, THE ELDERS HAVE REQUESTED THAT I NAME A SUCCESSOR.
AND AFTER CAREFUL DELIBERATION...
...I HAVE CHOSEN YOU, ZORDON OF ELTAR.
BUT I... I CAN'T.
ZARTUS HAS ALWAYS BEEN YOUR SECOND.
YOU'VE FOUGHT TOGETHER FOR YEARS. YOU SHOULD MAKE HIM CHIEF GUARDIAN.
IS THAT AN ORDER, GUARDIAN?
FOR SOMEONE WHO REFUSES TO LEAD, YOU SEEM TO HAVE NO PROBLEM GIVING COMMANDS.
OR PERHAPS I SHOULD OFFER YOU MY TITLE INSTEAD.

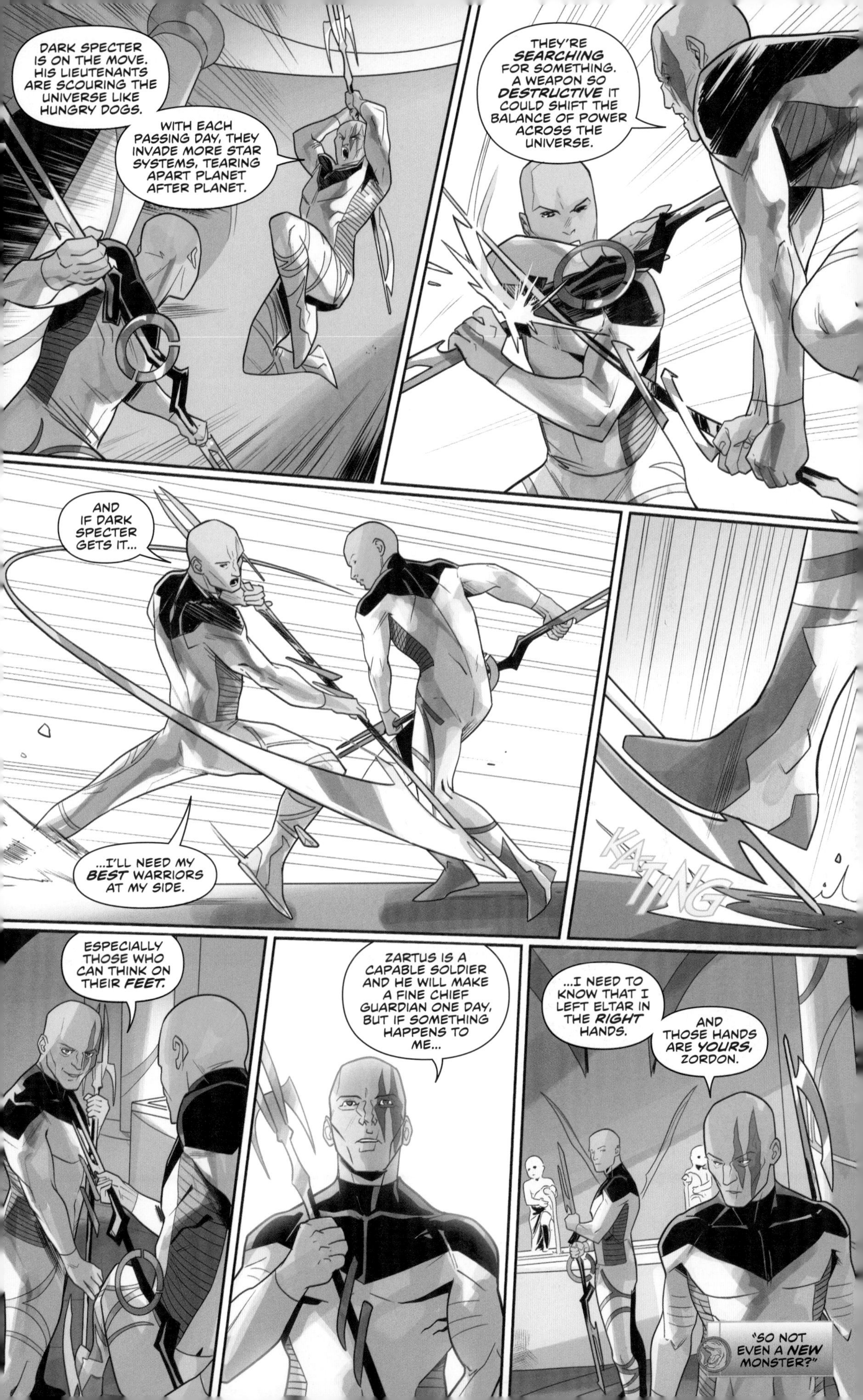
DARK SPECTER IS ON THE MOVE. HIS LIEUTENANTS ARE SCOURING THE UNIVERSE LIKE HUNGRY DOGS.
WITH EACH PASSING DAY, THEY INVADE MORE STAR SYSTEMS, TEARING APART PLANET AFTER PLANET.
THEY'RE *SEARCHING* FOR SOMETHING. A WEAPON SO *DESTRUCTIVE* IT COULD SHIFT THE BALANCE OF POWER ACROSS THE UNIVERSE.
AND IF DARK SPECTER GETS IT...
...I'LL NEED MY *BEST* WARRIORS AT MY SIDE.
KATING
ESPECIALLY THOSE WHO CAN THINK ON THEIR *FEET.*
ZARTUS IS A CAPABLE SOLDIER AND HE WILL MAKE A FINE CHIEF GUARDIAN ONE DAY, BUT IF SOMETHING HAPPENS TO ME...
...I NEED TO KNOW THAT I LEFT ELTAR IN THE *RIGHT* HANDS.
AND THOSE HANDS ARE *YOURS,* ZORDON.
"SO NOT EVEN A *NEW* MONSTER?"

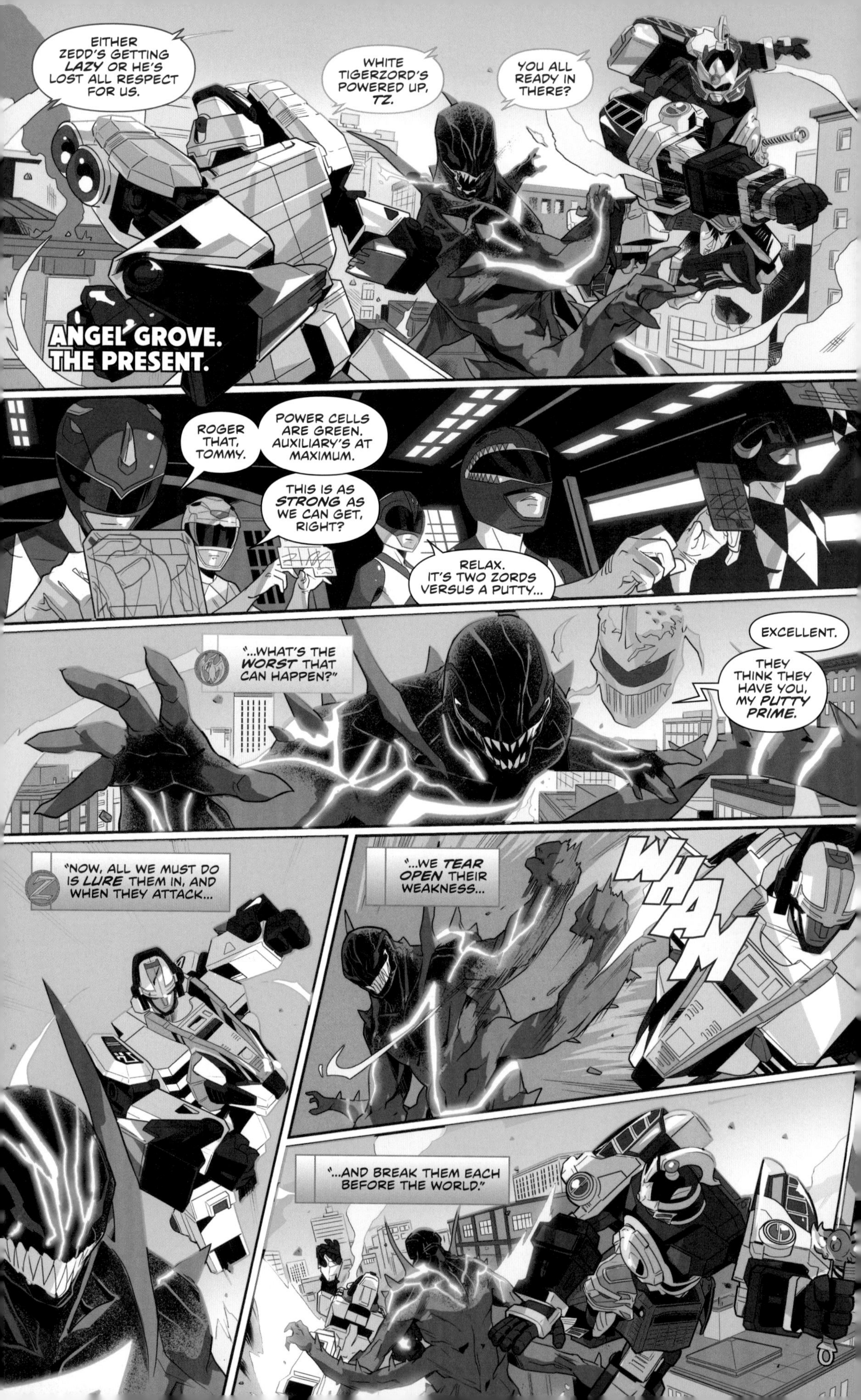
EITHER ZEDD'S GETTING LAZY OR HE'S LOST ALL RESPECT FOR US.
WHITE TIGERZORD'S POWERED UP, TZ.
YOU ALL READY IN THERE?
ANGEL GROVE. THE PRESENT.
ROGER THAT, TOMMY.
POWER CELLS ARE GREEN. AUXILIARY'S AT MAXIMUM.
THIS IS AS STRONG AS WE CAN GET, RIGHT?
RELAX. IT'S TWO ZORDS VERSUS A PUTTY...
"...WHAT'S THE WORST THAT CAN HAPPEN?"
EXCELLENT.
THEY THINK THEY HAVE YOU, MY PUTTY PRIME.
"NOW, ALL WE MUST DO IS LURE THEM IN, AND WHEN THEY ATTACK...
"...WE TEAR OPEN THEIR WEAKNESS...
WHAM
"...AND BREAK THEM EACH BEFORE THE WORLD."

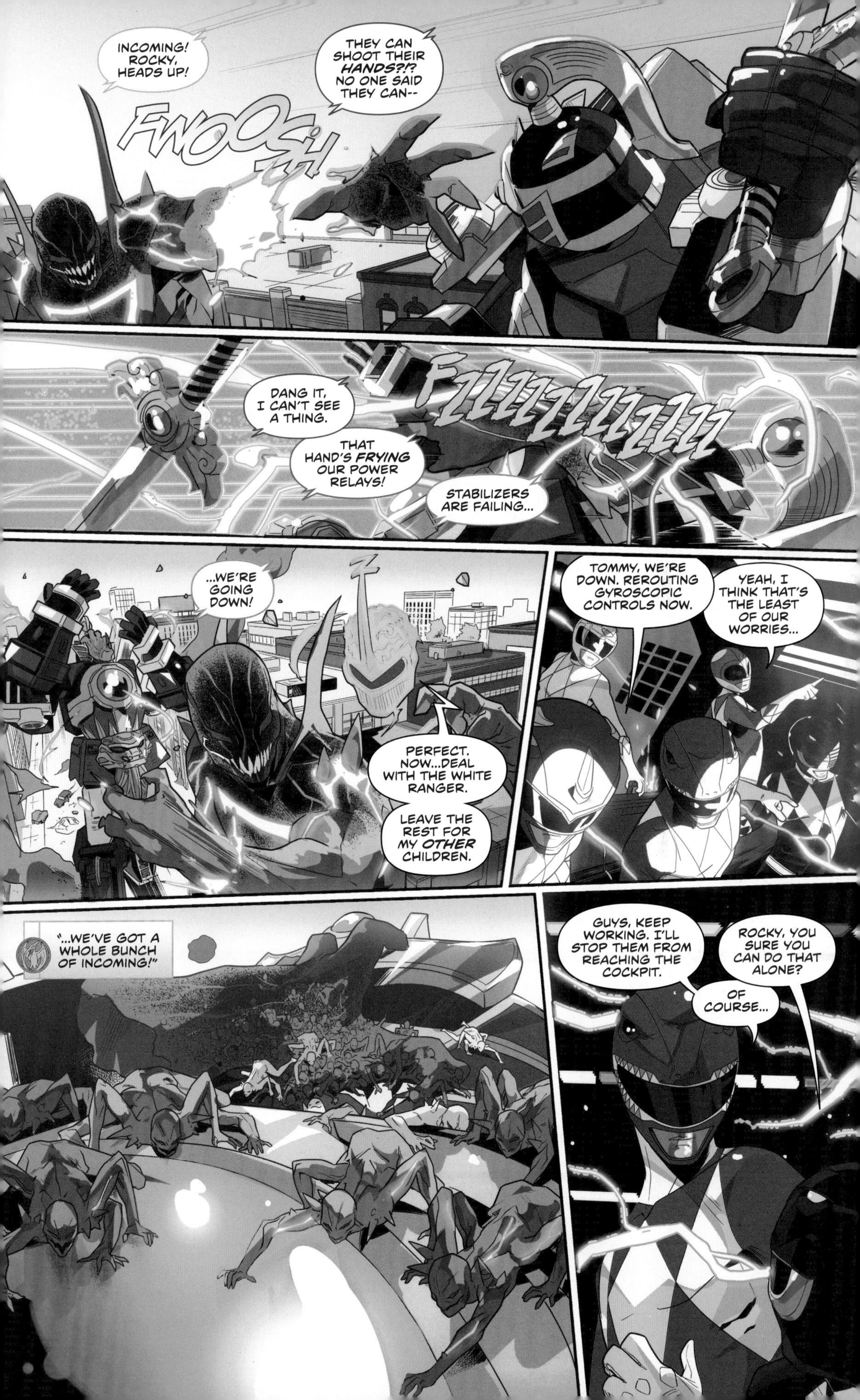
INCOMING! ROCKY, HEADS UP!
THEY CAN SHOOT THEIR *HANDS?!?* NO ONE SAID THEY CAN--
FWOOSH
DANG IT, I CAN'T SEE A THING.
FZZZZZZZZZZZZZZ
THAT HAND'S *FRYING* OUR POWER RELAYS!
STABILIZERS ARE FAILING...
...WE'RE GOING DOWN!
PERFECT. NOW...DEAL WITH THE WHITE RANGER.
LEAVE THE REST FOR MY *OTHER* CHILDREN.
TOMMY, WE'RE DOWN. REROUTING GYROSCOPIC CONTROLS NOW.
YEAH, I THINK THAT'S THE LEAST OF OUR WORRIES...
"...WE'VE GOT A WHOLE BUNCH OF INCOMING!"
GUYS, KEEP WORKING. I'LL STOP THEM FROM REACHING THE COCKPIT.
ROCKY, YOU SURE YOU CAN DO THAT ALONE?
OF COURSE...

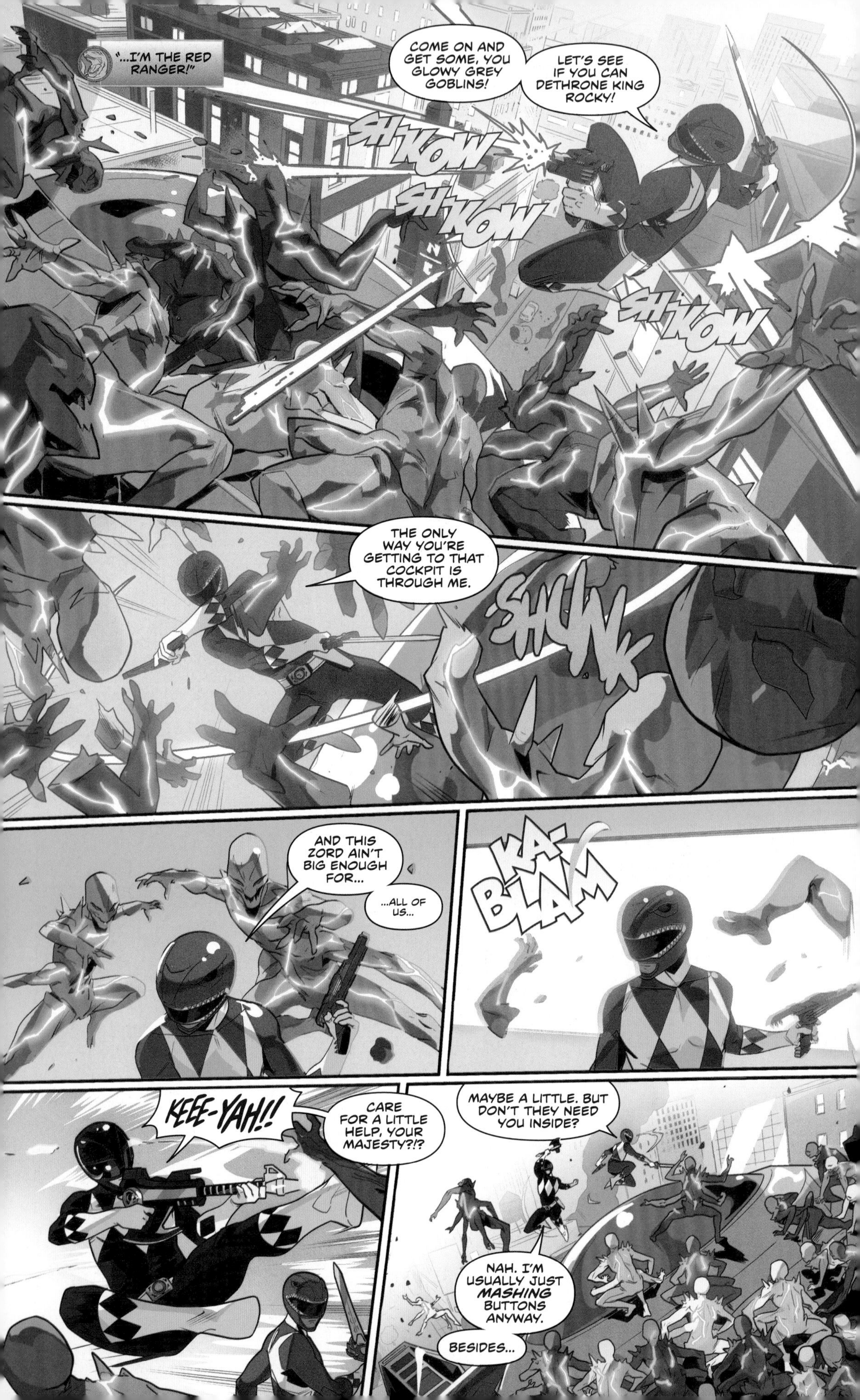
"...I'M THE RED RANGER!"
COME ON AND GET SOME, YOU GLOWY GREY GOBLINS!
LET'S SEE IF YOU CAN DETHRONE KING ROCKY!
SH'KOW
SH'KOW
SH'KOW
THE ONLY WAY YOU'RE GETTING TO THAT COCKPIT IS THROUGH ME.
SHUNK
AND THIS ZORD AIN'T BIG ENOUGH FOR...
...ALL OF US...
KA-BLAM
KEEE-YAH!!
CARE FOR A LITTLE HELP, YOUR MAJESTY?!?
MAYBE A LITTLE. BUT DON'T THEY NEED YOU INSIDE?
NAH. I'M USUALLY JUST *MASHING* BUTTONS ANYWAY.
BESIDES...

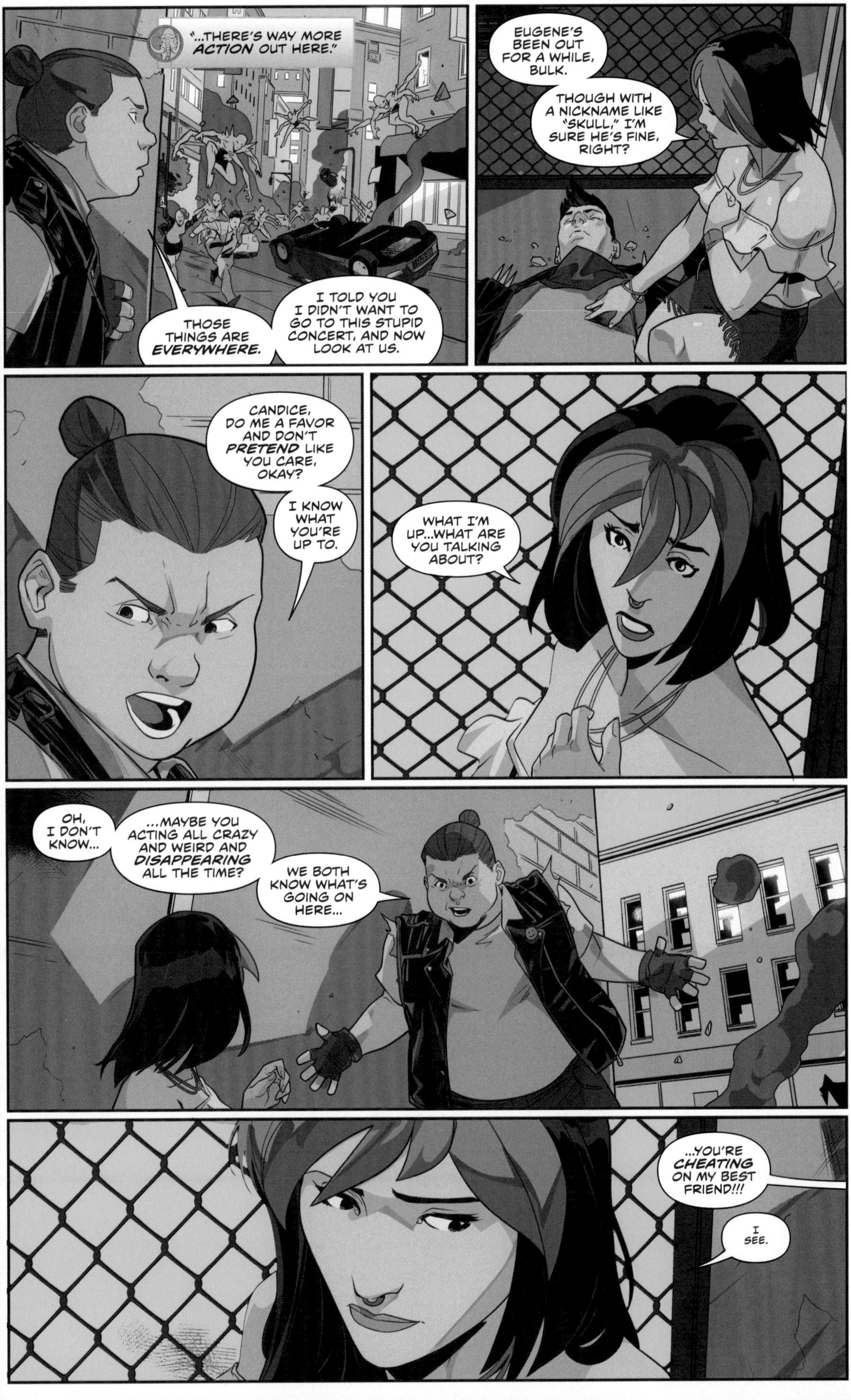
"...THERE'S WAY MORE ACTION OUT HERE."
THOSE THINGS ARE EVERYWHERE.
I TOLD YOU I DIDN'T WANT TO GO TO THIS STUPID CONCERT, AND NOW LOOK AT US.
EUGENE'S BEEN OUT FOR A WHILE, BULK.
THOUGH WITH A NICKNAME LIKE "SKULL," I'M SURE HE'S FINE, RIGHT?
CANDICE, DO ME A FAVOR AND DON'T PRETEND LIKE YOU CARE, OKAY?
I KNOW WHAT YOU'RE UP TO.
WHAT I'M UP...WHAT ARE YOU TALKING ABOUT?
OH, I DON'T KNOW...
...MAYBE YOU ACTING ALL CRAZY AND WEIRD AND DISAPPEARING ALL THE TIME?
WE BOTH KNOW WHAT'S GOING ON HERE...
...YOU'RE CHEATING ON MY BEST FRIEND!!!
I SEE.

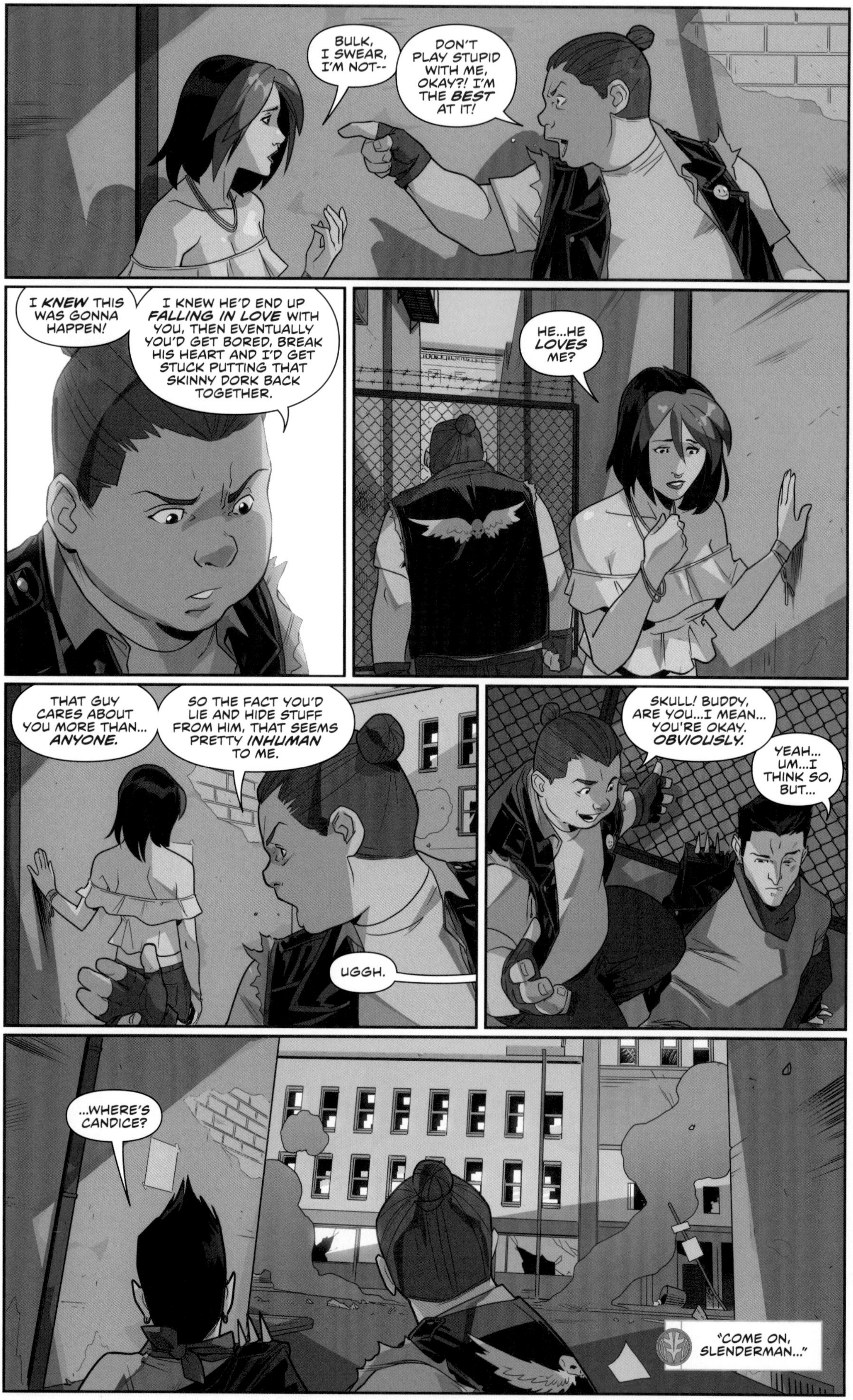
BULK, I SWEAR, I'M NOT--
DON'T PLAY STUPID WITH ME, OKAY?! I'M THE BEST AT IT!
I KNEW THIS WAS GONNA HAPPEN!
I KNEW HE'D END UP FALLING IN LOVE WITH YOU, THEN EVENTUALLY YOU'D GET BORED, BREAK HIS HEART AND I'D GET STUCK PUTTING THAT SKINNY DORK BACK TOGETHER.
HE...HE LOVES ME?
THAT GUY CARES ABOUT YOU MORE THAN... ANYONE.
SO THE FACT YOU'D LIE AND HIDE STUFF FROM HIM, THAT SEEMS PRETTY INHUMAN TO ME.
UGGH.
SKULL! BUDDY, ARE YOU...I MEAN... YOU'RE OKAY. OBVIOUSLY.
YEAH... UM...I THINK SO, BUT...
...WHERE'S CANDICE?
"COME ON, SLENDERMAN..."

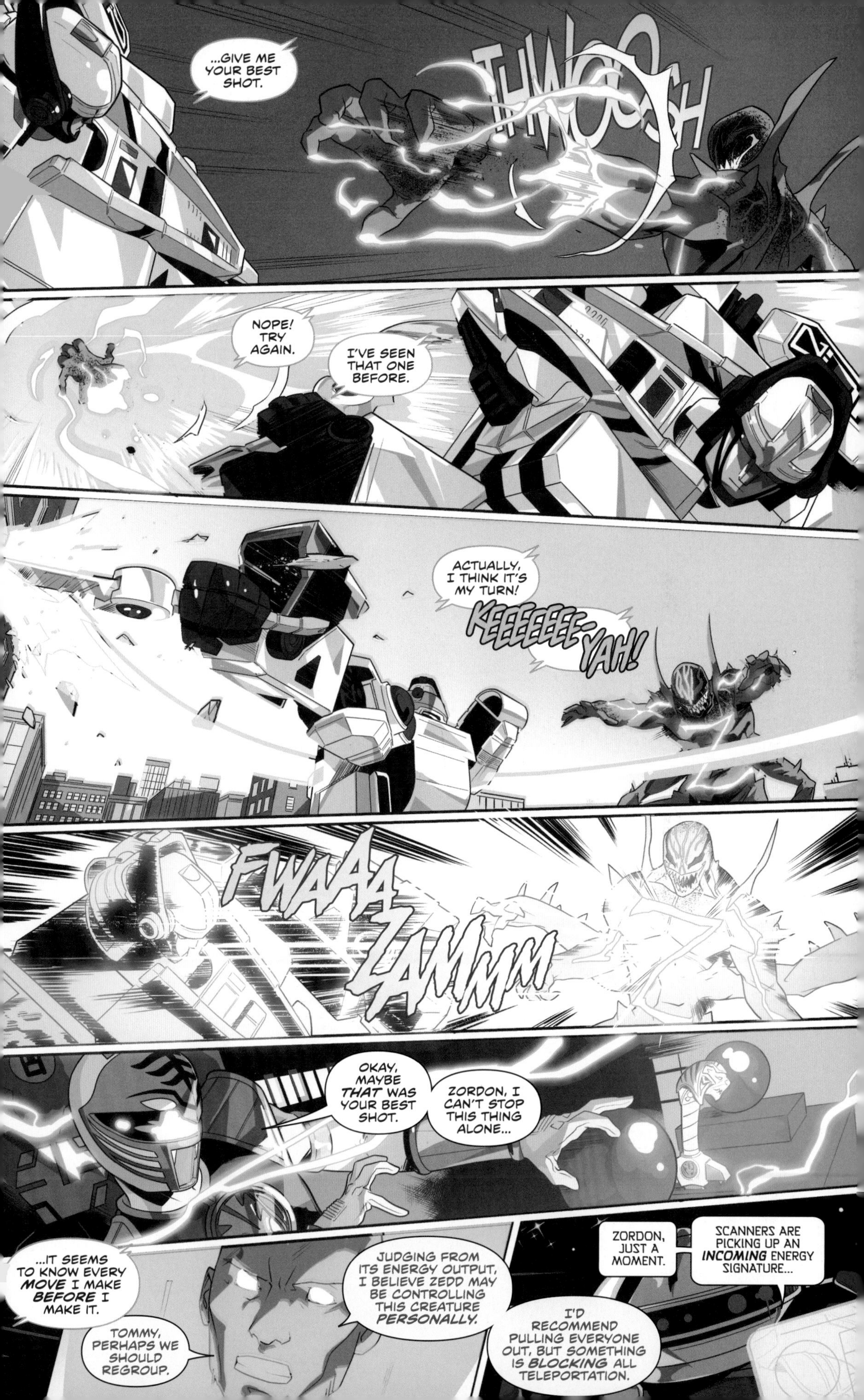

...GIVE ME YOUR BEST SHOT.
THWOOSH
NOPE! TRY AGAIN.
I'VE SEEN THAT ONE BEFORE.
ACTUALLY, I THINK IT'S MY TURN!
KEEEEEEE-YAH!
FWAAAAAMMM
OKAY, MAYBE *THAT* WAS YOUR BEST SHOT.
ZORDON, I CAN'T STOP THIS THING ALONE...
...IT SEEMS TO KNOW EVERY *MOVE* I MAKE *BEFORE* I MAKE IT.
TOMMY, PERHAPS WE SHOULD REGROUP.
JUDGING FROM ITS ENERGY OUTPUT, I BELIEVE ZEDD MAY BE CONTROLLING THIS CREATURE *PERSONALLY.*
I'D RECOMMEND PULLING EVERYONE OUT, BUT SOMETHING IS *BLOCKING* ALL TELEPORTATION.
ZORDON, JUST A MOMENT.
SCANNERS ARE PICKING UP AN *INCOMING* ENERGY SIGNATURE...

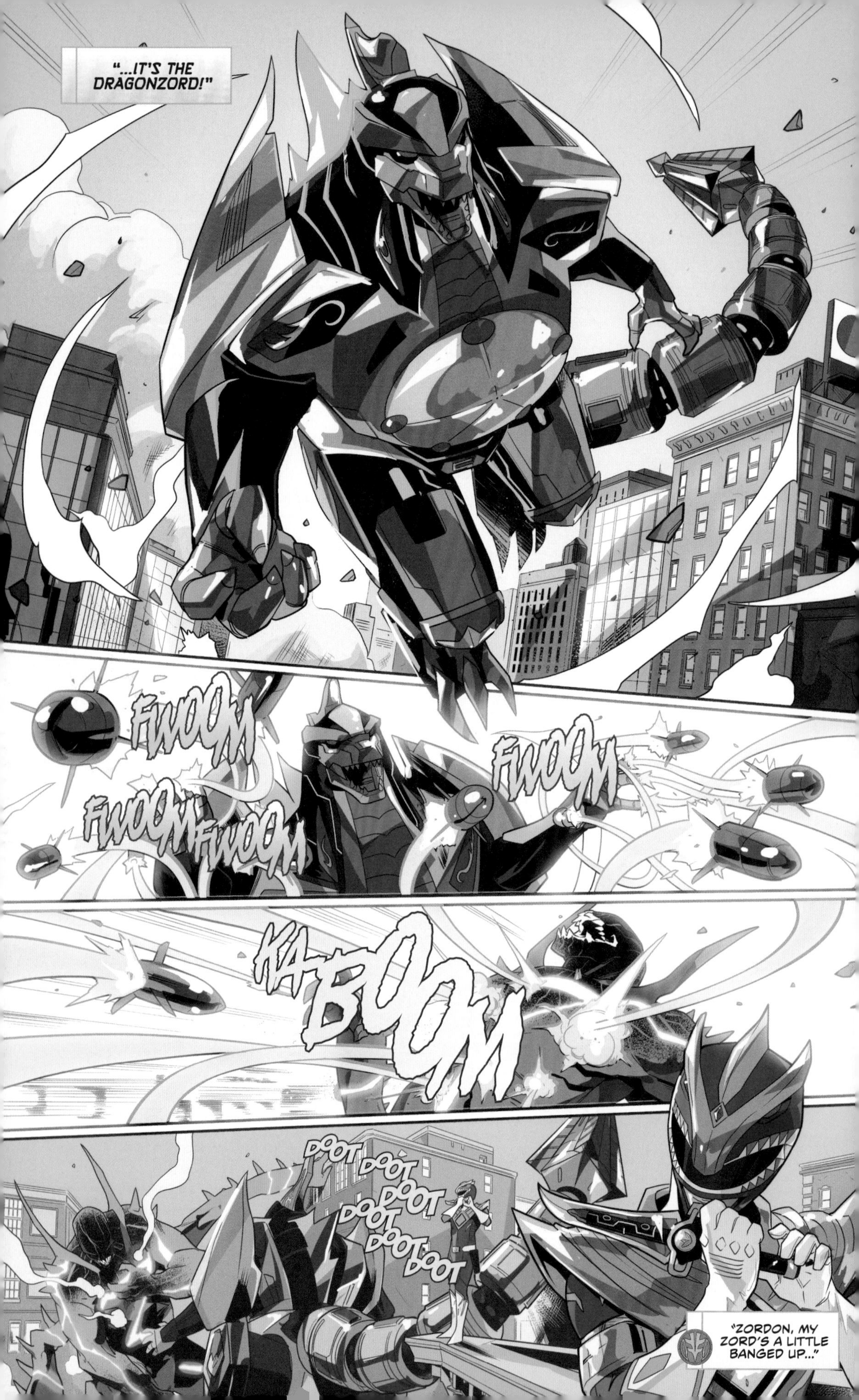
"...IT'S THE DRAGONZORD!"
FWOOM
FWOOM
FWOOM
FWOOM
KA-BOOM
DOOT DOOT DOOT DOOT DOOT DOOT
"ZORDON, MY ZORD'S A LITTLE BANGED UP..."

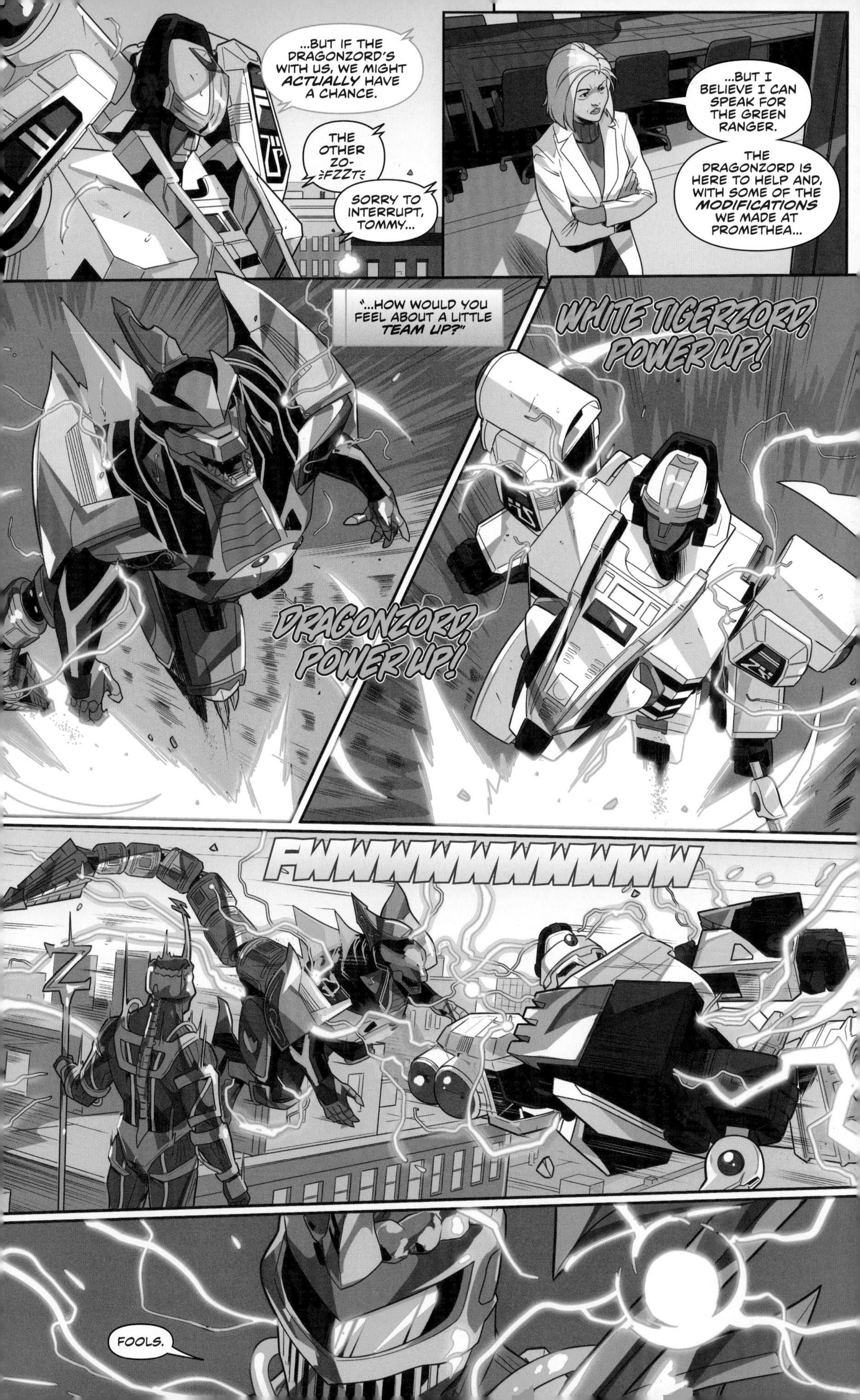
...BUT IF THE DRAGONZORD'S WITH US, WE MIGHT *ACTUALLY* HAVE A CHANCE.
THE OTHER ZO- ≈FZZT≈
SORRY TO INTERRUPT, TOMMY...
...BUT I BELIEVE I CAN SPEAK FOR THE GREEN RANGER.
THE DRAGONZORD IS HERE TO HELP AND, WITH SOME OF THE *MODIFICATIONS* WE MADE AT PROMETHEA...
"...HOW WOULD YOU FEEL ABOUT A LITTLE *TEAM UP?*"
WHITE TIGERZORD, POWER UP!
DRAGONZORD, POWER UP!
FWWWWWWWWWWWW
FOOLS.

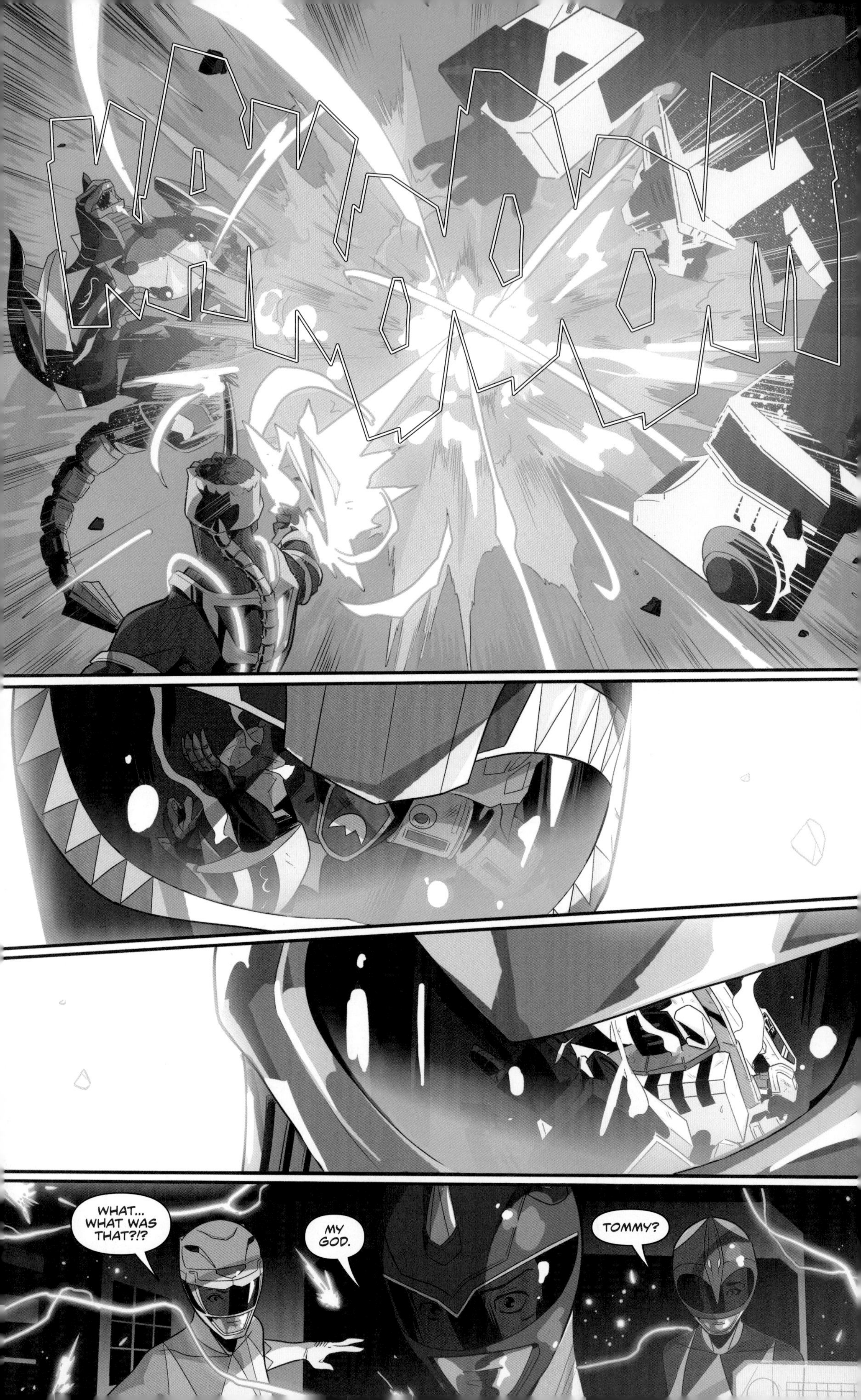
WHAT... WHAT WAS THAT?!?
MY GOD.
TOMMY?

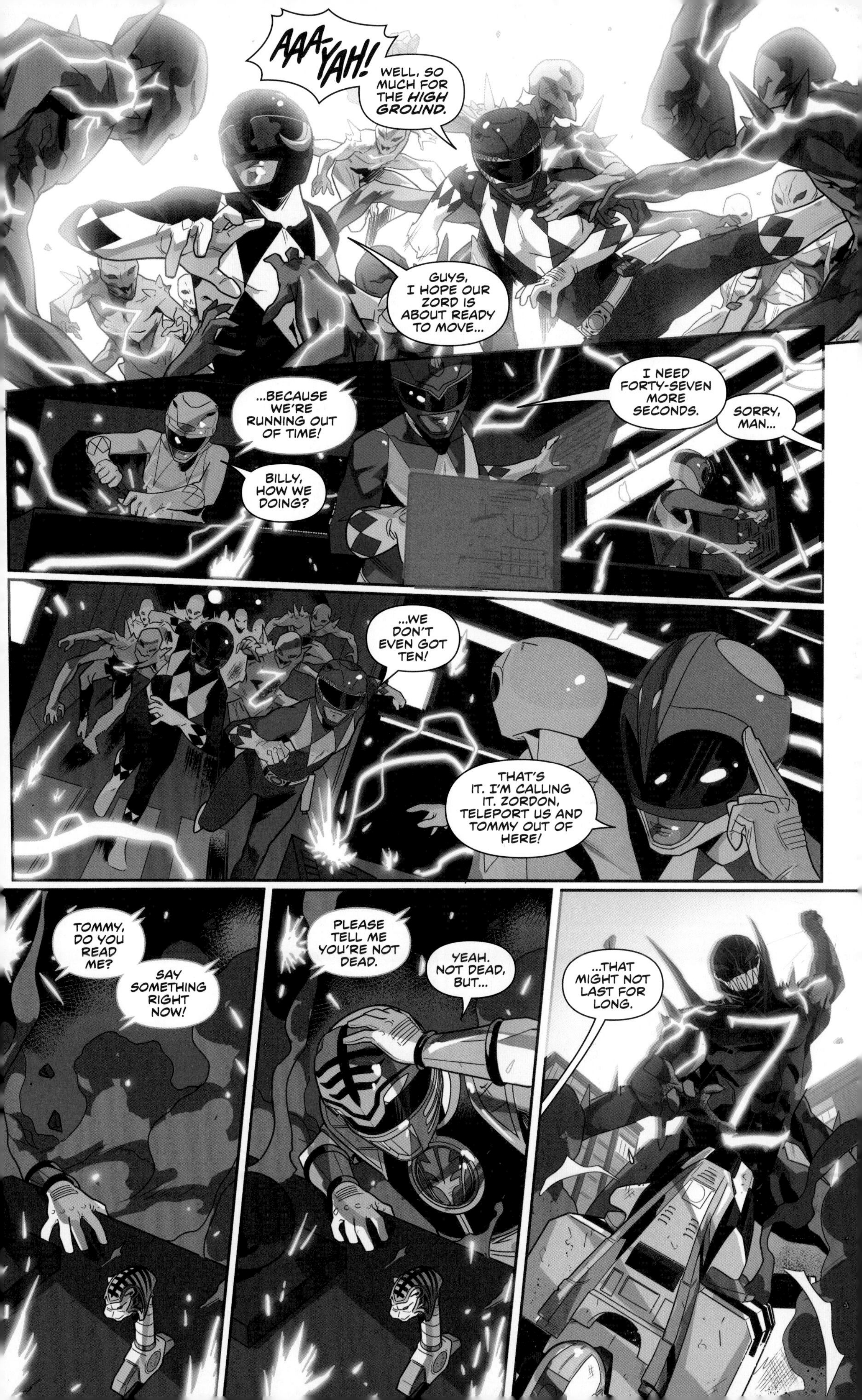
AAA-YAH!
WELL, SO MUCH FOR THE HIGH GROUND.
GUYS, I HOPE OUR ZORD IS ABOUT READY TO MOVE...
...BECAUSE WE'RE RUNNING OUT OF TIME!
BILLY, HOW WE DOING?
I NEED FORTY-SEVEN MORE SECONDS.
SORRY, MAN...
...WE DON'T EVEN GOT TEN!
THAT'S IT. I'M CALLING IT. ZORDON, TELEPORT US AND TOMMY OUT OF HERE!
TOMMY, DO YOU READ ME?
SAY SOMETHING RIGHT NOW!
PLEASE TELL ME YOU'RE NOT DEAD.
YEAH. NOT DEAD, BUT...
...THAT MIGHT NOT LAST FOR LONG.

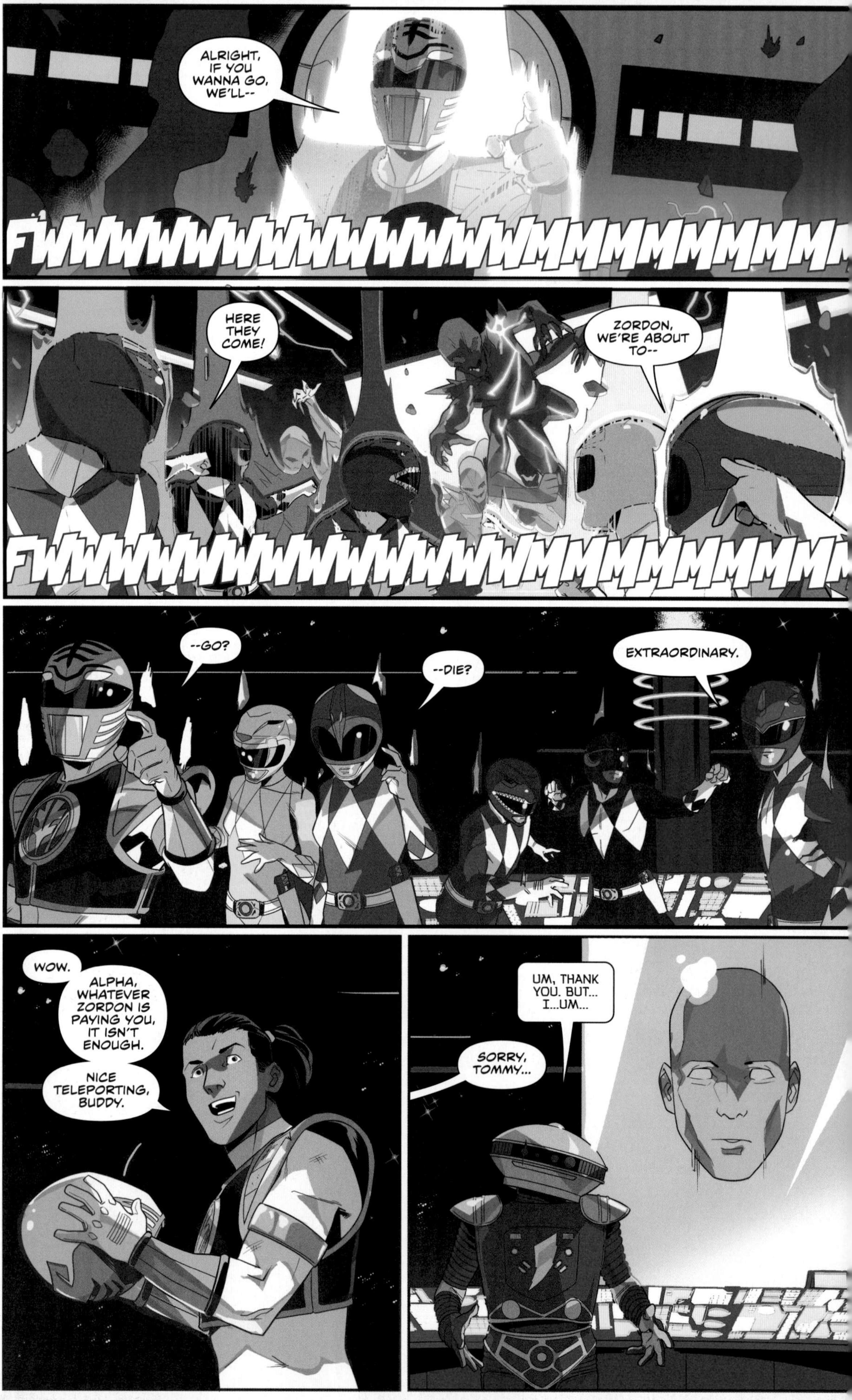

ALRIGHT, IF YOU WANNA GO, WE'LL--
FWWWWWWWWWWWWWWWWMMMMMMMMM
HERE THEY COME!
ZORDON, WE'RE ABOUT TO--
FWWWWWWWWWWWWWWWWMMMMMMMMM
--GO?
--DIE?
EXTRAORDINARY.
WOW.
ALPHA, WHATEVER ZORDON IS PAYING YOU, IT ISN'T ENOUGH.
NICE TELEPORTING, BUDDY.
UM, THANK YOU. BUT... I...UM...
SORRY, TOMMY...

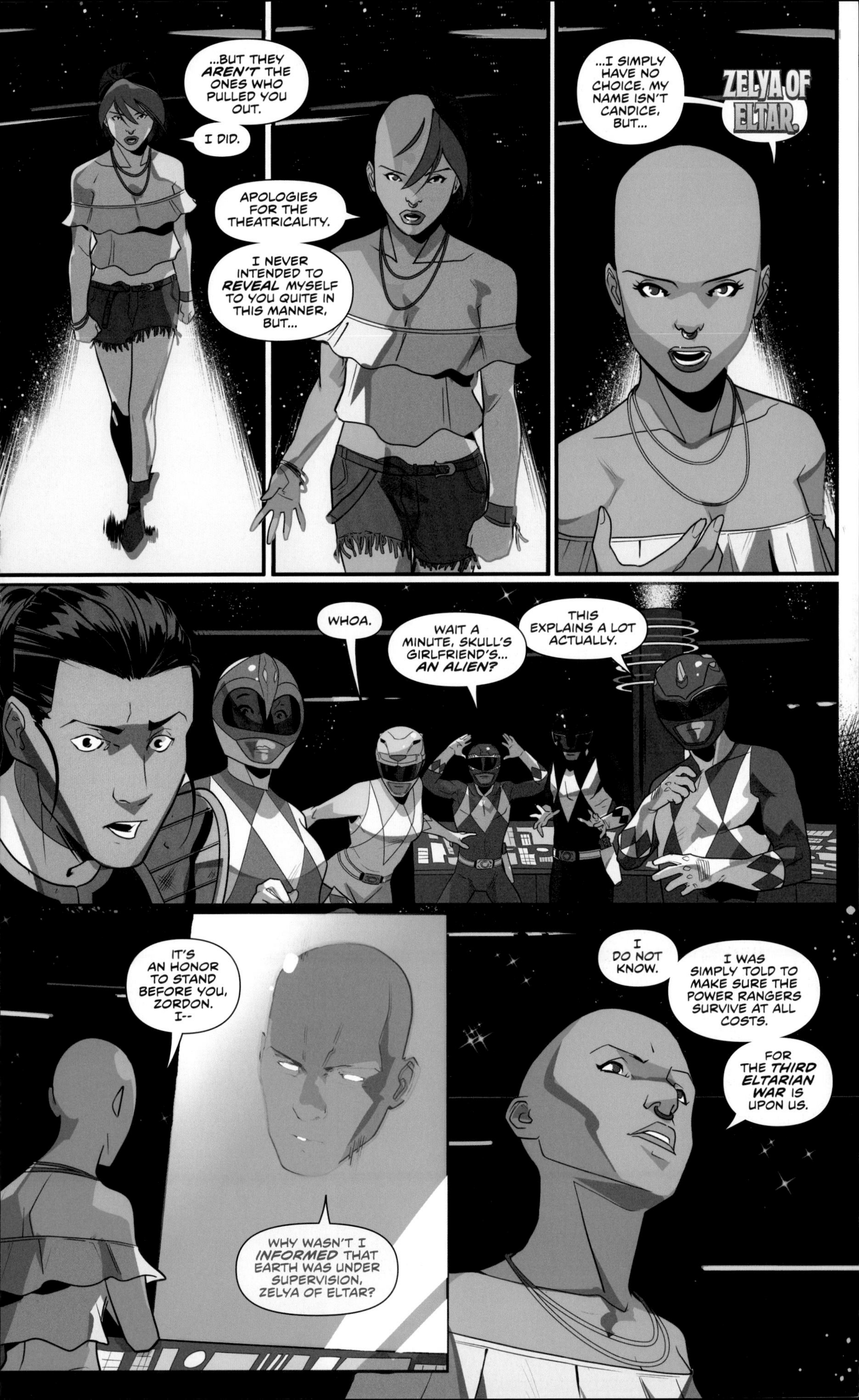
...BUT THEY AREN'T THE ONES WHO PULLED YOU OUT.
I DID.
APOLOGIES FOR THE THEATRICALITY.
I NEVER INTENDED TO REVEAL MYSELF TO YOU QUITE IN THIS MANNER, BUT...
...I SIMPLY HAVE NO CHOICE. MY NAME ISN'T CANDICE, BUT...
ZELYA OF ELTAR.
WHOA.
WAIT A MINUTE, SKULL'S GIRLFRIEND'S... AN ALIEN?
THIS EXPLAINS A LOT ACTUALLY.
IT'S AN HONOR TO STAND BEFORE YOU, ZORDON. I--
WHY WASN'T I INFORMED THAT EARTH WAS UNDER SUPERVISION, ZELYA OF ELTAR?
I DO NOT KNOW.
I WAS SIMPLY TOLD TO MAKE SURE THE POWER RANGERS SURVIVE AT ALL COSTS.
FOR THE THIRD ELTARIAN WAR IS UPON US.

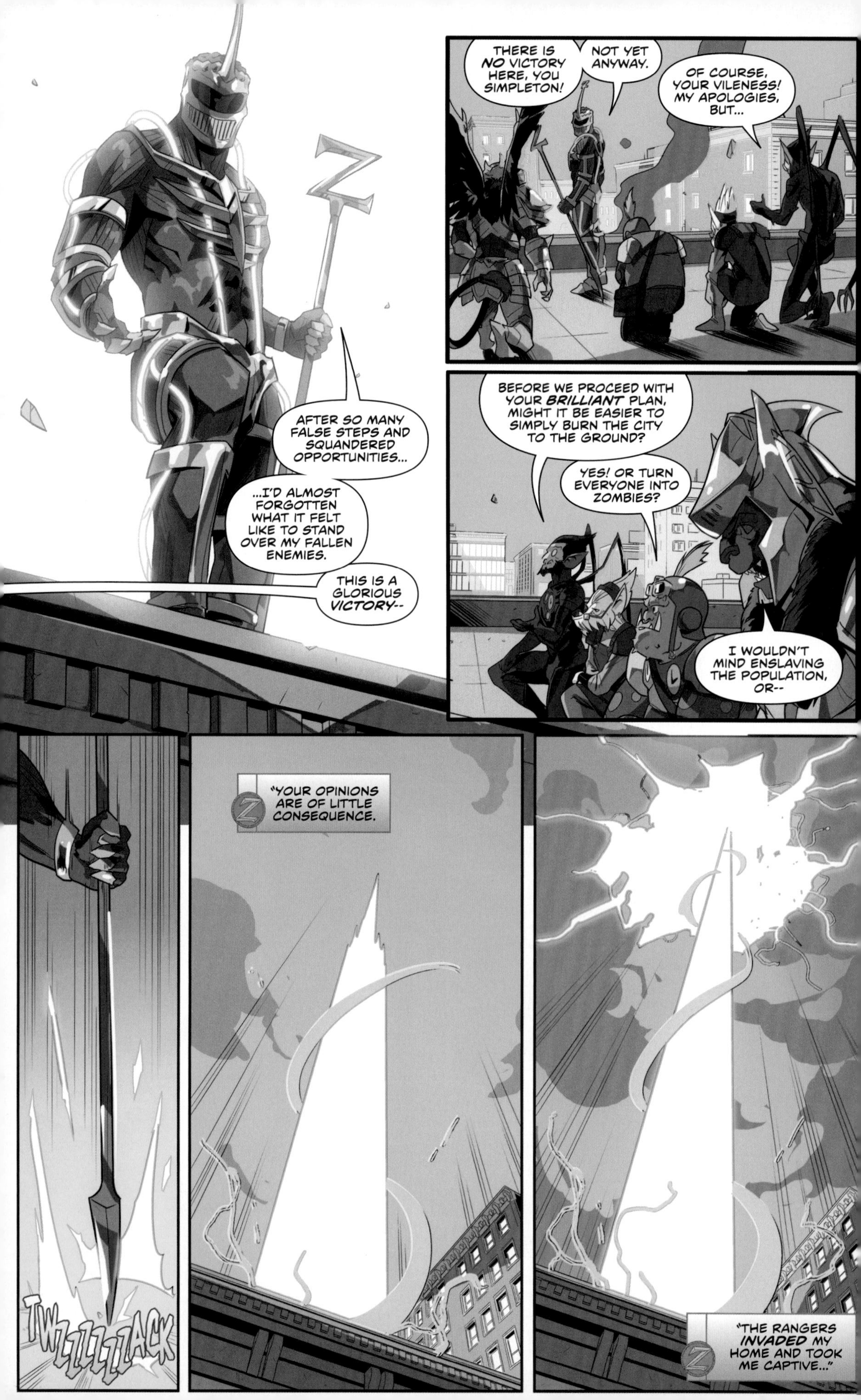
AFTER SO MANY FALSE STEPS AND SQUANDERED OPPORTUNITIES...
...I'D ALMOST FORGOTTEN WHAT IT FELT LIKE TO STAND OVER MY FALLEN ENEMIES.
THIS IS A GLORIOUS VICTORY--
THERE IS NO VICTORY HERE, YOU SIMPLETON!
NOT YET ANYWAY.
OF COURSE, YOUR VILENESS! MY APOLOGIES, BUT...
BEFORE WE PROCEED WITH YOUR BRILLIANT PLAN, MIGHT IT BE EASIER TO SIMPLY BURN THE CITY TO THE GROUND?
YES! OR TURN EVERYONE INTO ZOMBIES?
I WOULDN'T MIND ENSLAVING THE POPULATION, OR--
TWZZZZZZACK
"YOUR OPINIONS ARE OF LITTLE CONSEQUENCE.
"THE RANGERS INVADED MY HOME AND TOOK ME CAPTIVE..."

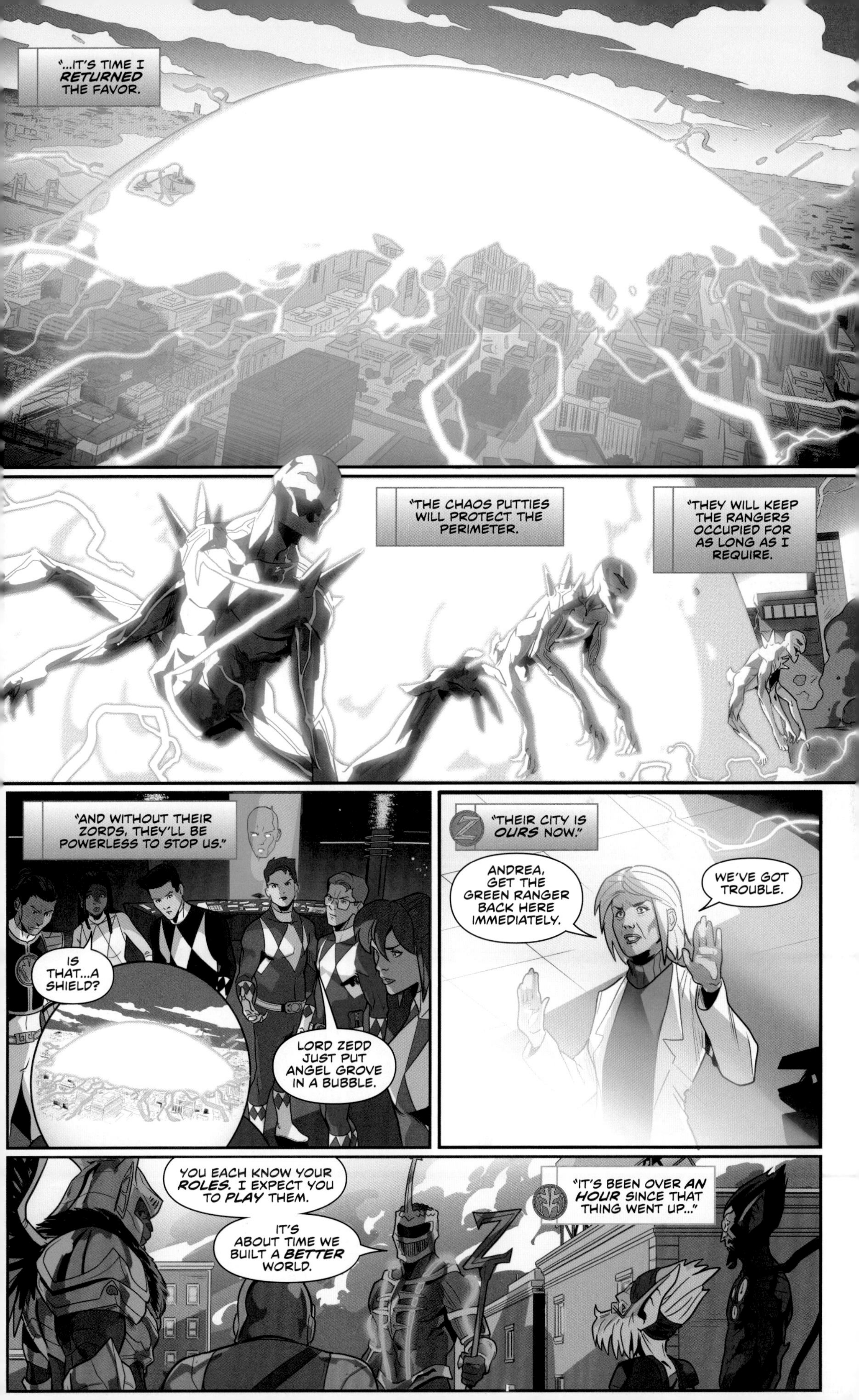
"...IT'S TIME I RETURNED THE FAVOR.
"THE CHAOS PUTTIES WILL PROTECT THE PERIMETER.
"THEY WILL KEEP THE RANGERS OCCUPIED FOR AS LONG AS I REQUIRE.
"AND WITHOUT THEIR ZORDS, THEY'LL BE POWERLESS TO STOP US."
IS THAT...A SHIELD?
LORD ZEDD JUST PUT ANGEL GROVE IN A BUBBLE.
"THEIR CITY IS OURS NOW."
ANDREA, GET THE GREEN RANGER BACK HERE IMMEDIATELY.
WE'VE GOT TROUBLE.
YOU EACH KNOW YOUR ROLES. I EXPECT YOU TO PLAY THEM.
IT'S ABOUT TIME WE BUILT A BETTER WORLD.
"IT'S BEEN OVER AN HOUR SINCE THAT THING WENT UP..."

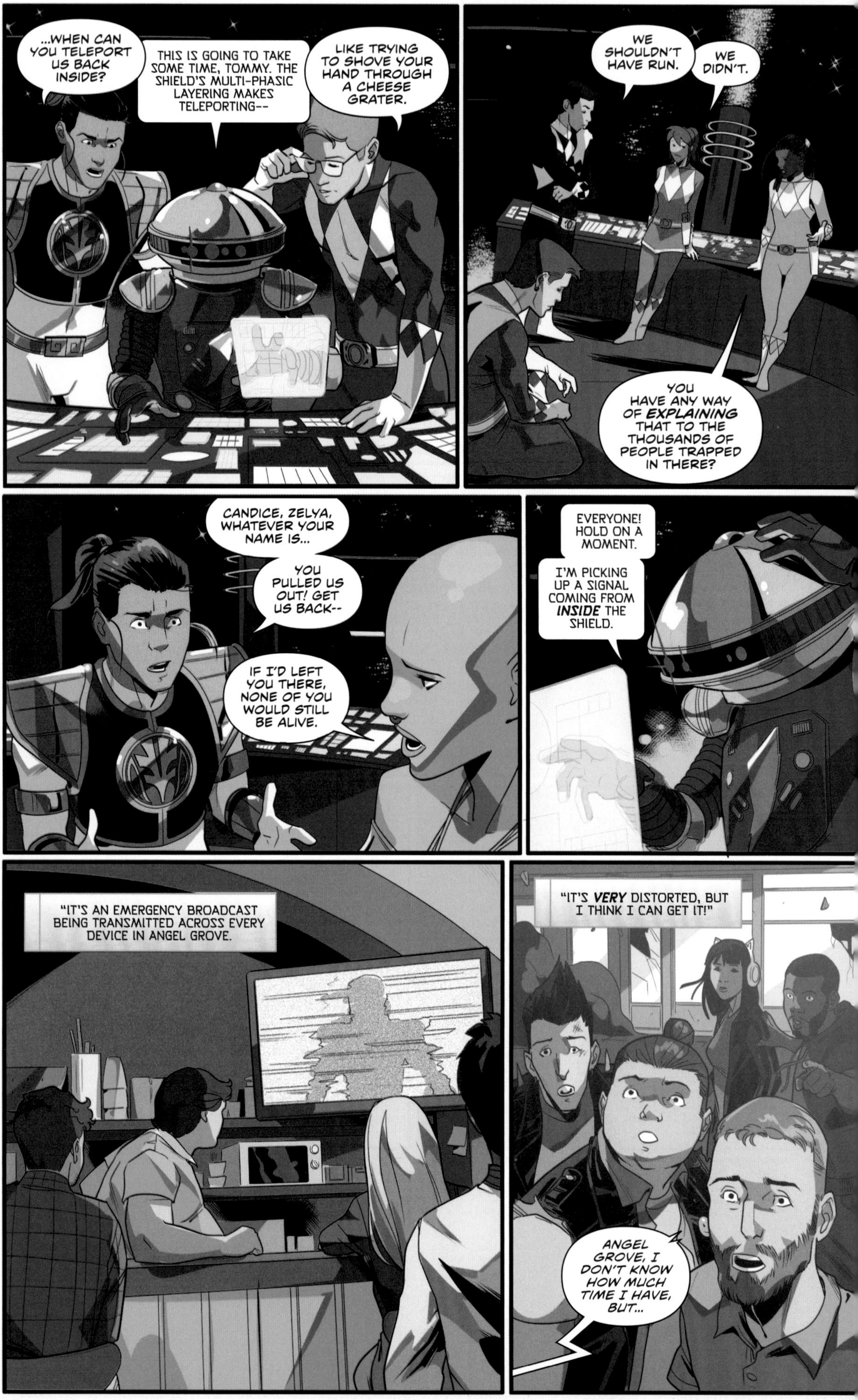
...WHEN CAN YOU TELEPORT US BACK INSIDE?
THIS IS GOING TO TAKE SOME TIME, TOMMY. THE SHIELD'S MULTI-PHASIC LAYERING MAKES TELEPORTING--
LIKE TRYING TO SHOVE YOUR HAND THROUGH A CHEESE GRATER.
WE SHOULDN'T HAVE RUN.
WE DIDN'T.
YOU HAVE ANY WAY OF **EXPLAINING** THAT TO THE THOUSANDS OF PEOPLE TRAPPED IN THERE?
CANDICE, ZELYA, WHATEVER YOUR NAME IS...
YOU PULLED US OUT! GET US BACK--
IF I'D LEFT YOU THERE, NONE OF YOU WOULD STILL BE ALIVE.
EVERYONE! HOLD ON A MOMENT.
I'M PICKING UP A SIGNAL COMING FROM **INSIDE** THE SHIELD.
"IT'S AN EMERGENCY BROADCAST BEING TRANSMITTED ACROSS EVERY DEVICE IN ANGEL GROVE.
"IT'S **VERY** DISTORTED, BUT I THINK I CAN GET IT!"
*ANGEL GROVE, I DON'T KNOW HOW MUCH TIME I HAVE, BUT...*

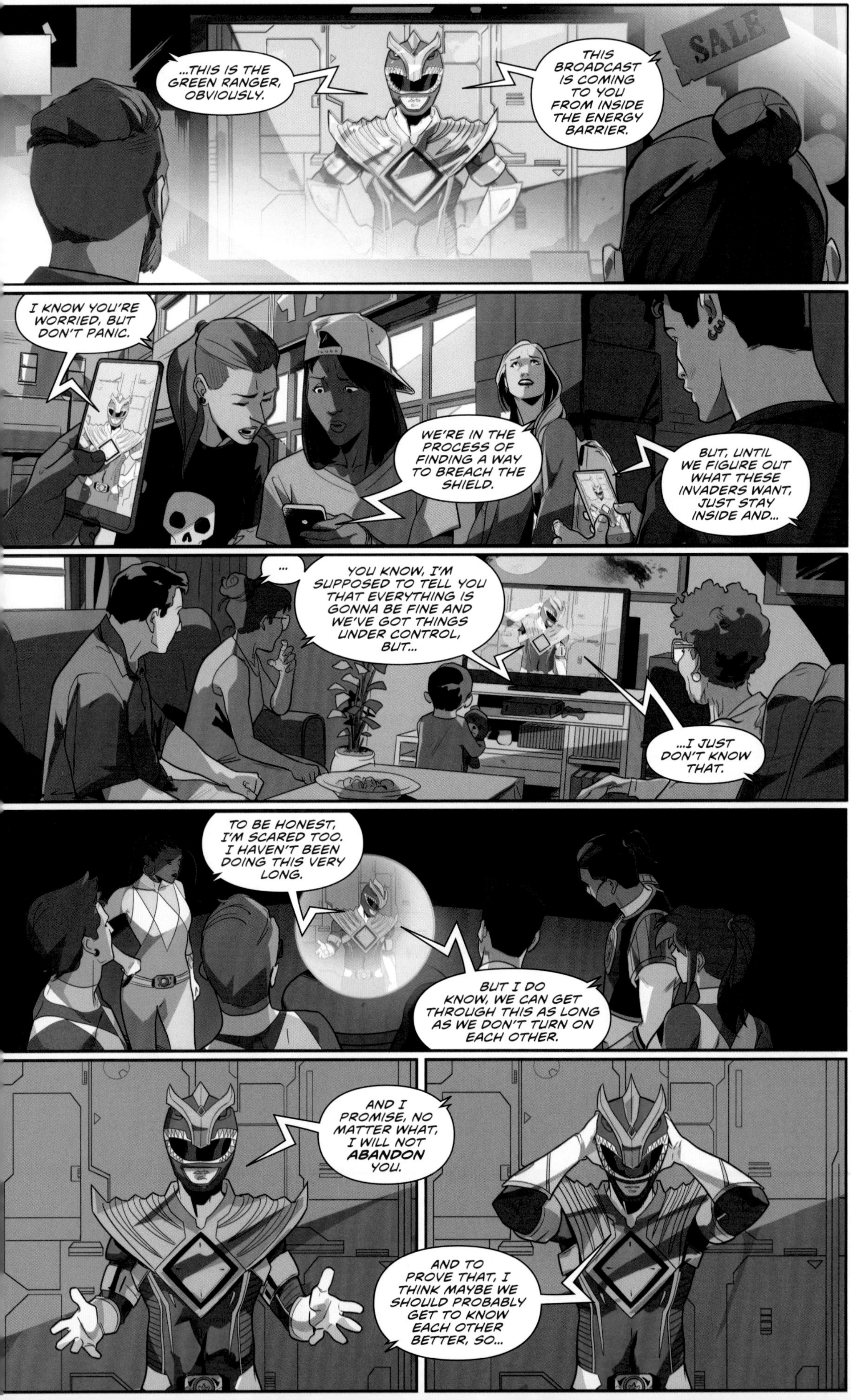

...THIS IS THE GREEN RANGER, OBVIOUSLY.
THIS BROADCAST IS COMING TO YOU FROM INSIDE THE ENERGY BARRIER.
SALE
I KNOW YOU'RE WORRIED, BUT DON'T PANIC.
WE'RE IN THE PROCESS OF FINDING A WAY TO BREACH THE SHIELD.
BUT, UNTIL WE FIGURE OUT WHAT THESE INVADERS WANT, JUST STAY INSIDE AND...
...
YOU KNOW, I'M SUPPOSED TO TELL YOU THAT EVERYTHING IS GONNA BE FINE AND WE'VE GOT THINGS UNDER CONTROL, BUT...
...I JUST DON'T KNOW THAT.
TO BE HONEST, I'M SCARED TOO. I HAVEN'T BEEN DOING THIS VERY LONG.
BUT I DO KNOW, WE CAN GET THROUGH THIS AS LONG AS WE DON'T TURN ON EACH OTHER.
AND I PROMISE, NO MATTER WHAT, I WILL NOT **ABANDON** YOU.
AND TO PROVE THAT, I THINK MAYBE WE SHOULD PROBABLY GET TO KNOW EACH OTHER BETTER, SO...

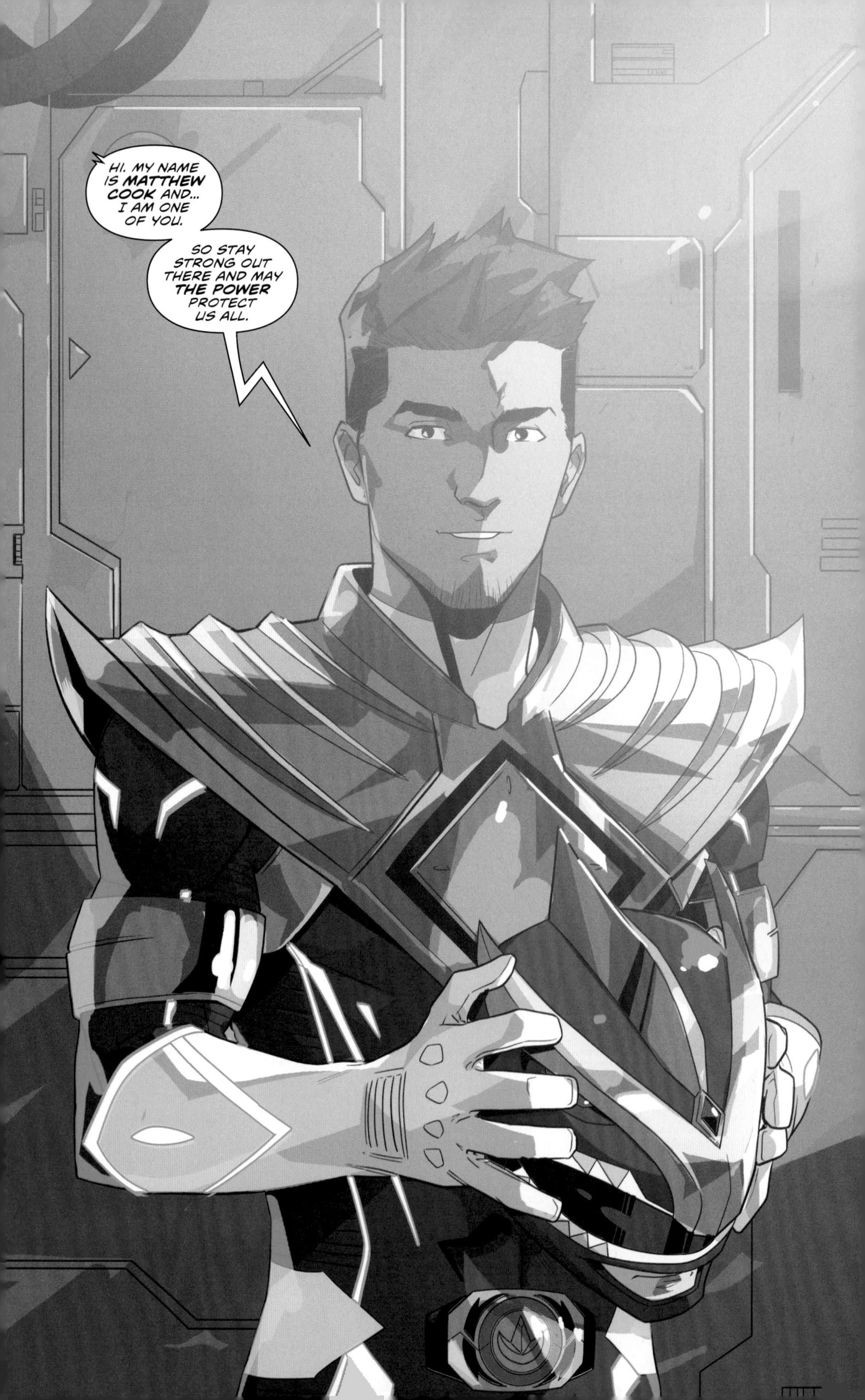
HI. MY NAME IS **MATTHEW COOK** AND... I AM ONE OF YOU.
SO STAY STRONG OUT THERE AND MAY **THE POWER** PROTECT US ALL.

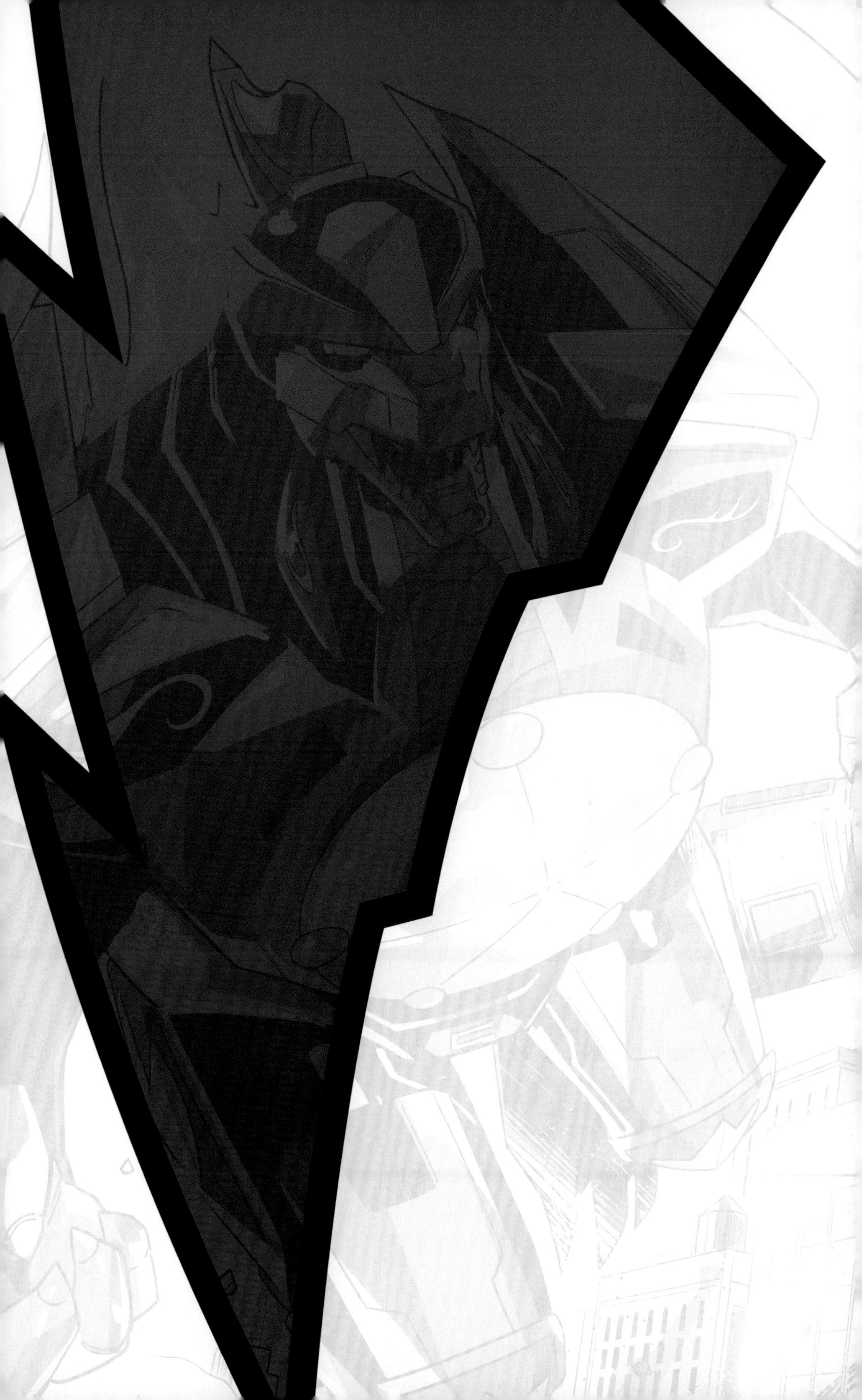

# COVER GALLERY

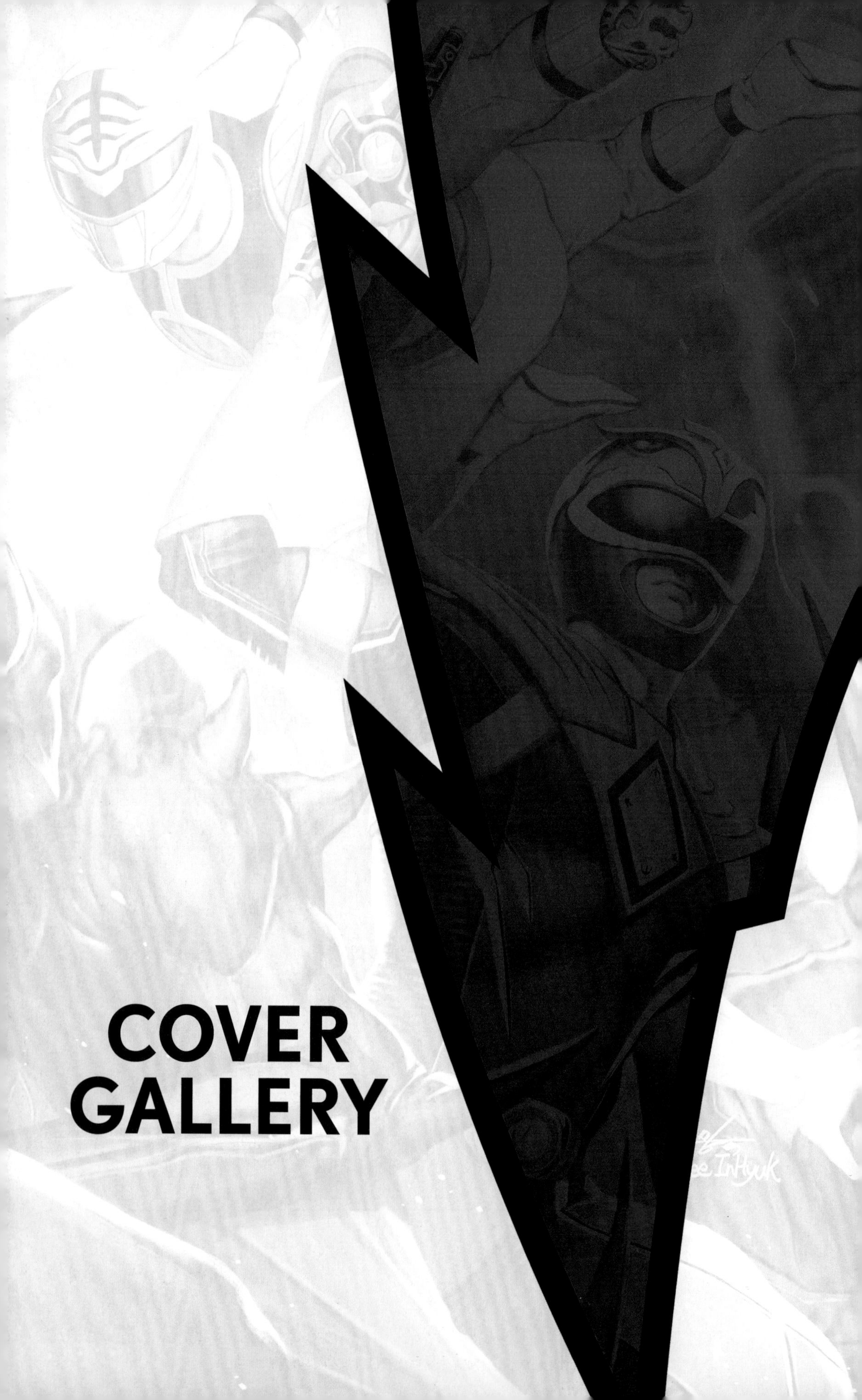

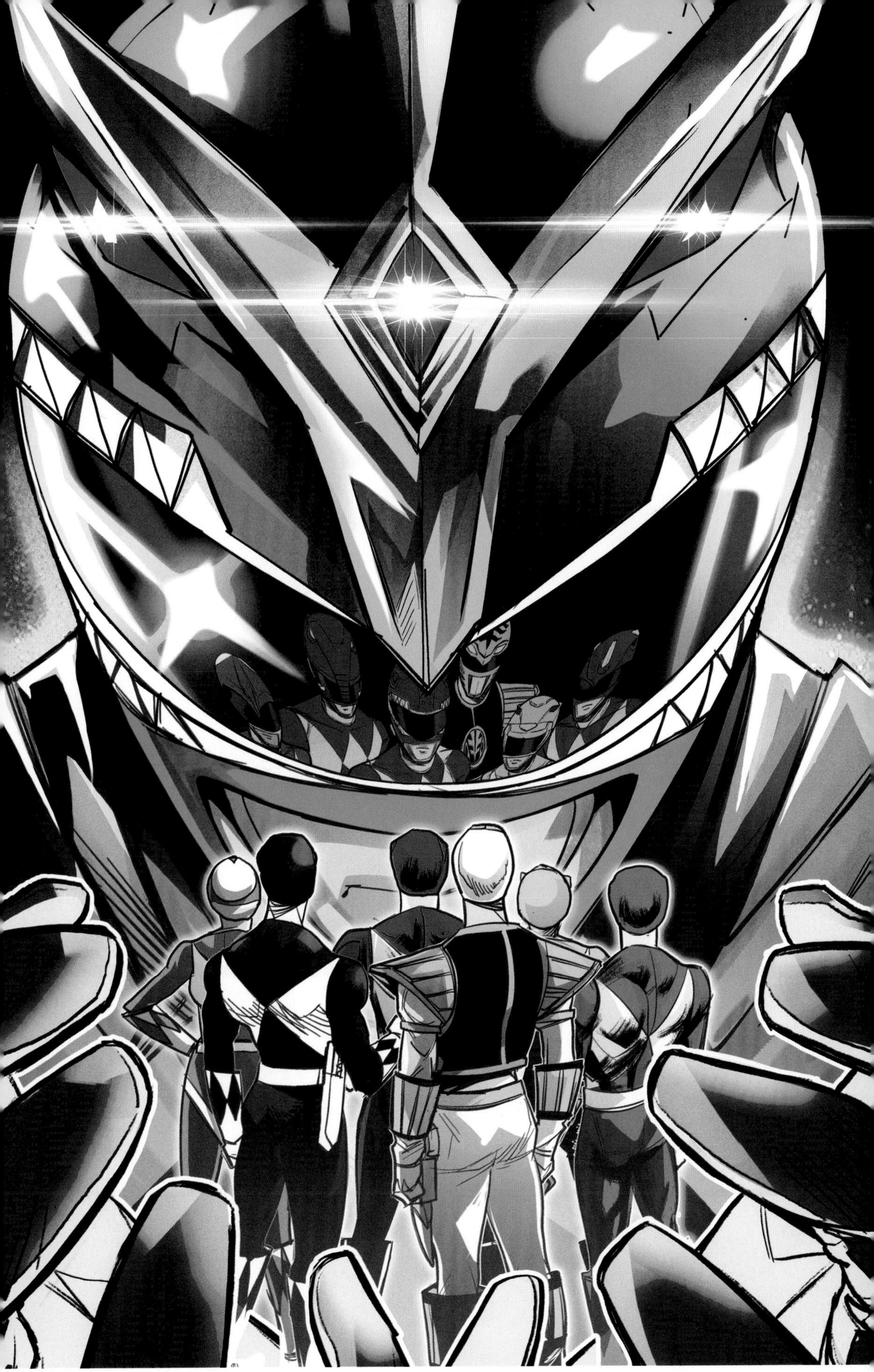

ELEONORA CARLINI | MIGHTY MORPHIN #1 VARIANT COVER

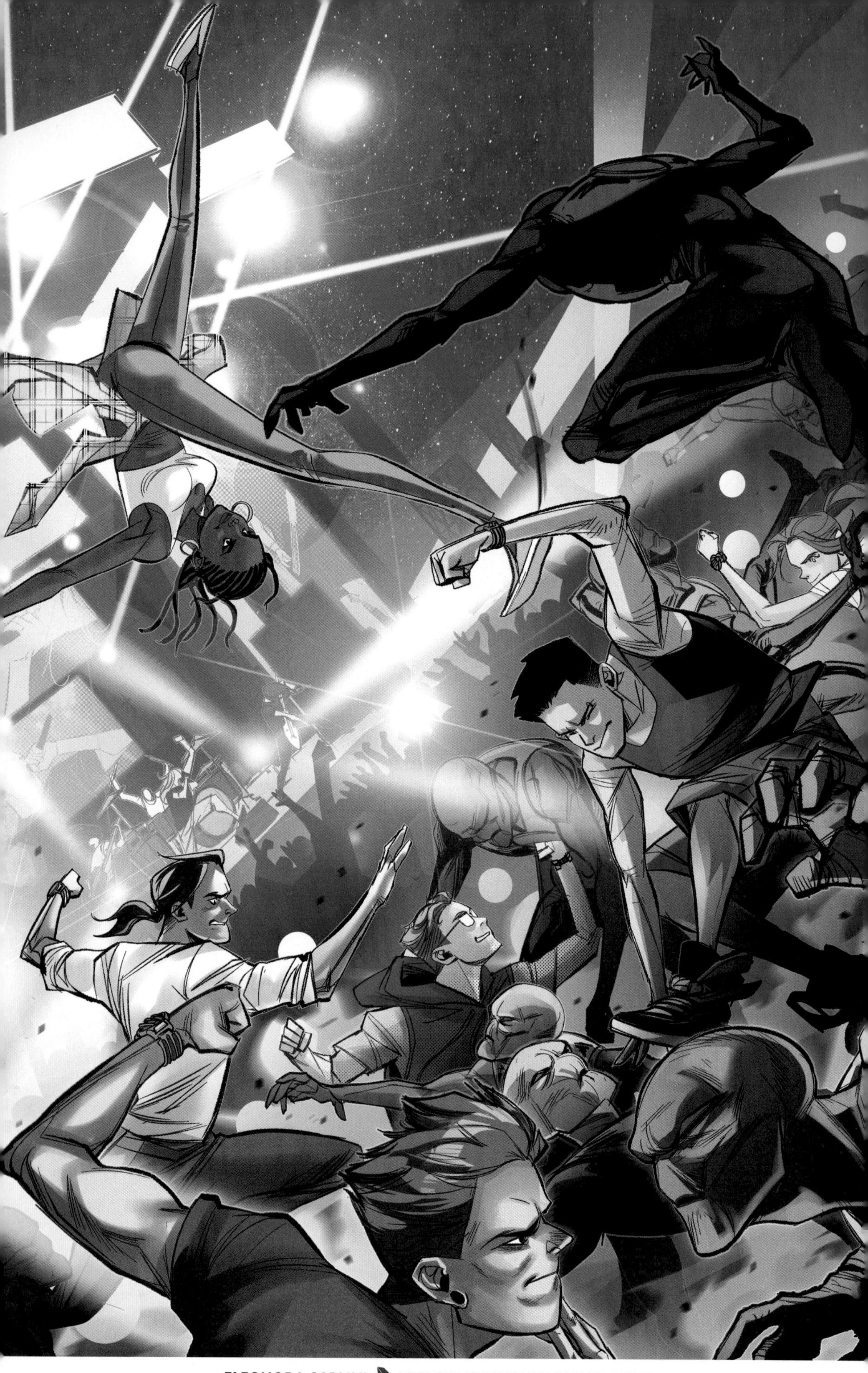

**ELEONORA CARLINI** MIGHTY MORPHIN #2 VARIANT COVER

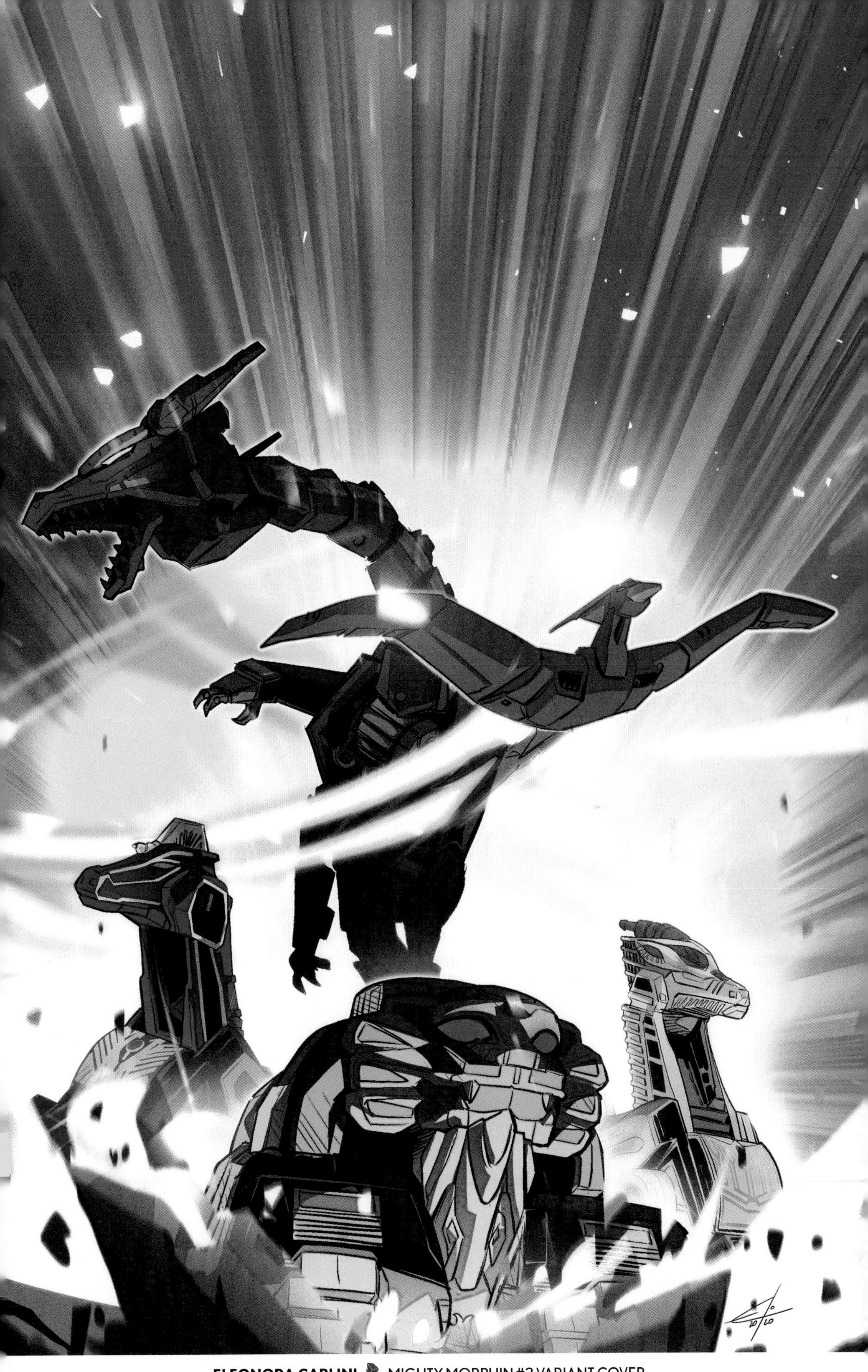

**ELEONORA CARLINI** MIGHTY MORPHIN #3 VARIANT COVER

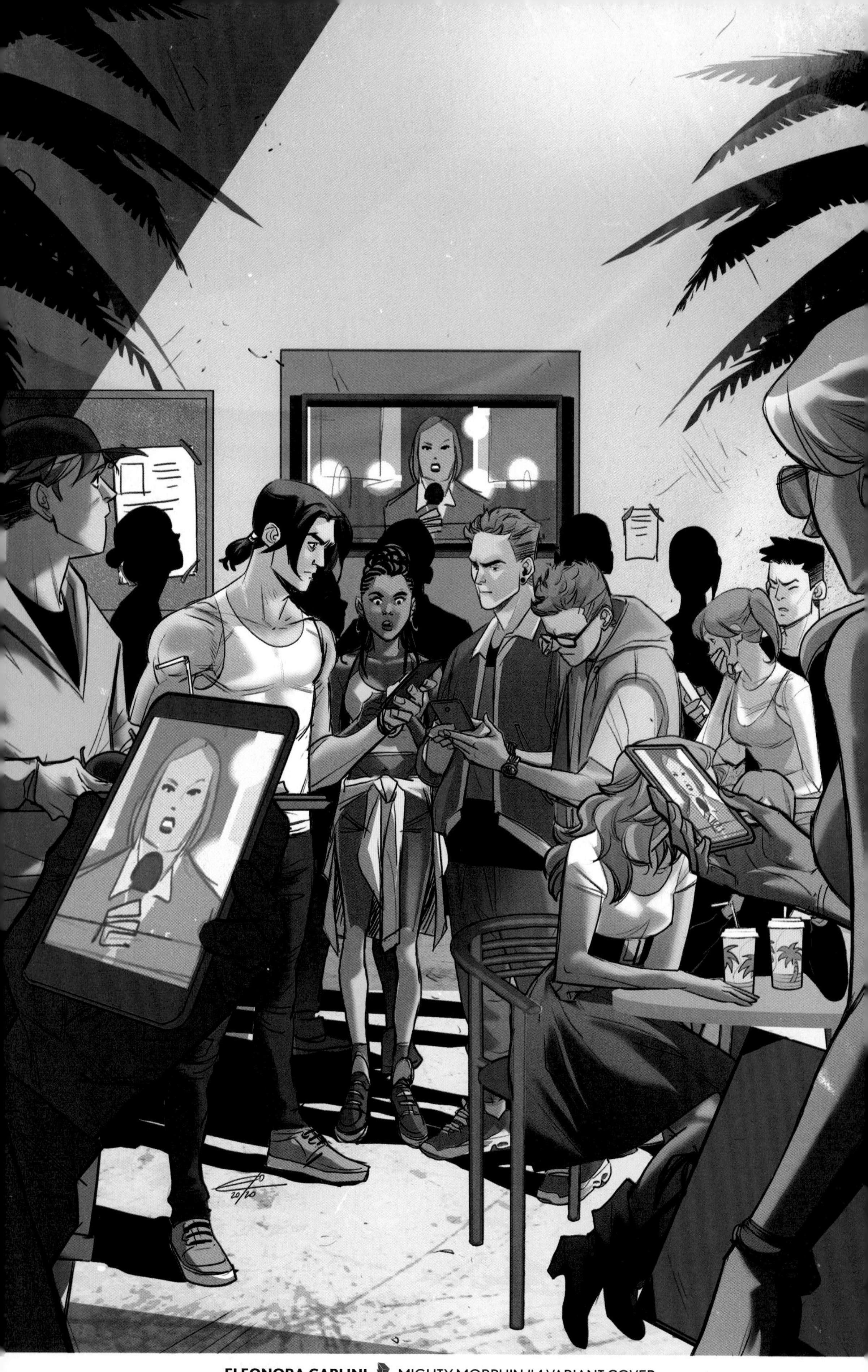

**ELEONORA CARLINI** MIGHTY MORPHIN #4 VARIANT COVER

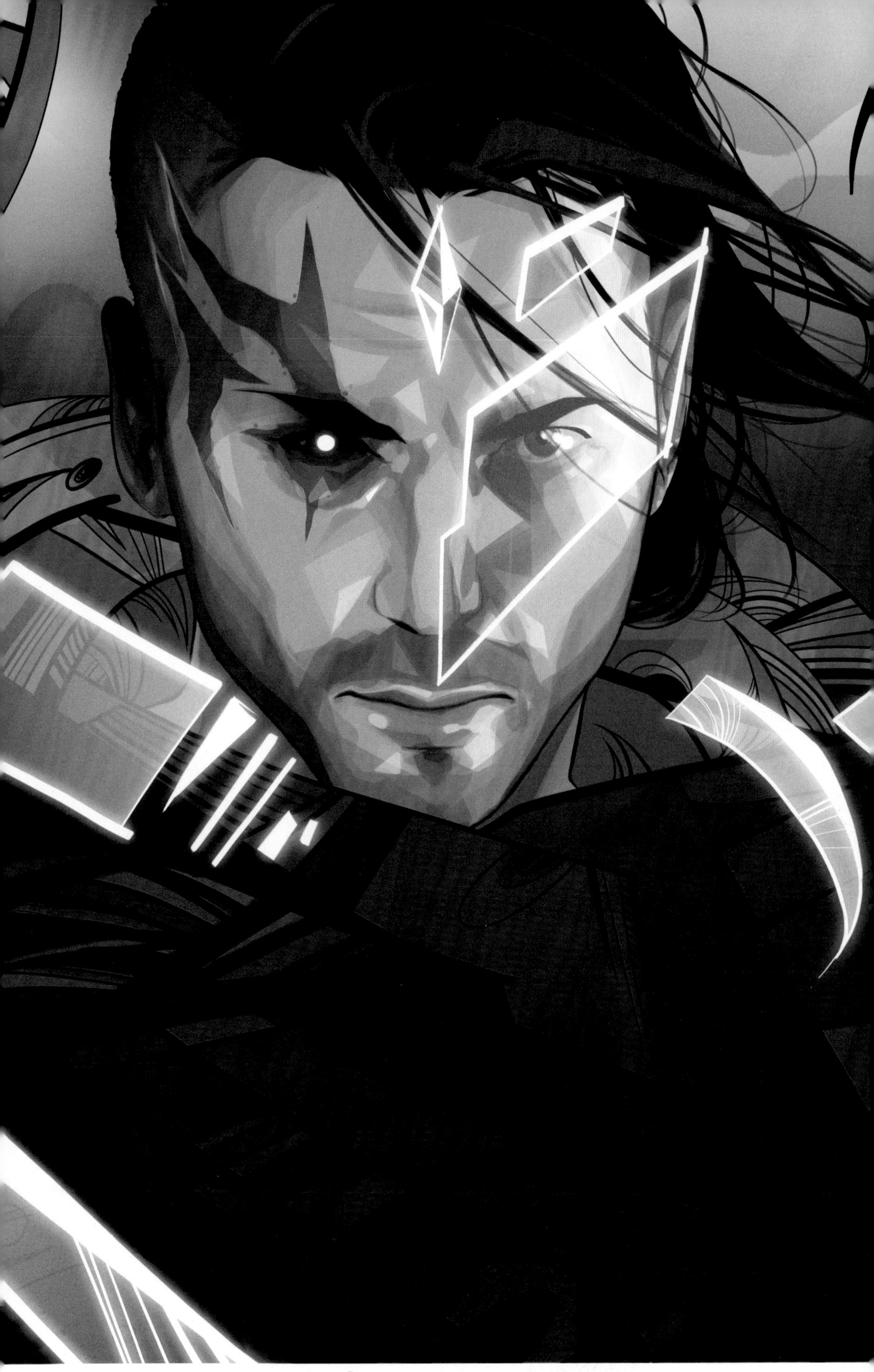

**GOÑI MONTES** MIGHTY MORPHIN #1 VARIANT COVER

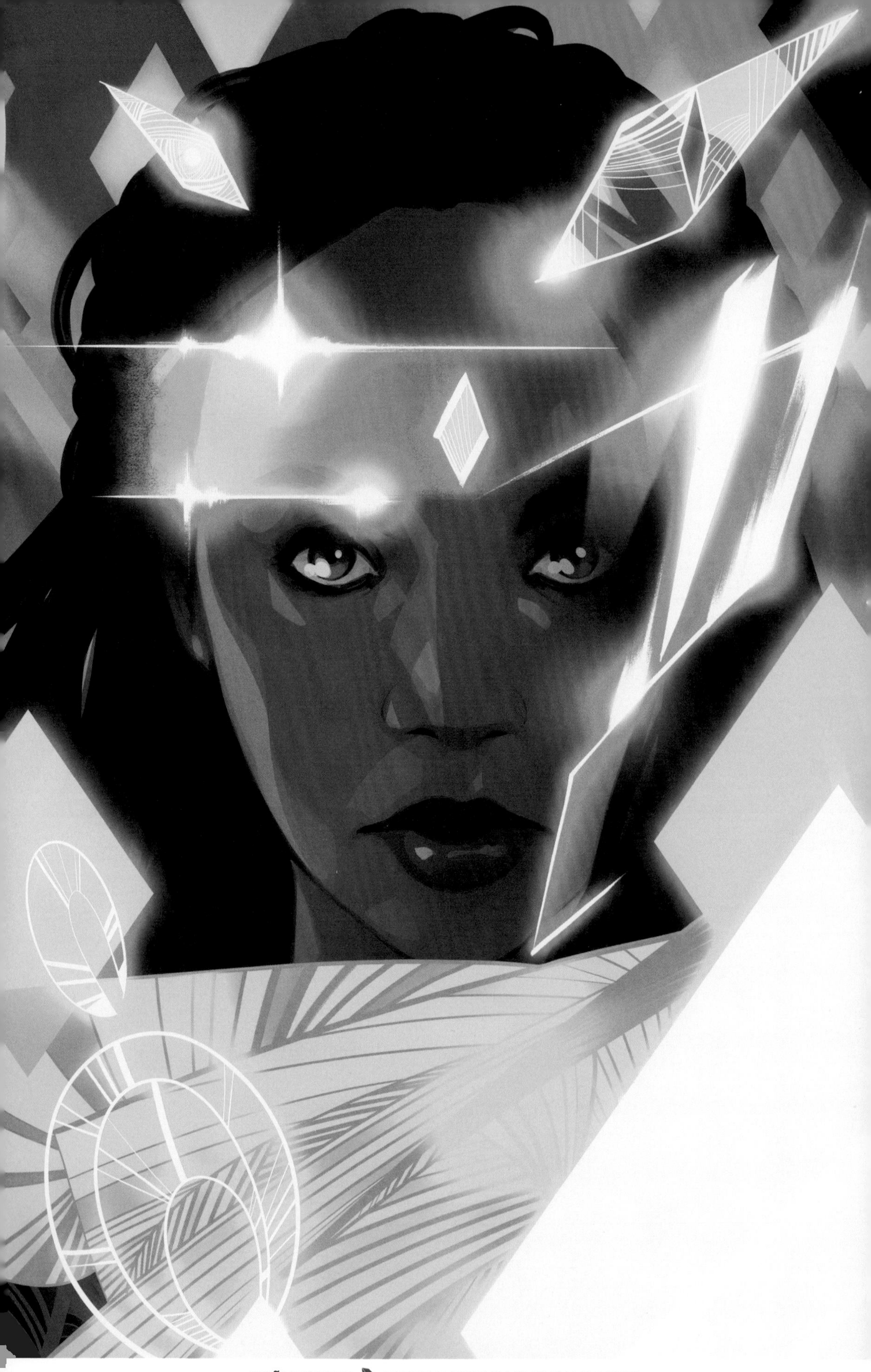

**GOÑI MONTES** MIGHTY MORPHIN #3 VARIANT COVER

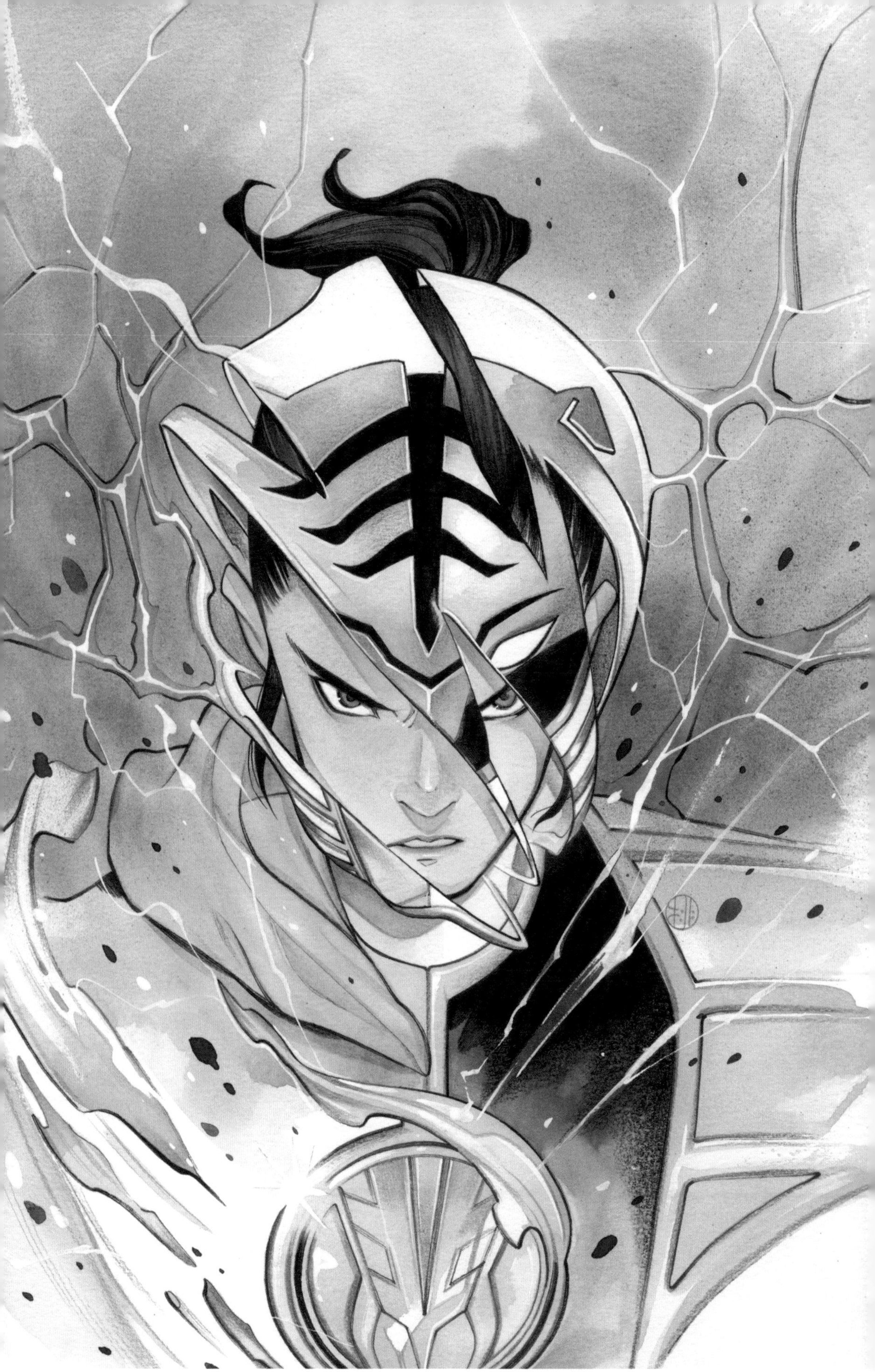

PEACH MOMOKO | MIGHTY MORPHIN #2 VARIANT COVER

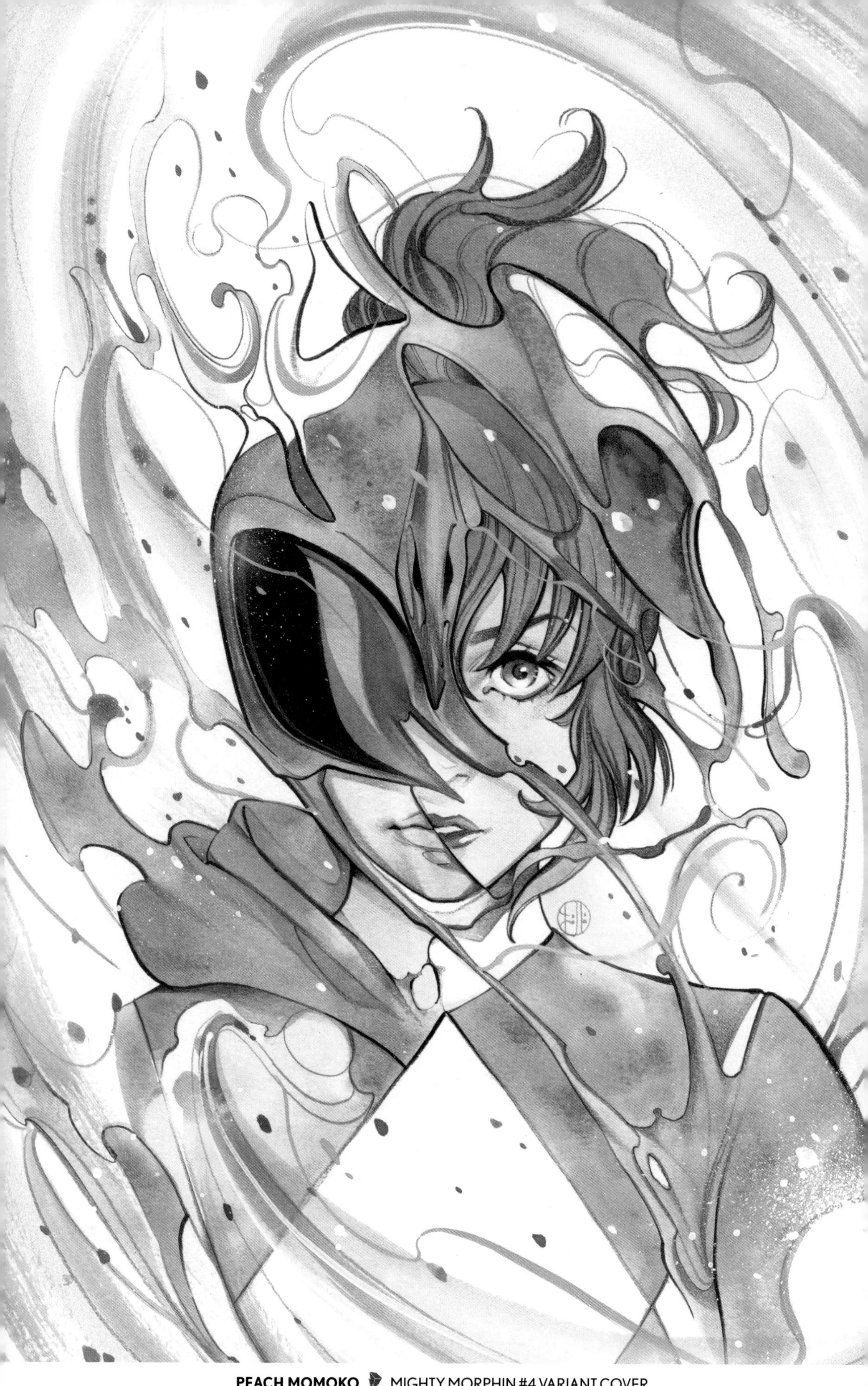

PEACH MOMOKO | MIGHTY MORPHIN #4 VARIANT COVER

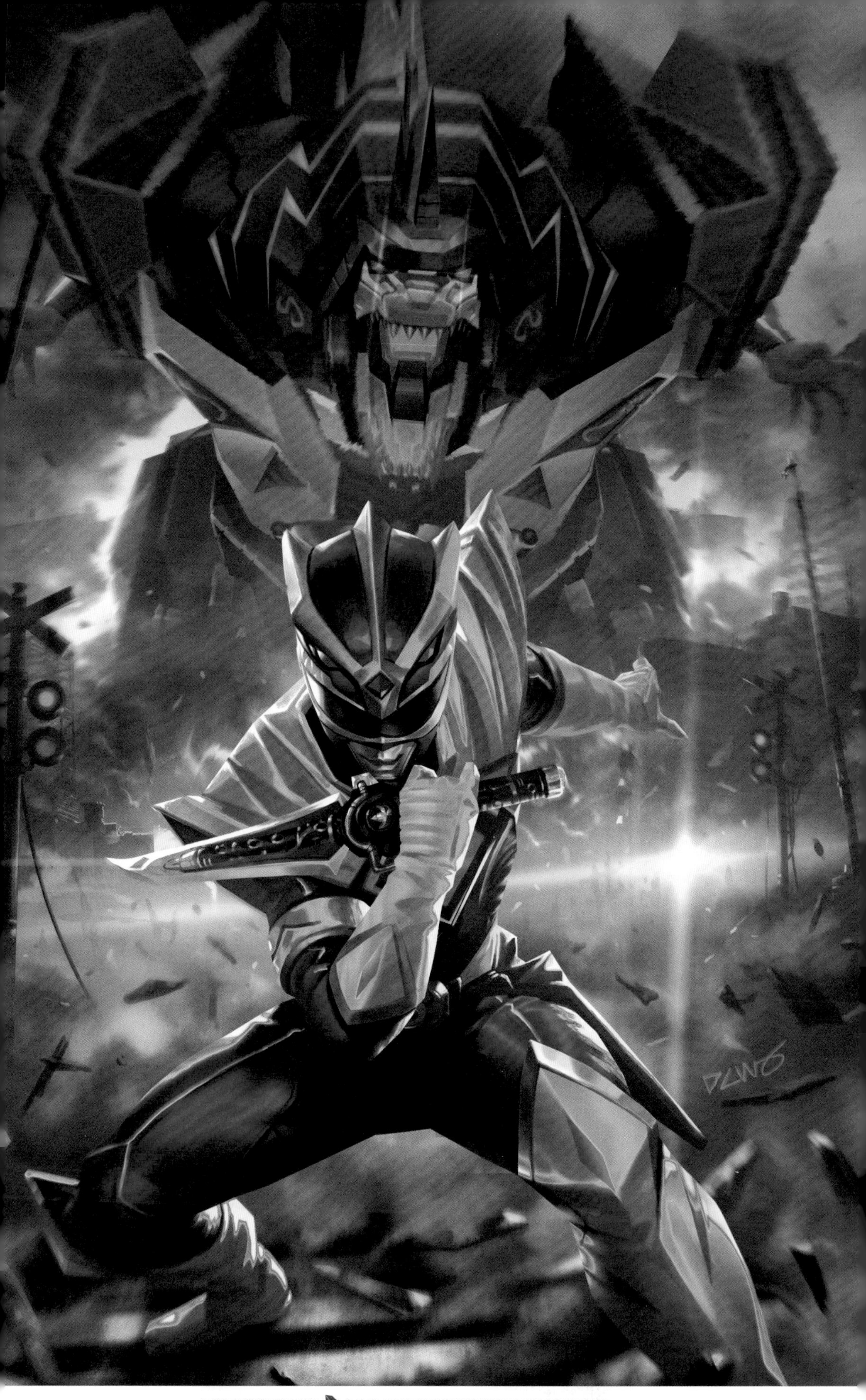

**DERRICK CHEW** MIGHTY MORPHIN #3 VARIANT COVER

# DISCOVER
# MORE POWER RANGERS!

HIGGINS • PRASETYA • HERMS
ORLANDO • HOWELL • LAWSON
MIGHTY MORPHIN POWER RANGERS
VOLUME ONE
INTRODUCTION BY POWER RANGERS EXECUTIVE PRODUCER JUDD "CHIP" LYNN

HIGGINS • PRASETYA SILAS • HERMS
VALENZA • ORLANDO HOWELL • LAWSON
MIGHTY MORPHIN POWER RANGERS
VOLUME TWO

FLETCHER THOMPSON HOWARD DI NICUOLO STERN
MIGHTY MORPHIN POWER RANGERS
PINK
INTRODUCTION BY AMY JO JOHNSON KIMBERLY HART, THE ORIGINAL PINK RANGER

POWER RANGERS
AFTERSHOCK
RYAN PARROTT LUCAS WERNECK JOANA LAFUENTE

MIGHTY MORPHIN POWER RANGERS
POSTER BOOK
FEATURING 20 REMOVABLE POSTERS

PARROTT • MORA • ANGULO
SABAN'S
GO GO POWER RANGERS
VOLUME ONE

**Mighty Morphin Power Rangers**
*Kyle Higgins, Hendry Prasetya, Matt Herms*
**Volume 1**
ISBN: 978-1-60886-893-3 | $19.99
**Volume 2**
ISBN: 978-1-60886-942-8 | $16.99
**Volume 3**
ISBN: 978-1-60886-977-0 | $16.99
**Volume 4**
ISBN: 978-1-68415-031-1 | $16.99

**Mighty Morphin Power Rangers: Pink**
*Kelly Thompson, Brenden Fletcher, Tini Howard, Daniele Di Nicuolo*
ISBN: 978-1-60886-952-7 | $19.99

**Saban's Go Go Power Rangers**
*Ryan Parrott, Dan Mora*
**Volume 1**
ISBN: 978-1-68415-193-6 | $16.99

**Saban's Power Rangers: Aftershock**
*Ryan Parrott, Lucas Werneck*
ISBN: 978-1-60886-937-4 | $14.99

**Mighty Morphin Power Rangers Poster Book**
*Goñi Montes, Jamal Campbell, Joe Quinones*
ISBN: 978-1-60886-966-4 | $19.99

**Mighty Morphin Power Rangers Adult Coloring Book**
*Goñi Montes, Jamal Campbell, Hendry Prasetya*
ISBN: 978-1-60886-955-8 | $16.99

**Mighty Morphin Power Rangers Year One: Deluxe HC**
*Kyle Higgins, Hendry Prasetya, Steve Orlando*
ISBN: 978-1-68415-012-0 | $75.00

BOOM! STUDIOS

**AVAILABLE AT YOUR LOCAL COMICS SHOP AND BOOKSTORE**
Find a comic shop near you at www.comicshoplocator.com
WWW.BOOM-STUDIOS.COM

Licensed by: Hasbro

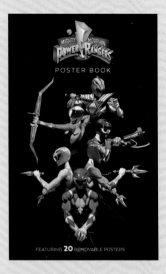